IT WASN'T A WASTE OF TIME

The Story of the Most Important Decade in Indian Cricket

Nikhil D. Samant

Leadstart
INKSTATE

ISBN 978–93–90266–84–5

First published in India 2021 by Leadstart Inkstate
A brand of One Point Six Technologies Pvt. Ltd.

123, Building J2, Shram Seva Premises,
Wadala Truck Terminal,
Mumbai 400022, Maharashtra, INDIA
Phone: +91 96999 33000
Email: info@leadstartcorp.com
www.leadstartcorp.com

Editor: Abhishek James Chandran
Cover: Dhiraj Navlakhe
Photo Credit: Julian Smith
Layouts: Kshitij Dhawale

To Sports. May your ability to unite people of all castes, colours and religions be the guiding light.

ABOUT THE AUTHOR

Nikhil D. Samant is a Chartered Accountant by profession, running his business in Pune. Fascinated by the art of storytelling, his writing quest began in a usual way; essay writing competitions. Years later, he found his passion again when he chanced upon a pan–India contest WRITE INDIA.

He participated in the 'WRITE INDIA CONTEST' conducted by Times Group which was a short story contest based on the prompts given by India's 11 prominent authors who then picked 3 stories each. His story titled 'SOMETIMES LOVE IS NOT ENOUGH' was selected by Mr. Ravinder Singh and it was published by Times Group in its anthology 'WRITE INDIA STORIES'. In Write India Season 2, another of his stories has been selected by Mr. Anand Neelakantan in the TOP 50.

This led him to complete his first Non–Fiction manuscript titled 'IT WASN'T A WASTE OF TIME – THE STORY OF THE MOST IMPORTANT DECADE IN INDIAN CRICKET.'

As all Indians, He is a huge fan of the game of cricket. Three years ago, He appeared for an Umpiring examination conducted by Maharashtra Cricket Association and cleared it. Then again last year, he cleared LEVEL–1 and LEVEL–1 Refresher examinations conducted by the BCCI. His passion and need to be associated with the game have culminated in this manuscript. This book is his tribute to Indian Cricket and all the players who have had the privilege to wear the Indian cap.

CONTENTS

TO BEGIN WITH

Dear Readers,

Like millions of others, I was fascinated by the game of cricket very early on my life, but it was ICC World Cup 1996 when I truly fell in love with the game. One man was responsible for it to a great extent. Sachin Tendulkar's ridiculous dominance over the world's best bowlers mesmerized me. Since then, I followed almost each and every game India played. Game after game, my fascination turned into addiction. Before I could know it, I got emotionally involved with the team. I wept and wept and wept when India lost to Sri Lanka in that Semi Final of World Cup 1996. I danced like I was insane on the sofa when Sachin demolished the Australian bowling attack in Sharjah. I was watching the match in the house of my cousin's neighbor, a complete stranger. Considering my dancing abilities, the obvious awkwardness of the situation did not occur to me. I did not utter a word for two days after India's unbelievable loss to Pakistan in the Chennai test in 1999. I was laughed at for my 'absurd' behavior, but the sorrow weighed more than the ridicule I faced. I would be lying if I said I never imagined myself playing for India even though I faced my first leather ball at the age of 28.

My world came crashing down with news of match fixing. My mother hated the sport and I cannot even count the number of times I had lied to her to watch matches. All had been in vain and my heart could not accept it. I felt so puny and helpless. I could not do anything for the game I cared for so much. To everyone who told me that cricket was just a waste of time, I could not answer back. For the first time in my life, I could not look into the eyes of those who made fun of my intense passion for the game.

Then in the year 2000 began the transformation. The following eleven years made my belief in the game stronger and stronger. The next 252 pages take account of Indian cricket's greatest journey. From the sickening feeling of betrayal to unstoppable tears of joy, from the lows of match fixing to winning the ultimate prize in world cricket, this is not only the journey of individuals who played for India in these eleven years but also mine as a cricket fan. **The emotions depicted in the book as well as the theories put forth are my perceptions of the players' thoughts and may not be correct at all times. Even though the statistics and events are true and correct,**

the thought processes I put forward from time to time in the book are my perspectives on the situation and cannot be attributed to any of the players or individuals.

India has a new generation which has not witnessed the match fixing phase. I hope this book conveys the level of efforts and hard work that has gone through to take Indian cricket where it is today. For those of us who have lived through this epic tale, I hope the book takes you back nineteen years and helps you relive those years. I, for one, have taken a long trip down memory lane.

As Sehwag announced his intentions to bat for 50 overs with 175 against Bangladesh; as Sachin bestowed the cricketing world with his genius centuries against England and South Africa; as Yuvraj triumphed over his inner demons and ill–health against the Netherlands, Ireland, West Indies and Australia; as the Indian bowlers countered the extreme pressure of a Pakistan Semi Final, only one sentiment filled my mind – we are finally here!

As forty five thousand people sang Rahman's Vande Mataram together in chorus to give all of India goose–bumps; as Dhoni hit that six and did his 'bat swivel' Rajinikanth style; as Yusuf Pathan carried Sachin on his shoulders for a victory lap around the Wankhede Stadium, after seeing Yuvraj, Harbhajan, Sehwag and Sachin in tears, one could not help turning a few pages of the story of Indian Cricket back. One could not help missing one man. After all that had happened in the shocking summer of 2000, how did we end up here?

PROLOGUE

THE WARNING

During the 1987 World Cup, rumors were rife about the team's performance but sometimes it seemed so obvious that it had me wondering. I also distinctly remember that match at Sharjah in 1991 when I was at the crease with Sanjay Manjrekar, when we decided to walk off because of failing light. To our surprise we received a signal from the team management to play on. This decision still baffles and angers me. Unfortunately, in situations where monkey deals are made in the dark and no proof is available, we can only shake our heads in disbelief. I noticed that such dealings seemed to be manipulated right from the top and players, who had reached the pinnacle, did not seem to be doing the right thing at crucial times.

Somewhere in the same period I was also approached by certain quarters to perform below par in a certain match. Before the India–Pakistan match in Sri Lanka for the Singer Cup in '94, I was offered Rs 25 lakh by an Indian team member for sabotaging the match in Pakistan's favour. I was told to play below my usual standards. I told him to get out of my room. I told him that I would never do what he was telling me to do. Because of this I soon acquired the tag of spoilsport in that group.

This did not stop the offers though, which flowed in regularly. There are times that things are so obvious; the entire nation watched it happen. In Kanpur, when we were chasing the West Indies score, Mongia came in to bat and conveyed the management's instruction to try and get as close to the target. The resultant bullabaloo about my going slow would be directed at the team management and not me as I was doing so under their instructions. Of the 48 balls in that period, I played just 11. I scored nine of those 11 balls. In fact, due to someone else's fault, I was dropped and humiliated.

Commercialization of cricket has changed its face–it's no longer just a game; it's a game where money is the main motivator. Sponsors and bookies have started exerting pressure and games are now being increasingly fixed. I remember the incident at Sharjah when Amir Sohail and Azhar went out to toss and both came back claiming that the other had won it. I feel that the day is not far when if the board is not vigilant enough, a major scandal might erupt."

• ***Excerpts from Manoj Prabhakar Interview***

Cronje – I had a look at pitch today, it can turn big.
Sanjay – it can turn big? Is (Pieter) Strydom playing?
Cronje – Yeah, he is playing. Yeah.
Sanjay – (Nicky) Boje?
Cronje – Boje is playing.
Sanjay – Boje is playing..... And who else is playing? (Herschelle) Gibbs?
Cronje – Gibbs and myself.
Sanjay – Okay. Just tell me. You have only four with you and not anybody else?
Cronje – No
Sanjay – And tomorrow I can deposit the money in your account. It is not a problem because of the time difference. Tomorrow itself I can deposit the money.
Cronje – Ok. I have spoken to Gibbs, and to (Henry) Williams, and Strydom. Everything is fine.
Sanjay – Okay. And how many runs for Gibbs?
Cronje – Less than twenty.
Sanjay – Okay. So everything is according to plan. They have to score at least 250.
Cronje – Yeah.
Sanjay – and if you score 270, it is off?
Cronje – Okay. And financially the guys want 25. They want 25 each.
Sanjay – Alright. Okay.
Cronje – So that's 75 for those three &.... What can you pay me? I do not know how much you pay me....
Sanjay – You say.
Cronje – if you give me..... 140 for everybody.
Sanjay – Okay that's fine.
Cronje – Okay.
Sanjay – We will sort something out for the previous one as well.
Cronje – Okay, sure. So we definitely are on.

- ***Excerpts of alleged conversation between a London–based NRI, Sanjay Chawla, and the South African cricket captain, Hansie Cronje***

THE CONFESSION

"I would like to apologise to all my family members who stood right behind me through this, especially (his wife) Bertha and all the other Christians who prayed for me.

"It has been a tough weekend but also a great weekend for me in that I now have the opportunity to face myself in the mirror again for the first time since the (1999/2000) Indian tour.

"On my way to the nets (before the first one–day international against Zimbabwe in January) I was stopped by Hamid (Cassim), a bloke who has been hanging around the team for a few years now, always handing out biltong (dried meat) to the guys in return for some tickets. He told me that if only he knew I was going to declare (in the fifth test against England at Centurion Park) he could have made himself some good money and my reply was: 'Why don't you ask?'

"Since that day, in a moment of stupidity and weakness, I allowed Satan and the world to dictate terms to me, rather than the Lord. Hamid called me almost four times a day from then on.

"He later introduced me to a friend called Sanjay during the one–day international series with England and Zimbabwe. Together, they told me that I could also make some cash if we could maybe cook a match. I told them that I was not prepared to do this unless we were assured of a place in the final.

"Of course, we only narrowly got through to the final and the opportunity never came. I had in my possession at that stage 10,000 to 15,000 U.S. dollars that Sanjay gave me just in case I had a change of mind.

"I told him that maybe (in) the first one–day international in India I could see what could be done, thinking that if we could get the match out of the way, we'd get rid of them and could then focus purely on cricket. My idea was never to involve other players.

"I would like to make it absolutely clear to any member of the South African team, whether player or management, about this: I lied to him (Sanjay) by saying certain players were involved when in fact I had never spoken to any of them. I couldn't face asking them to do it. I can't recall all the names that I mentioned and I can't remember the figures that were mentioned.

"I ignored him the night before the (opening India) match but early the next morning, Hamid phoned me again and urged me to go ahead with the plan. I phoned him up and suggested we go for it. All this time, I had in the back of my mind: Pride to play for South Africa and my team mates, whom I all respect. It was a difficult period for me before the match and I then decided I won't not try,

I'll give it my best shot and see what happens.

"As it happened, we got 301 for three. I got 19 off 20 balls and India knocked it off quite comfortably after (Mornantau) Hayward got injured. I can honestly say that I tried to win the match, even at that stage.

"When I got back to the hotel, Sanjay was upset because we got too many runs and I blamed the Indian keeper for three chances that he missed. I did not accept any money for that match.

"On the evening of the third day of the third Test against India at Kanpur, I received a call from Mohammed Azharuddin, who was friendly with a number of South African players. He called me to a room in the hotel and introduced me to Mukesh Gupta ('MK'). Azharuddin then departed and left us alone in the room. MK asked me if we would give wickets away on the last day of the Test to ensure that we lost. He asked me to speak to the other players and gave me approximately U.S. $30,000 in cash to do so. I led him to believe that I would. This seemed an easy way to make money, but I had no intention of doing anything. I did not speak to any of the other players and did nothing to influence the match. In the event, however, we lost the Test. I had effectively received money for doing nothing and I rationalised to myself that this was somehow acceptable because I had not actually done anything"

"The moment I took my eyes off Jesus, my whole world turned dark and it felt like someone had stuck a knife through my chest.

"I'll be back. Better off than I am now, once I have been punished."

• ***Partial Text of Hansie Cronje's Confession***

THE ACTION

"The former India captain Mohammad Azharuddin, Former Test player Ajay Sharma has been banned from cricket for life. Both are also barred from holding any position with the cricket board for life and would not be eligible for benefit matches. The Board's contribution to their benevolent fund would be withheld. Board Officials said they did not accept Azharuddin's denials on match fixing."

"Ajay Jadeja and Manoj Prabhakar, two other former test players are suspended for five years. Ali Irani, a former team physiotherapist, is also suspended from all cricket related activities. The wicket Keeper Nayan Mongia is admonished."

"This is a sad day in the annals of Indian Cricket. There is clear evidence of match fixing against Azharuddin. There is also evidence that Sharma acted as a conduit for match fixing. That's why we clubbed the two of them together and gave life bans. Others had nexus with bookmakers and introduced players to bookmakers, which is a serious breach of cricketing codes."

"These hard decisions have been taken after careful consideration. They will set an example for future."

• *Excerpts of the statement issued by the Chief of the BCCI*

PART I

OLD MONKS AND THEIR NEW GUNS

Betrayal is the only truth that sticks, observed the legendary American playwright Arthur Miller. At the cusp of the new millennium, murky clouds of betrayal put the nation of a billion cricket frenzied people into despair. Their reverence to the demi–god cricketing stars was rendered worthless in a matter of few days. The joy they felt when India won, the pain and agony they underwent when India lost, the long debates on India's performances, felt like a waste of time. The Match–Fixing scandal devastated a diehard Indian cricket fan's faith in the game. The value of the words belief and faith appeared hollow.

Nature has granted every specie one peculiar trait that sets it apart from rest. For humans, it is the mind, capable of undergoing so many emotions without which we are frivolous. We feel ecstasy, grief, envy, dejection, and each emotion enriches our lives in its own way. Faith, the strongest of them all, empowers you to achieve wondrous things but when shredded to pieces, it can pull you down to the deepest and darkest corners of anguish. How do you get up when despair subjugates you? How do you face the realisation that the team you believed in, the sport you put your heart in, was a scripted drama?

Hansie Cronje's confession and the possibility of the involvement of Indian players raised many unrelenting and uncomfortable questions which hounded Indian cricket and its fans. The CBI report and eventual decision by BCCI to ban the Indian captain and a few others made it official. India's biggest sport, its supreme passion had become its greatest shame. Fans found it difficult to come to terms with these happenings. The match–fixing saga brought Indian cricket to the brink of losing its charm; its fans and their unconditional support. Indian cricket called for a new radical mind–set and extraordinary resolve to reinstate its pride and glory; a miraculous endeavour to bring back people to the beautiful game which was worshipped in every nook and corner of the country till just a few days back. A few good men in the Indian dressing room, enduring similar angst as the fans, coupled with humiliating question–marks on their integrity, signed up for the task of restoring the image of Indian cricket.

THE OLD MONKS

JOHN WRIGHT

Year 1990. Stories were going around in the Indian cricket circles. "The boy has exceptional talent. He will in future become one of the greatest ever."

The boy himself came close to proving it in as early as his 6th test match. He fell 12 runs short of his first international test century. At a tender age of 16, he could not hide his tears. Danny Morrison could not hide the excitement of claiming a batsman on the verge of scoring a century. But the catcher had only a hint of a smile on his face; no extravagant celebration but his smile conveyed every bit of his passion. He had contributed equally in the dismissal but he chose to stay in the background and let Danny Morrison hog the centre–stage. Indian fans were aghast to see the young boy come so close to achieving such a monumental feat. They hated the catcher. Little did they know that the quiet man, who denied Sachin Tendulkar from being the youngest player to score an international century, would a decade later become the backbone of India's revival story! And of course, he would do it in his own way; all the while staying behind the curtain.

Each batsman who has played the game can be broadly classified into two categories; tenacious or flamboyant. John Wright belonged to the former. Together with Bruce Edgar, he formed one of the most successful opening pairs for New Zealand. His style of batting complimented and on many occasions nurtured his ability to be an unsung pillar. His failures as a sales executive, after he retired from international cricket, were inevitable as aggressive sales targets seldom comprehend a quiet way of achieving them. Only one job suited his approach. Unlike in football, the coach of a cricket team is not expected to take the front seat. He tasted success as the coach of an English County, Kent. The natural progression was to then coach an international cricket team but the pertinent question was – which team required his style of coaching the most? Which team could use his composure and poise to its advantage? Every question pointed towards one destination. Coaching the Indian team was considered to be the most challenging job in the cricketing world. John Wright, India's first foreign coach, faced two more difficult challenges though– to mould himself into a culture alien to him, and second to take charge of the Indian cricket team, embroiled in the ugliest turmoil in its history. The formidable asset of John Wright, his calmness, was going to be tested in the toughest possible environment. Even with such enormous odds stacked against him, he assumed his responsibilities with a calming smile, similar to the one he wore when he had caught Sachin Tendulkar out in 1990. His infectious smile gave the Indian team members much required motivation and a sense of trust in him.

V.V.S. LAXMAN

After trailing by 2 test matches in a three–match series and facing a deficit of 402 runs in the third test, it was safe to say that nothing had gone India's way in the 1999 Australia Tour. Indian fans had been through anguishing 4 months of pathetic cricket by their team and demanded something to cheer. That's when Vangipurapu Venkata Sai Laxman laid bare his true love for Australian bowlers. His innings of 167 on Sydney Cricket Ground was perhaps the finest Innings by an Indian down–under till that date considering the quality of bowling at the disposal of Australian captain. The Indian domestic circuit was already abuzz about his remarkable talent. The SCG innings put him on a pedestal of a potential legend.

Born in Hyderabad to a Telugu Brahmin family, Laxman had a noble lineage of academics. Abiding by the Indian tradition of choosing your parents' profession, he enrolled for medical studies. It is a mystery how a studious fellow fell in love with the game of cricket, but within a few months of his admission he made the tough choice of following his heart than his brain.

An inconsistent domestic season threatened to end his dream of representing India. A failed debut series and a poor test series in South Africa further hampered his chances to feature in the star–studded Indian middle order. But such a talent could not be wasted and hence the then team management asked him to open the innings, to fit him in the Indian team. It was his only chance to keep his place. Though he fared well as an opener, his scores were not good enough to secure a place against the forthcoming New Zealand series. His dismal ODI form virtually sealed all entry points.

Whispers of match fixing in Indian cricket were beginning to take a hideous shape. Meanwhile, V.V.S. Laxman broke the record for the most runs in the Ranji Season. He amassed 1415 runs at an average of 108, scoring 8 centuries in 9 matches. The numbers became impossible to overlook and Laxman got his ticket to Australia and Sydney happened. He took a courageous decision soon after his Sydney master class. He chose domestic cricket over continuing as an opener in the international cricket. Even after scoring quality runs as an opener, he believed the role did not suit him and the decision cost him his place in the Indian side.

He had to wait for an entire year to get his recall. A lot had come to pass in that year. He had scored tons of runs in domestic cricket and yet his heart ached. The love of his life for which he had sacrificed a promising career in medicine was getting tarnished day by day. He vowed to bring back respect to his love. The determination to prove his worth and cement his place in the Indian team had resulted in a wonderful innings at SCG a year ago. India needed a determined, disciplined knight whose integrity was unquestionable. For the first time in his international career of 5 years, V.V.S. Laxman fit into the team management's vision to the tee. He got his opportunity to darn the image of the game he so dearly loved.

ANIL KUMBLE

By the time the new millennium arrived, Anil Kumble was a veteran of 10 years in International Cricket and a legend already. He was a captain's delight because of his fighting spirit and unyielding attitude. His exploits of picking 10 wickets in an innings had elevated him to a different platform. But after the match–fixing scandal, India desired more than his cricketing abilities. It looked for a symbol of honor, honesty and dignity. Anil Kumble played his cricket in its truest spirit and his Karnataki roots guaranteed a dignified presence in the dressing room. He was required to lend his face to Indian cricket. As always, he was ready before anyone even asked.

RAHUL DRAVID

One man's loss always becomes someone else's opportunity. Sanjay Manjrekar injured his ankle in England which gifted Rahul Dravid a chance of a lifetime; a debut on the first ground of cricket, Lord's. His first innings in test match cricket highlighted two of his principal strengths. His technique was pure textbook, and he had loads of patience. From being the No. 7 batsman for India to India's regular number three, Dravid's journey and growth as a test match batsman was exemplary, akin to his batting. The shorter version of the game troubled him in the early part of his career but with an outstanding ICC World Cup 1999, he overcame that challenge to a considerable extent.

Every challenge thrown at Dravid was given an empathetic answer. That was the mark of a special player, a potential legend. Now, a new challenge awaited him. After playing International cricket for merely 4 years, he had to assume the responsibilities of a senior member of the team. One key character to conquer the darkest phases of life is patience. Rahul Dravid had it in abundance. His patience was India's strength. He was the guard that a young batting line–up required. In the true sense, he was India's guarding wall.

SACHIN TENDULKAR

Sachin Tendulkar encountered fame and recognition at an early age of 15 when his partnership of 664 runs with Vinod Kambli grabbed the attention of the entire nation. Legends like Gavaskar and Vengsarkar used to come to the grounds to watch him play. Till 2000, he had 46 international centuries to his credit. He had already enrolled his name in the list of all–time greats. Strong middle class roots never let success and fame go to his head. His humility stood above his godly stature which helped him connect with the average Indian fan.

However, India's best batsman never got it right as captain. External forces and petty politics appeared to stifle him. The pressure of delivering results affected his batting. India could not afford to lose Sachin Tendulkar, the batsman. Sachin Tendulkar the batsman was an inspiration to millions. Indian cricket needed an inspirational figure to cleanse itself of the dirt it was in. Sachin Tendulkar's presence was enough to rekindle hope. He always let his bat do the talking. He always answered criticism with huge scores. This time around, he needed to wield his bat to bring back hope in Indian cricket.

SOURAV GANGULY

The legend of Sourav Ganguly began in India's tour of Australia in 1992 with the infamous story of him refusing to carry water. It created an image of an arrogant rich brat who never had to struggle for anything in his life. Bagging the precious India cap wasn't easy though. But when he finally got his hands on it in 1996, he grabbed it in style with back–to–back centuries. Ever since his grand test debut, the man never looked back. His silky timing and glorious cover drives became India's most treasured possession. He formed one of the most successful opening pairs in ODI cricket with Tendulkar. Till 2000, he was known as a rich spoilt brat, an accomplished batsman and one half of the great opening pair. In those 4 years of his career, he never looked aggressive, dominant and showed no signs of leadership ability.

After the match fixing scandal and Sachin Tendulkar's stepping–down as captain, being the vice–captain of the team, he had to step up and take the wheel. 'Being the Vice–captain' was perhaps his only qualification for becoming Indian captain. As his compatriots, he was hurt, angry and frustrated by the events going around the team. The turmoil forced Ganguly to discover the angry man inside him. He decided to channel his anger. He glanced around him and saw a bunch of great players with big reputations but shy personalities. He found determination in Laxman, a fighter in Kumble, solidity in Dravid and inspiration in Tendulkar. One essential quality to rise above the filth India found itself in was lacking though. India was in desperate search of a little aggression and a bold 'in your face' attitude. It was very unlikely that these great players would be able to provide it. Ganguly had acquired his good boy image after four years of tireless efforts. Now, he needed to shed that image and become arrogant and blunt for real. For his vision, he knew he would have to take on established systems of Indian cricket, be it domestic cricket, the selection approach or the authority itself. To take on these mighty institutions, he needed to be that arrogant brat who refused to carry water. How hard he had tried to alienate himself from that perception that the state of Indian cricket now compelled him to be!

Indian cricket had not seen such outrage before. To steer out of it, Sourav Ganguly needed to be the captain India had never had before. He identified the first task even before taking over captaincy. The big names were all by his side. To succeed, he needed fearless, raw talent with fresh exuberance. He wanted players who did not give a damn about the world. The existing selection system did not allow him to have his way but the new arrogant Sourav Ganguly did not pay heed to the selection system. He convinced the authority to back his method of functioning. It was Sourav Ganguly's first altercation with the system and it was his first victory over the system. He now could focus on domestic cricket to select the new young guns.

THE YOUNG GUNS

THE SPEED MACHINE

Kapil Dev, India's best fast bowler of all time was not a 150 kmph bowler. He enjoyed the elusive skill to swing the ball both ways but his pace was medium. Every fast bowler produced by India in the past bowled at around 130 km/hr. While there seemed to be a factory churning out genuine speedsters just across the border, India battled to find even one but at the turn of the millennium, India finally caught sight of one.

In the Ranji Trophy season, there was a rare talent on display, a fast bowler who looked like a fast bowler with strong shoulders and a muscular physique. There was an unusual jump in his delivery stride but the decisive feature was the consistency of the speeds at which he bowled. The Indian domestic circuit had not seen a guy who bowled above 140 kmph. Zaheer Khan possessed two gifts that no former Indian fast bowler had, consistent high speeds and an ability to bowl yorkers at will. The Indian think–tank had identified its first soldier. Zaheer had ample ability to be the leader of Indian bowling attack someday. His impressive 35 wickets in Ranji Trophy season 1999–00 validated the team management's faith in him.

THE LIVEWIRE

A random dive from Ajay Jadeja, a few magical catches by Mohammad Azharuddin and an all heart effort from Robin Singh summed up India's fielding capabilities in 1990's. Even the likes of Kenya and Zimbabwe outperformed India in fielding. The fielding standards in international cricket were going up a few notches every day. India could not afford to lag behind. So, when Mohammad Kaif displayed his radiant agility in the field in the ICC Under–19 World Cup 2000 in Sri Lanka, the Indian team's captain and coach fell in love with him instantly. Kaif also brought an uncanny enthusiasm and energy in the team. How dearly India desired such positivity after the match fixing saga!

It was not only his fielding abilities that contributed to Kaif's recognition. His captaincy skills in India's Under–19 World Cup triumph were par excellence. It is very difficult for a captain to bring out the best in his team if he himself is struggling. Kaif was an exception. Despite his failures with the bat, he inspired his players to win the title. India needed such a calm head in the middle order. A fraction of the selection committee put a question mark on his ability to score in big pressure matches. With scores of 90 and 93 for India–B in probably the toughest Domestic tournament, Challenger Trophy 1999–00, he quashed every single doubt hurled at him!

THE DASHER

There was a man, fixated with the game of cricket. He could think of nothing else. His sole purpose in life was to represent India. He perhaps had the talent too to do so but in a country of a million lives, playing for India required something more than talent. He got selected to make his debut against New Zealand but it turned out to be his last test match for India. Just like millions of other aspirants, his dreams were shattered but unlike many, his hopes were not.

A few years after his dreadful debut, he took his son to his friend, Navjot Singh Sidhu and asked him to watch him play for a while. The poor kid's heart was in skating. His father hated the girly sport. He had thrown away the kid's medals, and a warning had followed," From now on, you play cricket, not this stupid game. If you don't, I will break your legs." But the threat had negligible effect on the kid as he didn't middle even a single ball. Navjot Singh Sidhu felt the pain of a father when he told him, "Sorry Yog, the boy does not have it in him."

The father was quiet the entire time while returning. The kid could not face the fact that he had failed his father. The realization of letting his father down made the boy take a decision; the decision to be a cricketer but his father had already decided it. He was constantly telling himself, 'Let's see how you do not become a cricketer.'

The same kid hit 5 fours and 5 sixes to the pace–laden Australian bowling attack in the semi–final of the ICC U–19 World Cup 2000 to score 58 from 25 balls. Yuvraj Singh possessed the flamboyance and hitting power the revamped Indian middle–order craved for. India had found the perfect boy for the new vision. Yogiraj Singh had made a cricketer out of his kid after all.

THE MAGIC MAN

Despite consistent performances in domestic cricket, Harbhajan Singh found it troublesome to perform at the international level but difficult was an apt adjective to describe the story of Harbhajan's life. At a tender age of 18 when a young player only wants to be on the ground every single day, Harbhajan Singh underwent tests to justify his bowling action. At 20, he became the head of his family after the death of his father. It brought him face to face with the harsh realities of life. The stark contrast in his domestic heroics and international performances was inexplicable. Sometimes, he went for plenty of runs. Other times, he went wicket–less for countless overs. Soon he saw himself out of favour for Indian selection. After a prolonged exile of more than 12 months from International Cricket, he faced another difficult choice. There was an opportunity of earning a livelihood in America, driving trucks. The task of taking care of his mother and five sisters was becoming harder each passing day which made the job offer more lucrative. He needed someone to guide him past his confusion in taking a decision. He found his saviour, albeit in a complete stranger till that point of time.

Sharjah 1998, is still remembered for the two blazing centuries by Sachin Tendulkar but there was another incident that captured the imaginations of Indian fans. After beating Ricky Ponting all ends up, Harbhajan, the aggressive Sardar, went out of his way and showed Ponting the direction of the Australian dressing room. An angry Ponting shoved his elbow in Harbhajan's chest. The incident faded from the memories of fans but one man remembered the spark Harbhajan had shown that day. When Harbhajan contemplated the most significant decision of his life, a theory rumoured to be backed by Sourav Ganguly, helped him take that decision.

"In Anil Kumble's absence, India needs wicket–taking spinners to pin Australia back. Harbhajan Singh is one such bowler who brings that aggression. He could be India's next frontline spinner." The statement put forward by the Indian think–tank made Harbhajan's choice easy. In fact, it left him with only one choice. Harbhajan Singh from that moment became India's leading spinner.

THE ENIGMA

"Agar ball mere zone main hai toh main marunga. Mujhe farak nahi padata main 1 pe hoon, 99 pe hoon ya 299 pe hoon." (If the ball is there to be hit, I will hit it. It does not matter if I am on 1, 99 or 299.) World cricket over the years had seen the demise of batsmen with such a philosophy. Batting is not so easy and someone with such a brazen approach was bound to fail. It did not matter to the purists that Virender Sehwag had scored 274 in a Duleep Trophy match (Season1999–00), the highest score of the tournament. It also did not matter that 15 days earlier, he had scored a merciless 187 from 175 balls against Punjab in a Ranji match. Cricketing

logic shouted at the top of its lungs that Virender Sehwag was bound to fail; that Virender Sehwag did not belong to international cricket. It would be foolish to pin your hopes on such an unpredictable batting approach but his domestic performances made him hard to ignore. One had to be insane to include him. Sourav Ganguly volunteered. When purists pointed out flaws in Sehwag's batting, the captain saw a huge star in the making.

The team looked ready. It comprised established players and gen–next identified by the captain, coach and selectors. There was a perfect mixture of experience and young exuberance. The job of these individuals was not only to take Indian cricket forward but also to demolish the demons of the last seven months. They had to make India believe in them again. The old monks and their new guns had to bring back the charm of India's most loved game. A near perfect setting awaited them. Away from the attention and questioning glares of Indian cricket fans and media, this new team was about to start a new crusade. In the unknown conditions of Nairobi, India started its hardest battle, the battle to win back its respect.

ICC CHAMPIONS TROPHY 2000
–
THE FIRST SPARK

A man stood outside his boss's cabin for a while. He was nervous and in a dilemma. His decision to raise an alarm was impulsive but as he approached the newly appointed President's cabin, he had started having second thoughts about it. Maybe he needed to do more legwork before bringing up the issue. He had not taken the President's prior appointment but the crisis at hand was severe and called for immediate attention. The man heard footsteps nearing his cabin door. The boss came out, gave a nodding smile and started walking away. His moment had arrived. Everything depended upon his efficiency in conveying the problem to the boss. Telling the boss about the failures of his own organization was a difficult task. The course of his discussion was going to decide the future of cricket's governing body. He gathered all the courage possible and said," Sir, if you have a minute or two, I would like to talk to you about something."

Jagmohan Dalmiya could not believe what he had just heard. The International Cricket Council was running short of funds to meet its expenses! He had been briefed on the financial troubles of the ICC but failed to judge the severity of the crisis. How could things have come to this? The situation commanded swift action. He was an astute businessman and a resourceful thinker. He required every ounce of his acumen to find a way. The governing body of an international sport faced financial problems and to get to know the gravity of the problem from somebody else embarrassed him even more. As the man kept talking, Jagmohan Dalmiya scanned various ideas in his mind to solve the problem. Of the many ideas which ran through his mind during that discussion, one fascinated him the most. He assured his colleague he would look into the matter. As soon as the fellow left the conference room, he took out a pen and paper and started writing something. A blurred idea to revive ICC's financial condition transformed into a master plan within a few minutes. In half an hour, Jagmohan Dalmiya chalked out the blue print of the solution to ICC's financial woes. A Knock–Out ODI tournament involving all test playing nations was his genius plan. The name,' ICC Mini– World Cup' was his masterstroke.

INDIA VS KENYA – PRE–QUARTER FINAL – 2000 EDITION

The Wills International Cup 1998 was a grand success as Jagmohan

Dalmiya had anticipated. He took it one step further in the next edition. Besides the 9 Test playing nations, two leading associates, Bangladesh and Kenya took part in the Year 2000 edition. To spread the game of cricket to these associate countries, ICC chose Kenya to host the tournament. For Kenya, the event offered a sense of belonging to international cricket. For India it was the beginning of a new dawn. An unexplored venue and a new format generated good buzz around the tournament. The tournament was bifurcated in two parts. The top 5 teams in ICC Rankings qualified for Quarter–Finals. The bottom four teams and two associate nations had to play pre–quarterfinals to fill out three vacant spots. The format reflected the appalling state of Indian cricket. India's first match was a pre quarter–final against the hosts.

Indian teams of the past, on most occasions, used to play with two medium pacers and two spinners irrespective of the venue and conditions. The Indian squad for the Champions Trophy 2000 included two experienced medium pacers in Venkatesh Prasad and Ajit Agarkar and two experienced spinners in Anil Kumble and Sunil Joshi. Choosing these four bowlers was an easier choice. That's what any of Ganguly's predecessors would have done. Indian cricket was facing difficult times which entailed bold decisions that would set Ganguly apart from his predecessors and benefit Indian cricket. Sourav Ganguly made a brave selection call. Zaheer Khan responded in the best possible manner. His debut figures of 3 for 48, gave India an easy target of 209. Indian batting veterans chased it with utmost ease. 31 months ago, Kenya had stunned India in Gwalior. The match fixing scandal had made fans cynical about that result in hindsight. Though the Indian team felt redeemed by knocking Kenya out of the Champions Trophy 2000 in its home, Indian fans still looked skeptical and hurt. It was evident that India needed a much more consequential result than thrashing a minnow to earn the respect of hurt Indians.

INDIA VS AUSTRALIA

The last decade of the millennium witnessed the rise of two prominent players in international cricket. Sachin Tendulkar took the level of batting to new heights and Glen McGrath redefined the word accuracy. To the disappointment of world cricket, both never came face to face at their peak. Sachin had got the better of McGrath in the 1996 World Cup but McGrath was struggling with injuries in that phase. Glen McGrath had owned Sachin Tendulkar in the 1999 tour but back then, Sachin was troubled by criticism on his captaincy and team selection. ICC Champions Trophy 2000 was the first time both of them faced each other at their deadliest best.

The focal strength of McGrath was his accuracy. He seldom missed the good length spot. Back in time when the first 15 overs were vital to set up the tempo, Glen McGrath's miserly first spell often dented the opponent's chance of a good score. Sachin Tendulkar decided to test McGrath's accuracy. He had been working on a special technique to counter Glen McGrath. The 1st Quarter Final of the ICC Champions Trophy 2000 was when he decided to implement it.

He first tried to hit McGrath without moving his feet. His top edge carried the ball to the stands, fortunately. The intent was surprising and refreshing. He then gifted world cricket a method to counter Glen McGrath by using his feet and hitting him over his head for a massive six. Glen McGrath's consistent accuracy made his line and length predictable. Sachin Tendulkar exploited the predictability with a similar shot again, this time for a four. More than those two strokes, another pull shot for six and a glorious cover drive for four, what astonished India was Sachin Tendulkar's response to Glen McGrath's sledging. Sachin Tendulkar, who used to walk away from any bowler trying to sledge him, confronted McGrath and gave a few words back. That was something new. That was something different, but that felt good. Sachin Tendulkar, India's calmest monk had given a few words back to an Australian. The state of Indian cricket had made even Sachin Tendulkar angry but his anger was a good sign.

Sourav Ganguly had made a brave call by selecting Zaheer Khan against Kenya. He had made another bold call in that match but Yuvraj Singh did not get an opportunity to bat and prove his captain right. Against Australia, after the blistering start given by Sachin Tendulkar, India lost its way with the fall of four crucial wickets. Yuvraj Singh got the opportunity he was waiting for. All the senior batsmen were gone, and he faced the mighty Australian bowling.

Yuvraj Singh, apart from the traditional Indian gift of silken timing, also possessed a rare gift for an Indian batsman – the ability to play short pitch bowling. His flicks, cuts and drives assured India of a star in the making. His 84, against the best bowling attack in the world justified the captain's call. Yuvraj Singh's first innings gave India 265 runs to defend. It looked too easy for the legendary Australian batting line–up but it was not the same old India that Australia was dealing with. There was a new dawn in Indian cricket and Zaheer and Yuvraj were about to introduce Australia to it.

In a run chase that ebbed and flowed from one side to the other, four images got etched in the minds of Indian fans.

> For eternity, India had looked at Jonty Rhodes, Ricky Ponting and wished it had a fielder who could dive full length to take those brilliant catches and who could hit the stumps directly from any corner of the field. Yuvraj Singh produced both, to dismiss Ian Harvey and the ever so dangerous Michael Bevan.
>
> India had always looked in awe at the fierce fast bowlers of its opponents and hoped one day, it would find one of its own. Zaheer Khan's fast full–length ball shattered Steve Waugh's stumps and fulfilled India's hopes. India's search of a fast bowler was over at last.
>
> Sourav Ganguly gave Yuvraj a bone crushing hug when he ran Bevan out. Zaheer Khan received an even tighter embrace when he bowled Steve Waugh. India finally found a captain who expressed his emotions just like any of them would. They related to him instantly. The India V/s Australia game in the ICC Champions trophy achieved two results. Australia was knocked out of the tournament and Indian fans started to rediscover their lost love for the game.

INDIA V/S SOUTH AFRICA – SEMI FINAL

The new talent, on which Ganguly pinned his ambitions, carried India to the Semi Finals. Now was the occasion for the veterans to exhibit their prowess. The task ahead was monumental though as South Africa sported arguably the best all–round bowling attack in the world; comprising Shaun Pollock, Allan Donald, Jacques Kallis and Lance Klusener. Only one fact tipped the scales in India's favour; South Africa's disastrous record in ICC events. Sourav Ganguly was aware that he could not depend on such an unpredictable factor. For India, this tournament was a means to erase the memories of last few months. For Ganguly, it provided a chance to get

India out of the mudslinging taking place back home. Nobody inspires better than a captain. Sourav Ganguly played a sublime innings of 141 against South Africa to give India hope again. For the first time in the last 7 months, Indian fans cheered an Indian inning. The frustration of the last 7 months was visible in each of Ganguly's 11 fours and 6 massive sixes. His every single shot relieved Indian fans of the agony they had gone through in the last 7 months. Each and every shot of his brought them closer and closer to their first love. Sourav Ganguly carried India to the finals of an ICC event after 17 years. It gave Indian fans something to look forward to. After 200 days of sorrow, Indian fans awaited a cricket match like they used to, in the past.

INDIA V/S NEW ZEALAND – FINAL

ICC Knock–Out 2000 was India's story so far. It was pitted against New Zealand, another unexpected finalist which increased India's expectations. An ICC Trophy was an ideal way to get rid of the match fixing ghosts and nobody knew it better than the Indian team. The veterans again had to assume the chunk of responsibility. Young players lacked the experience to absorb the pressure of a final of an international tournament. Sourav Ganguly stood up to the challenge once again. His determined strokes had elegance and class. He caressed the off–side field as only he could. Sachin Tendulkar at the other end played at his dominating best. Both openers built a solid foundation of 141 runs in merely 26.3 overs by playing pure cricketing strokes; thus, assuming absolute zero risk.

New Zealand bowlers looked incapable of picking up a wicket. Run out seemed the only possible mode of dismissal. New Zealand hit jackpot with two. Two run outs and Sourav Ganguly's untimely wicket snatched the momentum away from India. India's earlier wins in the tournament were so dominant that its weaknesses were never exposed. The lower middle–order of Vinod Kambli, Robin Singh and Vijay Dahiya lacked the ability to give India a thrust again. The innings which promised over 350 runs at one time folded out for 264! New Zealand had crawled its way back into the match.

After Indian batting lost its course in the latter part of the first innings, the start given by Indian bowlers raised hopes. Venkatesh Prasad, Anil Kumble cut out half the New Zealand batting for half the runs required but a certain Chris Cairns had other ideas. He was on painkillers in the match but Indian bowlers looked in more pain when he smashed all of them to every part of Nairobi Gymkhana Club Ground. Along with Chris Harris, he conjured one of the most stellar fightbacks with a 122 runs partnership. Chris Cairns' 102 led New Zealand to its first ICC trophy. India had played extraordinary cricket in the tournament and it took a miraculous century from Chris Cairns to hand India its first loss of the tournament. India had set out to achieve two results in the tournament; to win the trophy and to win back Indian fans. Chris Cairns dented its first goal but India's performance in the tournament managed the second. Considering the circumstances surrounding Indian cricket, it was more important than winning a trophy. ICC Knock–Out 2000 achieved its bit. Indian cricket was brought back on the right path.

AUSTRALIA'S TOUR OF INDIA – THE EPIC SERIES

"Australia is scheduled to play here next in 2004. I am not sure whether Steve Waugh will be around at that time. This is the only place he is yet to conquer. This is going to be his final frontier." One of the Australian journalists signified the importance of Australia's tour of India, 2001.

THE HISTORY

It eventually occurred in 1995. The remarkable run of West Indies was at last broken. West Indies lost a test series and its number 1 ranking after 15 years. Mark Taylor's Australian side triumphed 2–1 and with that victory, Australia assumed the reigns. It was proclaimed to be the best test team in the world. Australia's next away test series after the heroic Caribbean win, was against India. How difficult could it be for a team who had demolished the strong West Indies! It turned out to be very difficult as Anil Kumble and company spun a web of spin around every Australian batsman. The team that dethroned West Indies lost to India 1–0. Its invincible tag was put to rest in a matter of 18 months. India had given Australia a wake–up call. It was not so easy to beat India in India.

In 1998, Australia came back to India as a fiercer champion. Invincibility was now its identity and it beamed with confidence to beat India in India and why not! It had one of the greatest leg spinners in its side, a rare luxury for a travelling captain. The battle of Sachin Tendulkar and Shane Warne had already gathered epic proportion. Poor Australia received a shock of life when Indian batsmen, led by Sachin, tormented Shane Warne. He had not suffered such a ferocious mauling ever; so much so that Shane Warne confessed to fears of having nightmares of Sachin hitting him for sixes. India's batting icon managed to unsettle a tough Aussie. His team put a question mark on Australia's invincibility. The invincible Australian side lost again 2–1.

WAR OF WORDS

Those two losses hurt. While Australia dominated every single country with ridiculous ease, winning a test series in India remained elusive. By the time the 2001 series began, Australia had transformed itself into the undisputed king of cricket. It had won 15 consecutive tests before it turned up in Mumbai. Steve Waugh's men possessed all elements to produce the impossible this time around. A shoulder injury and consequent surgery of India's leading spinner increased Steve Waugh's chances of realising Australia's long pending dream. In the absence of his main man, the Indian captain pinned his hopes on a rookie Off–Spinner. Though the condition of the pitches worried Steve Waugh a little, another very crucial factor was in his favour.

The Indian test team had no structure. The openers looked scratchy. Rahul Dravid, for the first time in his test career was going through the crisis of lack of form. V.V.S. Laxman's position and role in the team remained uncertain. Above all, it was Sourav Ganguly's toughest challenge in his young captaincy career. It was not yet fully known how he would meet it. His first press conference before the series served as an appetizer.

"They have won most of their games at home, beaten West Indies 5–0 at home, beaten India, Pakistan at home. They toured here in '96 and lost. They toured here in '98 and lost. So obviously that's going to be at the back of their mind. I agree they are playing good cricket for the last 12 months but it's going to be a different ball game when they come here," Sourav Ganguly retorted to a question on Australia's streak of 15 successive test wins.

"You will find out when the test match starts, I think. Enough of talk has been going on about the wickets. I didn't read that. I haven't read it. The only thing I'll say is how does he know what's happening from Australia? We've never said anything yet. I don't think it's possible for him to comment on that by sitting in Australia." Sourav Ganguly's blunt response to Steve Waugh's comment on Indian Board influencing the preparation of pitches threw light on how Ganguly would approach the series. He was going to give it back to the Australians despite his own worries of the composition of his team, untested openers and a novice leading spinner. It took the nation by surprise as it was not used to such forthright public answers. It did not matter to him that his team lacked the ability to back his talk. He had set the ball rolling. India was about to encounter the toughest chapter of its revival story. A win here was sure to roll a forward path. A loss was sure to trigger the murky past. In any prospect, a fascinating contest was guaranteed. Sadly, the best batsman of all time decided not to be witness to this epic series. One day prior to the eve of the Mumbai test, Don Bradman travelled to heavenly abode. Cricket lost its the most precious jewel but life had to resume two days after.

And so, it began. After all the press conferences, all the hype around the series, India and Australia finally faced each other on the field of play. What India witnessed for the next one month was cricket at an unparalleled level and a series that defined Indian cricket for the next era.

MUMBAI TEST – NIGHTMARES ARE RETURNED WITH PLEASURE

DAY ONE

Contrary to the murmurs of Ganguly influencing the preparation of the pitches, Steve Waugh received a pleasant surprise in the form of a seamer friendly Mumbai pitch. He had no hesitation in bowling first. He bore the risk of batting last on the Mumbai pitch because he knew he held a lethal fast bowling attack. India faced its first challenge on the first day of the first test. Shiv Sunder Das and Sadagoppan Ramesh had to confront Glen McGrath and company. Many experienced openers had found that task difficult. It was certainly beyond the competence of the current Indian openers. Australian fast bowlers sent the top three Indian batsmen back inside 14 overs. Ganguly himself could not back his talk as Australia steamrolled the first session. At 62 for 4, India had only one hope as Sachin Tendulkar looked in menacing touch for his 19 not out.

V.V.S. Laxman tried his best to stay with Sachin but looked a pale shadow of his Sydney outing. In the partnership of 75, he scored only 20 and then, the hope of a fightback came clattering down as Glen McGrath upstaged his arch rival. In India's 139 for 6, Sachin scored 76. Sourav Ganguly's attempt to change the perspective of Indian cricket seemed to go in vain. His big talks failed to inspire his team. Australia displayed another of its vintage performances, reminding Ganguly why it had won 15 consecutive tests. Shane Warne, who had had nightmares of Sachin 3 years ago, finished with inning's best figures of 4 for 47. India's capitulation at 176 on Day One warranted only one result.

DAY TWO

The Indian batting had worried many, even before the match started. Hence, its meek surrender did not come as a surprise. The bigger worry was its bowling. In the absence of Kumble, Ganguly had put his hopes on Harbhajan Singh, whose previous record did not suggest that he was worthy of it. But his first spell on day two gave foretaste of his talent.

In perhaps the best batting conditions, Harbhajan Singh got the ball to grip, bounce and spin. Justin Langer's lunging forward defense was a characteristic Australian response to an off–spinner and his edge to slip was a characteristic Australian dismissal on Indian pitches. The next ball saw a classic test match dismissal in India. Mark Waugh tried to flick a quick turning ball and Ganguly at leg slip latched onto a brilliant diving catch, continuing India's long lineage of splendid close–in catchers.

Australia's score of 99 for 5 brought loads of belief. Mathew Hayden and Adam Gilchrist had not played a test match in India till then and the cricketing world did not need a reminder of the hassles first timers faced playing in India but the world also did not need a reminder of the Australian spirit. Two left–handers started a counter attack of unbelievable quality. At 1.88 meters, Hayden was the tallest Australian batsman. He used his reach to his advantage by sweeping Harbhajan ferociously which put Harbhajan off the line. Harbhajan tried to induce him on the front foot and Hayden kept sweeping him. Hard–hitting sweeps rattled Harbhajan as he tried too many variations in his length and speed. Adam Gilchrist at the other end was ready to pounce on anything loose.

India was taken aback by the audacity of Gilchrist's counter–attack. It was unbelievable that the man was playing his first test in India, on a pitch that had started turning viciously. The energy infused by Harbhajan's brilliant spell turned into dropped shoulders and worried faces in no time. India began to feel the Mumbai heat whilst Hayden and Gilchrist made it seem like they were batting in Melbourne. Both scored outstanding centuries and put Australia in a commanding position with a lead of 173. The Indian openers' endeavour to apply themselves and to stay on the pitch in the second innings was credible but the challenge in front of them was monumental. Both lost their wickets on Day Two itself. Australia, in two days of ruthless cricket cast aside all doubts raised on its ability to perform in India.

DAY THREE

Mumbai in those days rarely received untimely rains and hence the only chance of India's escape was a distant dream. Dravid somehow survived the first session. He looked clueless throughout. Sachin Tendulkar again looked in absolute command. But soon after lunch, the result of the match became apparent. India came out blazing in the first seven overs of the second session as Sachin got some wonderful strokes going. But just when India nurtured a thought of a counter–attack a` la Hayden & Gilchrist, Sachin lost his wicket in the weirdest manner possible. Mark Waugh bowled a half tracker which cried to be hit out of the stadium. Sachin got everything right on the ball but his powerful shot hit short leg who was trying to get out of the line of fire. The ball rebounded off his back and looped up in the air. Ponting ran and dived to take an absolute stunner. The bizarre nature of the dismissal symbolized India's outing so far. It took Australia another 27 overs to wrap up the Indian innings and further 7 overs to chase the target. And with that, it equaled the record of 16 consecutive test match wins.

One episode in Mumbai test summarized India's performance. In India's second innings, Dravid stood his ground after Michael Slater claimed a catch. Replays showed that there was enough doubt over the fairness of the catch and hence Dravid was given not out. An angry Michael Slater charged towards Dravid, hurling furious words at him. A visibly shocked Dravid did not respond to Slater's outburst. He did not try to give it back to Slater who had violated the basic code of a sportsman's conduct. Was Dravid calm or could not gather the courage to answer Slater back? India similarly, was blown away by an aggressive Australian performance. Was India stunned or did it not have the metal to counter Australian aggression? The manner in which Australia whipped India worried Indian fans. The famous legend of India's invincibility at home ran a risk of getting reduced to a fiction. India needed to do something. Sourav Ganguly needed to do something.

KOLKATA TEST – THE MATCH THAT GAVE INDIA BELIEF

The Mumbai test brought the wound out in the open. India did not possess a team to take on Australia. India needed heroes and individual brilliance to steer it. It was an inherent problem in Indian cricket; individual heroism ahead of team performance. Ganguly had vowed to eliminate it. What a grim irony it was that he now depended upon individual performances to stay in the series. But to rattle the Aussies, India called for something more than on–field performances. Australia had toyed with India in Mumbai and Sourav Ganguly had hated every minute of it. He grew irritated with every passing day due to the extensive scrutiny of India's Mumbai debacle. He had to get on equal terms with the rampant Australian aggression.

A simple delay in turning up for the toss in Kolkata did the trick. It left Steve Waugh fuming as Ganguly took his time to appear. He won the mind game but was his team capable of winning the real game?

DAY ONE

Australia's opening stand of 103, after its Mumbai dominance was not at all surprising. A 90 runs partnership for the second wicket followed the big opening stand. Australia's score of 193 for 1, made India restless. Australia threatened to run away with the match and the series on Day One itself. When all expectations diminished, Ganguly asked the 21–year–old Harbhajan to save India. He threw a young off–spinner into the deep end. To the utter surprise of all, Ganguly discovered his first hero.

It commenced with a mistimed shot from Hayden and concluded with a hat–trick. Harbhajan Singh, the young spinner turned the game on its head with 5 wickets in just 18 overs. His hat–trick was the first ever by an Indian bowler in test cricket. It consisted of a plum leg before of Ponting, a dubious leg before of Gilchrist and an unbelievable diving short leg catch by Sadagoppan Ramesh. From 193 for 1 to 252 for 7, Australia began its infamous collapse in India. India, for the first time in the series held a commanding position.

DAY TWO & THREE

While the Australian batsmen came and went in a hurry at the fag–end of Day One, Steve Waugh stood at the other end and watched. But even in the frenzy of the collapse, his eyes told a different tale. He somehow seemed confident amidst the chaos at the packed Eden Gardens. His confidence perhaps stemmed from India's hapless batting in Mumbai. The real source of his assuredness turned out to be the gritty determination of Jason Gillespie who walked in next. He stayed at the crease for 147 balls to score 46. His partnership with Steve Waugh drastically changed the complexion of the game in Australia's favour. Jason Gillespie's stout resilience enabled Steve Waugh to score one of the bravest centuries. Even after Harbhajan's exploits on Day One, India stared at a first innings total of 445. Sourav Ganguly again, was in need of a hero.

The openers were not likely to be Ganguly's heroes. Dravid tried his heart out to be one but lack of confidence did not allow him to rise to the occasion. When India's ultimate batting hero fell to the same fate as that of the openers, Dravid and India's captain; no hero was left for India to salvage the match. After getting crushed within 3 days in Mumbai, India suffered the humiliation of a follow–on in its home. The heroes that India was so desperate to find to save its nose were nowhere to be seen. But what the entire country failed to notice in India's miserable 171 in the first innings captured Ganguly's imagination. V.V.S. Laxman's classy 59 reminded him of a 1975 classic film, Chupke Chupke.

The Hindi movies in the decades of 70s and 80s were dominated by India's angry young man, Amitabh Bachchan. He carried so many films on his shoulders but once in a while, films like Chupke Chupke released casting Amitabh in a supporting role. He blossomed in such roles as well. His performances in such films many times brought out the best from the man who played the lead role. Chupke Chupke is till date remembered as a Dharmendra film, despite an outstanding performance by Amitabh Bachchan. That was the trick, wasn't it? Give your lead player a supporting role and cast a new fellow into the lead role. Sourav Ganguly hit the nail on its head by identifying his Amitabh and his Dharmendra!

So, after following on, when Sadagoppan Ramesh's valiant effort (a 43–ball 30) ended at 16.4 overs, V.V.S. Laxman walked in at No. 3. Ganguly had given Laxman a lead role. The move ran a massive risk of India losing the series and Ganguly losing the captaincy but Ganguly trusted his new lead. Trust transformed into confidence as Laxman started showing flashes of his Sydney innings. The captain himself attempted to attain the highest levels of concentration and grit. His resolute 48 runs were not enough though, as India ended Day Three at 254 for 4. V.V.S. Laxman was unbeaten on a majestic 109 and Sourav Ganguly's Amitabh Bachchan, playing a supporting role this time, was on 7.

DAY FOUR

Australia had packed off India within just three days in Mumbai. It had enforced a follow–on in Kolkata on Day Three. It had been astonishingly easy for Australia so far. Many members of the Australian squad wondered what the fuss of playing in India was all about. For the sake of competition, Australia would have wished for an Indian fight back. So, when the first session on Day Four went wicket–less for 122 runs, Australia seemed to have enjoyed it. In the ten sessions played so far in the match, India won its second. Australia finally saw an opponent willing to fight. But when it could not scalp a single wicket in the second session for another 115 runs, Australia looked a tad bit worried. The Australian bowlers seemed tired. India led by 217 runs and playing last on an Indian pitch posed a considerable threat. India had staged a fightback but it was time for Australia to end the fairytale. However, when India scored another 98 runs without losing a wicket in the third session, Australia gauged the gravity of the situation. India had not only fought back but suddenly taken a commanding charge of the test. This was the day Australia was reintroduced to test cricket in India. This was the time Australia was introduced to 'Day Four miracles' at Eden Gardens. This was the day Australia was introduced to the pair of V.V.S. Laxman and Rahul Dravid.

India had begun Day Four in anticipation of a humiliating loss in its fortress. The only aspect to look forward to on Day Four was Laxman's batting. His century on Day Three was loaded with class and elegance. On Day Four, he continued from where he had left. On top of all his front foot drives to reverse swinging balls, his disdainful pull shots to lethal short pitch bowling, and his wrist flicks to the fast bowlers, stood the manner in which he attacked the greatest leg spinner of all time. Only an Indian could imagine dancing down the pitch to an away spinning ball and then placing it against the spin between mid–on and mid–wicket despite Shane Warne's round–the–wicket line which created an impossible angle for the batsman to hit. Where at one end Laxman made batting look as easy as sipping a cup of tea, Rahul Dravid at the other end faced an enormous challenge. The toughest test for any sportsman is to get hold of a mind muddled with low self–confidence. He had spent 6 hours and 47 minutes at the crease in this series so far which had yielded only 73 runs. Fortunately for him, he walked in a situation where minutes consumed in the middle were more precious than the runs he scored. The fluency and ease of Laxman's innings did wonders for Dravid, as it allowed him time to spend in the middle. He needed to hold one end up which was his favourite job. Gillespie's opening spell tested every ounce of his technique but he hung–in. With every minute spent on the pitch, Rahul Dravid's conviction grew which reflected in the strokes he played. The feet that searched the pitch of the ball so far, started to move with authority. When he played his signature flick to mid–wicket, India heaved a sigh of relief. Its mainstay of test batting was back and if there was any doubt about it, his flick to Shane Warne's full toss stamped his return to form. Significant it was because his tangled feet movement in the first innings had converted a similar ball into a yorker that had dismissed him. The decisiveness in the foot work this time around gave him a boundary.

The Rahul Dravid that the world knew was a calm person who had his head firmly on his shoulders. He never got carried away or pressurized by the bowlers' antics. How dearly India remembered his stone face when Allan Donald had come charging towards him, spitting fire! India had witnessed another such incident in the Mumbai test as well, when Michael Slater lost it but Dravid just stood at the crease, maintaining his composure. It was hence startling to see an angry Dravid showing his bat to the dressing room when he reached his century. As uncharacteristically animated Rahul Dravid celebrated his century on Day Four, he thought of the little pat his captain had given him 24 hours ago when he walked in to face the most difficult innings of his life till date. He did not have any confidence in himself but found his captain investing all the confidence in him. The captain had made him search for his self–belief and boy! He found it in grand style. The celebration reflected his frustration but even in that angry moment, not a single word was uttered by him. He had answered his critics and he had repaid the faith of his captain.

The television channel that broadcasted the match was a paid channel and many were not able to watch this historic day. In a time when '24X7 news channels' was an unknown phenomenon, Door Darshan (the national TV channel) was an angel. It aired the first and the last hour of each day's play. For all those who saw Dravid's struggle against Jason Gillespie in the first hour were speechless in disbelief when they caught sight of both the batsmen unbeaten before the commencement of the last hour on Day Four. Many mistook the live match for highlights. As it turned out, India had produced one of the mightiest days in its cricketing history. V.V.S. Laxman became the highest individual scorer for India, surpassing Sunil Gavaskar. Rahul Dravid scored his first test century against Australia. The unbeaten partnership of 357 runs was the highest for any wicket by an Indian pair against Australia. The record–shattering 4th day ensured that the side that followed on a day before, now led by 315 runs.

DAY FIVE

No team had ever scored 300 runs in the fourth innings of a test match in

India. Still, Ganguly decided not to declare. May be, he waited for Laxman's triple century. When Laxman fell on 281, Ganguly still did not declare. May be, it was Rahul Dravid's double hundred he waited for. When Dravid got out on 180, Ganguly still decided to continue. India consumed 13 overs on Day Five and many believed, lost the golden opportunity to level the series. As the Australian openers, after the Indian captain eventually declared, took the score to 74 in 23 overs in its second innings, the crowd began to panic. Sourav Ganguly, on the other hand, trusted his off–spinner to end the Australian innings in the remaining day's play.

Harbhajan threatened to take a wicket on every single ball he bowled before he found Michael Slater's inside edge to get Australia one down for 74. Justine Langer hit two massive sixes to Venkatapathy Raju but his discomfort against Harbhajan was visible. His half paddle–half sweep shot ended his miserable stay at the crease. Venkatapathy Raju was nonexistent for the large part of the match till a sharp arm ball, perhaps the best ball of his career, trapped Mark Waugh in front of his wickets reducing Australia to 116 for 3. Australia lost three wickets quickly but it also played out 43 overs. India still required 7 more wickets, and it had only one session to do so. The late declaration threatened to haunt Sourav Ganguly.

In the 3rd over of the third and final session of this epic test, began India's final surge to complete its greatest comeback. Steve Waugh's effort to flick Harbhajan to fine leg got intercepted by Hemang Badani. Steve Waugh's brave hundred had snatched the momentum from India in the first innings. Seeing his back brought joy to the Indian team. Ricky Ponting had looked lost ever since he stepped foot on Indian shores. Harbhajan Singh sensed his vulnerability and produced the best ball of his spell. Ponting's squat–sweep was hard to explain but the Indian team did not seem to bother for an explanation. Australia lost half its side for 166 and it still had 30 overs to play.

Even with the euphoria of two quick wickets, the captain sensed one glaring problem which had the potential of stealing this match away from him. Harbhajan Singh, Sourav Ganguly's lead spinner bowled with a lot of character but lacked support from the other end. A part–time bowler was bowling from the other end but with two wickets in Harbhajan's over, cricketing logic asked him to bring back his second specialist spinner. The previous two overs by India's part–time leg spinner had seen plenty of spin and grip. Sourav Ganguly had defied cricketing logic every single time in this match. He again decided to do so, even when it ran a risk of putting a part–time leg spinner against two left–handed batsmen known for their big hitting.

A good release of the ball is half the battle won for any leg spinner. To Ganguly's delight, Sachin got a brilliant drift on his first two balls. His third though was an absolute genius. It pitched on spot, turned to perfection and sneaked through Gilchrist's booming sweep. Ganguly's ploy to give Sachin another over paid off. He now could bring back his regular bowler, or so everybody thought. He persisted with Sachin. Sachin gladly obliged.

Mathew Hayden had scored runs for fun in the series so far and the sweep shot had fetched him a bulk of those runs. He had employed it well to the ball turning away from him. To play it to the ball turning into him was even simpler. But Sachin's enticingly tossed up ball slipped through his big sweep and India attained a real chance of winning the match. For anyone who thought the match had provided every bit of drama, twists and turns so far, Sachin provided another incredible moment. Sachin Tendulkar the batsman had proved his upper hand on Shane Warne. Sachin Tendulkar, the leg spinner, matched him.

When Shane Warne saw a half pitch ball pitching outside his off stump, he got into position and waited for the ball to turn away so he could cut it with all the power in the world. Somewhere between the moment he rocked on to his back foot to cut and the moment the ball pitched, he realised what he had done. He figured out why the ball was so short. Sachin had released it from the back of his hand. Warne changed his stance as quickly as possible to bring his bat to the ball but it was too late. By the time his bat came down, the ball had already hit his pads, the fielders had already appealed, and the umpire had already given him out. It was cricket's mischievous irony. Sachin Tendulkar dismissed Shane Warne on a googly. The drama reached a higher octane. Australia was 174 for 8.

Eden Gardens often provided such turnarounds but this by far was the most remarkable. Australia had controlled the first three days of the match but India's miraculous fourth day had restored the balance. The match deserved a fitting final hour and Australia's three fast bowlers, often ridiculed for their batting, obliged. Jason Gillespie teamed up with Michael Kasprowicz and devised a unique strategy for Harbhajan. Both of them planted their front foot way forward and started defending. It worked for 9 crucial overs until Jason Gillespie hit it straight in the hands of the short–

leg. Australia still required 15 overs to play out and Glen McGrath walked in. For the first seven of those 15 overs, India waited for McGrath to make a mistake. Instead, it got strenuous defending from the man. It takes courage to admit one's mistakes and correct them. Sourav Ganguly realised his error of waiting for things to happen. The lack of time was making Harbhajan Singh anxious as only 8 overs remained. Sourav Ganguly recognized Harbhajan Singh's anxiety. His last few balls were pushed through on to the pads of McGrath and Kasprowicz. Both found them easy to defend. Every ball played by both the tail–enders heaped the pressure back on India. In the tense atmosphere, Ganguly rolled out his final master–stroke. When India was in frantic search of the last wicket, he took his leading spinner out of the attack and brought himself on. With only 6 overs to survive, the last Australian pair was more than happy to face a medium pacer on a turning track. But the actual move happened elsewhere. As Kasprowicz defended the last ball of the next over and went to McGrath to have a chat, he saw Harbhajan walking to the other end. Sourav Ganguly had given Harbhajan a change of ends and a few minutes to regroup.

Harbhajan's first ball from the other end made the captain happy. Harbhajan had used those few minutes to reassess. He realized his mistake and returned to his original speed and flight. McGrath drove it well to extra–cover. A cover drive from a right–handed batsman is every off–spinner's delight. The risk is always higher for a batsman to play against the spin. He bowled the next one a bit quicker and McGrath padded it up. Now Harbhajan knew McGrath's response to a faster ball. He needed to be more accurate. The third ball of his over produced the loudest roar India had ever heard. The attendance at Eden Gardens was over a hundred thousand people and every single one of them roared like never before. It was only the third occasion in the history of test cricket that a team had won a match after being asked to follow on. Curiously, all three had been against Australia. The five days at Eden Gardens were more than a match for India. They gave India a reason to believe. They gave India a captain to trust. A simple uproar in the stadium did not do justice to the momentous occasion. A fitting celebration was needed to carve the moment for eternity. Every piece of paper in the ground was burned to raise a fire. The fire symbolized the determination of V.V.S. Laxman and Rahul Dravid to defy the inevitable on that fateful fourth day. The fire symbolized the eagerness and enthusiasm of Harbhajan Singh to perform at the international stage. The fire symbolized India's resurgence from the ashes.

CHENNAI TEST – THE FITTING END

Nobody wished to get over Eden Gardens. Nobody could stop raving about India's greatest test match so far. No doubt there were other contenders for the spot! There was the Madras Test of 1952, India's first test win or the first overseas series win in New Zealand in 1967–68. Then, there were tours of West Indies and England in 1971. But nothing matched India's fightback in Kolkata. The hysteria of the match made the nation forget about the 3rd Test in Chennai. India was not sure whether it could handle more tension and drama. Drama higher than Kolkata was not possible. Or was it? Chennai was ready for a fitting end.

DAY ONE

More often than not, cricket is driven by momentum. Kolkata had given India plenty of it. Australia realised how dangerous India could be at home with the momentum. It was imperative that Australia countered India's ascendency with aggression of its own. The giant accepted the responsibility as he hammered the Indian bowlers left, right and centre. India sported three spinners and only one fast bowler in Zaheer Khan, though it wasn't a secret who the real threat was. Hayden, unlike any other Australian batsman, had had a measure of Harbhajan in the series so far. He used an attacking route to unsettle him. For all the momentum India had, Australia shunned it on Day One of the Chennai Test. Australia's 326 on Day One left India stunned.

DAY TWO

Australia advanced on Day One as if Kolkata had not happened. India prayed for a helping hand to pull itself out of the hole. It came in the 6th over, in the least imaginable manner. Steve Waugh tried to sweep Harbhajan, failed, stood back up, saw the ball going on to the stumps and pushed it aside with his hand. He saved himself from getting out bowled but forgot the Cricket Law named 'Handled the ball'. Steve Waugh's right hand gave India the tiny opening it so badly wanted.

0, 1, 0, 0, 0, 3. Those were the scores of the next six Australian batsmen. Australia surrendered its last 6 wickets for 51 runs, out of which Mathew

Hayden alone scored 47 to register his first double hundred and continue his romance with India. But the Australian collapse stole the limelight away from one of the most destructive innings from an overseas batsman in India. Australia had snatched India's momentum on Day One. India won it back in the first session of Day Two. The stage was set for the genius to grace the scene. In India's celebrated win in Kolkata, India's greatest batsman had absolutely zero batting contribution. Chennai, his favourite hunting ground, provided him an excellent setting to have his say.

DAY THREE

Day Three belonged to one man. The ominous form he had shown in Mumbai had deserted him in haste in Kolkata. He found it again in Chennai. In the inhuman temperatures of Chennai, the man demonstrated his vintage best against his favourite bowling attack. Glen McGrath's superb reverse swinging deliveries were flicked with disregard. Jason Gillespie's inviting away–swingers were cover driven with authority. Collin Miller's gentle off spinners were dispatched to the stands. Shane Warne's big turning leg spinners were dominated one more time. Sachin Tendulkar played every single shot in the book, even some which did not feature in the book. His master–class 126 reinforced India's upper hand in the match. Sachin Tendulkar made a potential series–winning contribution.

Many memorable events came to pass on that day. It saw V.V.S. Laxman taking a giant step towards immortality. The day marked the transformation of Rahul Dravid from a man with zero confidence in his batting before the Kolkata test to a man who hit Jason Gillespie over his head for a huge six. His meticulous feet movement had found him once again. The day also witnessed Glen McGrath at his lethal best exploiting reverse swing. The day had a brilliant slip catch from Mark Waugh but when Sachin Tendulkar scores a chanceless century, everything else gets pushed to the periphery. One fact could not be ignored though. India led by 89 runs at the end of Day Three. On a Day Four and Day Five pitch, it was worth a goldmine.

DAY FOUR

Since Mumbai, the series had gone back and forth. Hence, India did not feel comfortable with the eventual lead of 110. An Australian comeback was inevitable. An opening partnership of 82 runs ate out almost the entire lead. Venkatapathy Raju had produced only one ball worth mentioning in the Kolkata match to take the most decisive wicket of Mark Waugh. Nilesh Kulkarni playing in Chennai had promptly followed Venkatapathy Raju's footsteps. He had done nothing in the match till the 19th over of Australia's second innings. Though Zaheer Khan's diving catch in the outfield was more responsible for the wicket than the quality of Kulkarni's ball, he got rid of the biggest threat. India finally saw the back of Mathew Hayden. He had come to India as a newcomer but was sure to leave India as an Australian stalwart.

Steve Waugh came up with his version of batting–order change by sending Gilchrist at number three. After his heroics in Mumbai, Adam Gilchrist had not managed to put his bat to ball for a decent length of time in the series. He had found Harbhajan unplayable since Mumbai and the humidity in Chennai made it worse for him. The move horrendously backfired and triggered the Australian collapse, one last time. The Waugh brothers tried their best to get Australia out of trouble. Even Ricky Ponting reached double figures for the first time in the series to register his highest score of the tour, 11, but could not stop Harbhajan who went on a rampage in the second and the last session, to end up with outstanding figures of 8 for 84. After the humiliation in Mumbai and the follow on in Kolkata, the Indian team was 155 runs away to end Steve Waugh's dream. As for Australia, they knew they had to fight harder but that was anyway the only way Australia played its cricket.

DAY FIVE

One word could describe the atmosphere in the packed Chepauk stadium – nervy. The Chennai crowd, noted for its cricketing acumen, acknowledged that the target of 155 was not as comfortable as it looked and considering the way the series had unfolded, it had realised that India required going through hell before making 155 runs. The openers posed no threat to the Australian fast bowlers. Australia got them both inside 20 overs. The real challenge for Steve Waugh was India's in–form middle order. For India, it required one composed innings to get the job done. V.V.S. Laxman arrived at the crease as early as the 5th over and as he had done in Kolkata and in the 1st innings in Chennai, he started playing his shots and appeared at absolute ease. The hardness of the new ball suited his natural timing and Australia's chief tormentor was at it again. Australia was quick to realise that it needed to control India's scoring pace and notched up its fielding to implausible accuracy. Indian batsmen have an inherent affinity for boundaries and the dearth of them started affecting both the batsmen at the wicket. It eventually resulted in a classic mix up and a run out. Though Sadagoppan Ramesh's dismissal did not hamper India's chances too much, the situation became tensed never the less.

The wicket brought two in–form batsmen at the crease with only 79 runs to win. The pressure Australia created by disciplined bowling and spectacular fielding made those 79 runs look like a mountain. Sachin engineered a simple solution to the problem. He tried to counterattack with three scintillating boundaries but Australia had devised a plan of its own. Gillespie bowled at his body from round–the–wicket. Sachin got his body out of the way but failed to get his bat out of the way. At 101 for 3, India looked shaky as only one of the remaining 7 batsmen was in–form. The captain had to assume the responsibility of guiding the team. He had the ability but his form suggested otherwise. So did Jason Gillespie's fast ball which took the edge of Ganguly's bat. The wicket brought the pair of Laxman and Dravid together again. How fitting it would be for both of them to guide India to a series victory, India thought; but Australia was in no mood to commit the same mistake twice. It tightened the noose and when the Kolkata pair was dismissed in a space of 6 overs and 13 runs, India came to a standstill, especially after seeing Mark Waugh's outrageous catch to get rid of Laxman. It took Laxman himself half a minute to believe the catch. India required 20 runs and still to come were two debutants, a three–match old bowler, a twenty–year–old hot headed sardar and another 20–year–old fast bowler. The match that was in the grasp half an hour ago, already looked lost.

Sameer Dighe, India's debutant wicket keeper was known in the domestic circuit for his 'back against the wall' performances. However, the stark contrast in quality in India's domestic cricket and international cricket posed a question–mark on Dighe's ability to make a difference in the match. He struggled to find the middle of his bat but his outside edge found a boundary to reduce India's target to 13. Another bottom edge from his bat reduced India's target to 9. Another outside edge took India 4 runs closer to the target. Meanwhile, Glen McGrath found Zaheer's outside edge at the other end. Zaheer was not as lucky as Dighe. His edge carried straight to the slips and then the moment arrived. With 32 wickets in 3 test matches, India had discovered a young spinner to carry the lineage and tradition of the famous Indian spinners. He had single–handedly torn the Australian batting apart. He now held a bat. India needed 4 more runs. With an edgy Dighe at the other end, the situation could not get any more tense. The pressure of the situation forced both sides in committing an almost terminal mistake in the next over. First, India attempted a foolish run which almost cost India its 9th wicket. Then a wayward throw almost gifted the match to India. A brilliant back up by Collin Miller saved a certain overthrow boundary and stretched the match to the next over.

Every time India looked to be in a winning position, Australia had grabbed a wicket and came back into the game. McGrath had the ball in his hand and India's number 10 on strike. A face–off between unequals! India's young off spinner faced the world's best fast bowler. The dying moments of the match provided the ultimate 'David v/s Goliath' story. McGrath bowled the most accurate yorker one could ever bowl. It headed towards the middle stump with leg before wicket or bowled written all over it. Then, it came. In the nick of time it came. Just as the ball crashed into Harbhajan's stumps, it came. Harbhajan Singh's bat guided a perfectly pitched McGrath Yorker towards point boundary. The geometrical improbability of the angle of his bat and the length of McGrath's yorker was the last thing India could think of. Everyone joined–in in the extravagant celebrations by both the Indian batsmen. The shot had created history. India, after getting floored for the first 8 days of the 3–match series, had won the Chennai Test and the series 2–1.

The series held significance on many counts. Steve Waugh could not conquer his final frontier. India defended its fortress once again against the invincible Australians. India found a spinner who showed signs of greatness and an elegant batsman who made India's middle–order more formidable. But the most significant aspect the series brought out was Indian captain's resolve in embracing the challenge and his emotional connect with his team which was evident in how he hugged Harbhajan after each of his 32 wickets, and the ardour with which he celebrated those last two runs in Chennai. The series win was important because the manner in which the team responded to his passion was a first in Indian cricket. The series was important because it provided the Indian team self–belief. It compelled the Indian fans to believe in its team once again. The epic series brought the charm of Indian cricket back. The series brought Indian cricket fans back home.

INDIA'S TOUR OF ENGLAND 2002 – THE TASTE OF OVERSEAS SUCCESS

India's momentous win over Australia achieved two results; another home series win and the other, a more precious one; rediscovery self–belief. In early 2000's, South Africa had handed a shock 2–0 defeat to India. Australia came close to repeating it but the fortress of India remained unconquered although home victories were not a priority for the current captain. India's wretched away record troubled him constantly. India had not won a single test match outside the subcontinent in the last decade. Winning test matches at home was not testimony to his captaincy and his team's caliber. The Australia series had brought Indian fans back to the game. It was time now to bring back their respect by winning abroad.

INDIA'S TOUR OF WEST INDIES – 2002

For many batsmen of the 20th century, facing the relentless West Indian fast bowlers (sometimes four of them in a match) was a dreaded prospect. In India's 1996–97 tour of the West Indies, despite India's obvious short–comings, it had sniffed a test match win in West Indies courtesy Abey Kuruvilla's unexpected five–for. India had required only 120 runs. The doubts on Sachin Tendulkar's captaincy were about to be put to rest but just then, Indian cricket witnessed a nightmarish batting display, getting dismissed for an appalling 81. The horrors of that loss stayed with every Indian fan forever. When Sourav Ganguly's team touched the scenic islands in 2002, it looked determined to erase that distressing memory once and for all.

Sachin Tendulkar's 29th test century, equaling the legend Sir Don Bradman, and inspired bowling led to a new memory to relish for India. India won a test match in West Indies after 27 long years but before the joyous feeling could sink in, old nightmares resurfaced as West Indies dismissed India for 102 in the next test. It dealt an irrecoverable dent to India's confidence in the rest of the series. India lost the series 2–1. There were ample positives from the series though. Indian bowling displayed its capability of taking 20 wickets in overseas conditions. Despite having two poor outings, Indian batting showed adequate quality to score huge runs. Sourav Ganguly had a team which could win overseas. He wanted his team to believe it and the tour of England presented him that stage.

India's previous tours to England had thrown up many famous individual performances. Dilip Vengsarkar had risen to prominence with his exploits in the 1986 series. Sachin Tendulkar had announced himself at the world stage with a century in England. India's last tour had given it two gems in Rahul

Dravid and Sourav Ganguly. A tour to England always carried a feel–good factor, despite a rare team success. Sourav Ganguly realised that this feel–good factor mixed with his team's performance to its potential could start a revolution. Apart from that, he had not forgotten 3rd February 2002.

It had all come down to the last match of the ODI series of England's tour to India 5 months back. A spectacularly tight ODI series, which swung from one side to another over the course of the last 5 games, was heading towards a befitting climax. India needed 11 runs in the last over to win the 6th ODI. England had exceeded its expectations in the series and a drawn ODI series was as good as a win. Andrew Flintoff, whose brilliant bowling had stirred English bowling attack to make a match out of the last ODI, found his chance to shine in the dying moments of the match. He picked up 2 wickets in 2 balls but after that; he did something that annoyed home fans. His shirtless sprint around the Wankhede Stadium did not go down well with the disappointed crowd. He seemed to care little because England, by levelling a series against India in India, had done the unlikely. It deserved a celebration and Flintoff celebrated it in his own way. Somewhere down in his mind, Sourav Ganguly took note of it. He was sure that his young team would give him an occasion to return the favour.

INDIA TOUR OF ENGLAND – 2002 – THE NATWEST SERIES

"Are we on to something here? Are we on to something here?" Harsha Bhogle articulated the question every spectator and viewer back home asked in unison. After blasting 109 runs in the first 15 overs in the NatWest Series Final, India had totally lost its way. Tendulkar was the 5th wicket to fall after Sehwag, Ganguly, Mongia and Dravid. Two 21–year–olds were the most improbable pair to chase down the target of 326. So, when the Indian score was 257 for 5 at the end of 40 overs, the question on Bhogle's mind was worth contemplating.

ONE MONTH AGO

India, after a remarkable 6 months of ODI cricket, landed in England with a talented pool of ODI players. It consisted of the usual suspects in Tendulkar, Ganguly, Dravid and Kumble but the rest of the bunch was visiting England for the first time. The new boys comprised of the adventurous but careless Virender Sehwag, the very talented but inconsistent Yuvraj Singh, Mohammad Kaif who had elevated Indian fielding standards to an unprecedented high, and a genuine quick bowler in Zaheer Khan. All these players had one crucial ingredient in common – the unconditional backing of the captain. But his backing also posed a challenge while picking India's playing eleven. The solution to his problem had resulted in two of the most crucial decisions of Sourav Ganguly's captaincy career.

Rahul Dravid's marathon innings in Kolkata had transformed him into the most important cog in India's test match set–up but he somehow struggled to carry his consistency in the shorter format. An unchartered responsibility awaited him in England. He was made India's ODI wicket keeper. The move looked more as a front for keeping Dravid in the ODI team than helping India's cause but that's how India's new captain was. Dravid formed an integral part of the team and he had to be in the team, come what may! The other decision invoked a fierce debate. The influx of young players resulted in an inexperienced middle order. Hence, India's opener premiere was asked to drop to the middle order and a rookie Sehwag took his place. The move did not go down well with anybody including the man himself. However, Sourav Ganguly stood firm and Sachin Tendulkar, being a team man, eventually accepted the role.

India began the tri–series in alien English conditions with an unproven approach and an untested team combination. These factors automatically rendered India least favourites to win the Tri series. Hence, when India chased down 271 at the Lord's in its first league match against England, India's highest run chase on that ground till that date, it was termed a fluke, overlooking some heartening positives. Rahul Dravid took two sharp catches and had a delightful stumping to add to his score of 73 runs at a strike rate of 85. There was a refreshing improvement in his fitness and his running between the wickets. Virender Sehwag blasted 71 runs in 65 balls, shooting warnings of his destructive abilities as an opener. Yuvraj Singh's 64 under pressure suggested that he was now getting into the groove.

India's 2nd match against Sri Lanka was a captain's joy. India had not seen such lethal new ball bowling in ages. It had pace, it had accuracy, and it felt soothing to see Sri Lankan batsmen jumping and fumbling. For far too long had Indian fans seen Sri Lankan batsmen decimate Indian bowlers with a preposterous ease but not anymore! A clinical bowling performance was followed by a matured chase. This match marked the turnaround in India's dismal past record against Sri Lanka. The new approach was worth discussing, the skeptics felt.

Sachin Tendulkar hogged the centre stage in India's 3rd and 6th match. Dropping him to 4th position meant he would no longer get those first 15 overs of the field restriction, hampering his scoring opportunities. Well! That's what mortals thought but not Sachin Tendulkar. He did not score because of the field restrictions; he scored because he loved only one thing, scoring runs. His centuries against England and Sri Lanka demonstrated his appetite for runs and his extraordinary ability to adapt. His centuries were laden with features of the middle order innings; lots of ones and twos to begin with and tremendous acceleration in the death overs. He structured his innings as if he had played all his life in the middle order. Both centuries helped India earn crucial points. India reached the final without breaking a sweat. An overseas tournament victory would have given the desired boost to India's rebuilding phase. India felt destined to win the trophy, but it all went horrendously wrong during the 1st half of the final. Marcus Trescothick barely put a foot wrong in his 109 runs. At the other end, Nasser Hussain barely found the middle of his bat in his innings but all his inside edges, outside edges, mistimed shots got him his 1st ODI century. He was cocky enough to forget the quality of the innings and show his batting number to some of his critics who had questioned his ODI batting position in England's batting line–up. The captain in him could not have asked for a better batting performance. His team had already asked India to chase its record total at Lord's earlier in the series. India had managed that with ease. Chasing 326 in a final was for sure not so easy.

"I have a gut feeling that this is going to be the captain's day," Alan Wilkins predicted at the start of India's innings. The sole aspect that had failed in India's new approach was Ganguly himself; managing only 89 runs in the league phase. But more than his personal form, the Indian team looked up at its captain in the hope of a leader's knock. For that, the Captain needed to rediscover his old self. Every batsman has his favourite shot, the one which eases his nerves. Caressing the bowlers through the off side was Sourav's. But over the years, bowling sides had found–out Ganguly. The strategy of cramping him outside his off stump was used against him but as all great batsmen do, Ganguly came up with a method of his own to counter it.

If the England bowlers did not allow him room outside his off stump, he created it by shuffling outside his leg stump. Such shuffling at the crease was not at all expected from a traditional batsman like him. By shuffling across, he created the room he wanted for his glorious bat swing which helped him in finding his old timing, his favourite gaps. When he did not find gaps, he chose to hit the ball over the infield. India caught England unawares by its counter–attack and Ganguly's innovative technique. At the other end stood Virender Sehwag and there was no second guessing his approach. Sehwag matched Ganguly's shot for shot. As Ronnie Irani, who had troubled the Indian batsmen throughout the series, was hit for 4 fours in an over, India looked uncontainable. The England bowlers had no answer to Ganguly's 'shuffling across the crease' and Sehwag's 'stand and deliver'. They tried bowling short but Ganguly cut them over the off side. They tried bowling full and Sehwag smashed them to all parts of the historic Lord's. Astonishingly, in India's surprising 'Blitzkrieg', the Indian captain outscored Virender Sehwag. That was a hell of an achievement! After 14 overs of annihilation, India was running away with the match. Alan Wilkins's prediction appeared to hit bull's eye.

England surrendered to India's devastating attack, hoping for India to make a mistake. It was the Indian captain who blinked first. He attempted a big heave across the line but missed the ball and it kissed his off stump. Big run chases often depend upon the momentum. Ganguly's untimely dismissal snatched India's momentum. India required rebuilding again but at a brisk run–rate. Sehwag found it difficult and a strange looking shot cost him his timber. Dinesh Mongia never looked comfortable in his 18 minutes stay and was put out of his troubles by Ronnie Irani. Rahul Dravid had transformed himself into a wonderful ODI batsman in this series. He had looked fitter, hungrier for ODI success. His wicket–keeping had resulted in an evident improvement in his approach. India now trusted him to be as dependable in ODIs as he was in test matches. Unfortunately for him and India, he managed only 5. Sachin Tendulkar looked confused about the strategy to adopt. The situation was so precarious that another wicket would have gifted the game to England but the asking rate did not allow India to take its time. Confusion won over him as his half–hearted attempt to hit Giles over covers failed miserably. With Sachin's wicket, 90% of India switched off the television sets. India had played quality cricket in the series but the final now looked beyond it. The young Indian team required more grooming to adjust to International cricket. India required being patient to allow the young team to settle in international cricket. Two young men begged to differ. For them, the rebuilding was over. Now was the time to deliver. They had been chosen in the Indian set up for a reason. The Indian captain had chosen them because they understood what winning signified for this Indian team. They knew that this Indian team was playing for its pride.

For the next 10 overs, Yuvraj Singh and Mohammad Kaif scored runs in a quiet demeanour showcasing calmness and resolution in their body language. England mistook their approach for inability to accelerate. The pair scored 60 runs in those 10 overs consisting only 4 boundaries and a single six. India had not witnessed such intense running between the wicket ever before. After the 34th over though, all of a sudden, the pair shifted gears. The intent was announced by Yuvraj with three consecutive boundaries off Flintoff and Kaif joined in with a huge six and a boundary in the next over. England again was caught sleeping as India scored 51 runs in the next 6 overs. At this moment, the rest 10% of India, which had still kept its television sets on, agreed with Harsha Bhogle. India indeed looked on the course of accomplishing something special.

At 146 for 5 in the 24th over, India had nothing to lose. Perhaps the circumstances permitted two young minds to play their natural game. At the end of the 40th over, India required 69 runs in 10 overs which looked achievable and hence heaped real pressure on the pair. With the finishing line within sight, both youngsters needed to steady their nerves. Yuvraj Singh could not, as he top–edged a sweep that went straight to short fine leg. Nobody was more dejected than Yuvraj himself. India felt his pain. He had conjured one of the most incredible fight–backs in Indian cricket but fell short of completing it but if Yuvraj's agony made India cry, Kaif's confident existence at the other end gave India hope. Yuvraj was the aggressor in his partnership with Kaif. Kaif now had to assume the lead. He showed his eagerness for it by hitting a six within 3 balls of Yuvraj's dismissal.

Harbhajan Singh's only objective was to get Kaif on strike and stay unbeaten at the non–striker's end. It was amusing to see a 22–year–old Sardar curbing his aggressive Punjabi instincts for his team. In the partnership of 35 balls in which India added 47 vital runs to take its score to 314 runs, he faced only 13 balls. The Punjabi instincts led to Harbhajan's eventual downfall and with Kumble lasting only 2 balls after Harbhajan's departure, the match had a twist again. At the end of the 48th over, England had a golden opportunity to seal the match. Zaheer Khan, India's No. 10 faced

England's best death over bowler, Darren Gough with India still 11 runs away. Zaheer by any means required putting his bat to ball and running to the other end but India knew how difficult that was for an Indian tail–ender. The historical Chennai test of 1999, Venkatesh Prasad's inability to survive for one ball against Zimbabwe in that crucial World Cup 1999 loss ran before Indian fans' eyes in a flash, although another of India's young turks was determined to convince Indian fans that this team differed from its predecessors.

Zaheer managed to score a single on the first ball. It looked clumsy but the style was the least of the expectations from India's No.10. Kaif handed another chance to Gough by giving the strike back to Zaheer on the 4th ball. Zaheer again scored a run on the 5th which brought India's target to 6 runs. Then, Kaif, for the 1st time in the match, swung his bat mindlessly and managed a thick edge to the boundary. The boundary brought India within just 2 runs but it also brought Zaheer Khan on strike. The young Indian players had managed something extraordinary thus far. All of them had shown maturity, courage and desire beyond their ages. Even after facing 2 dot balls in the last over, India's on field pair exuded a sense of assuredness. On the 3rd ball of the 50th over, Kaif ran, one last time, he ran. He ran as if his life depended upon it. He dived as if it was his last deed on the earth and with an overthrow, India achieved its greatest moment of joy since the match–fixing saga. Kaif appeared confused about how to react to the win. The Indian balcony did not know how to celebrate the win either. One man, who had pinned his trust on a bunch of newbies, the man who took on the world for including young players in the Indian team, knew the precise way to celebrate the win. On 3rd February 2002, he had made a note in his mind. On 13th July 2002, the shirt came off. It was waved just like it was waved 5 months ago. Sourav Ganguly, with one gesture, highlighted the attitude of modern India. The new Team India dared to give it back. The new Team India was ready to fight hard. The new Team India was ready to win.

LORD'S TEST

The Indian cricket teams of the last decade never sported a bowling attack capable of taking 20 wickets in bowler–friendly overseas conditions. The defensive mindset of bowling on flat Indian pitches was so deeply imprinted that Indian fast bowlers never extracted bounce or swing from friendly overseas pitches. In the conditions where a spinner could only play the role of holding up one end; Indian spinners were expected to take wickets. Poor Anil Kumble tried his best every time but seldom succeeded. Overseas batsmen found it humiliatingly easy to score huge runs against Indian bowling and put pressure on Indian batting.

India's fast bowling was the rising star in the league phase of the NatWest Series. India enjoyed the luxury of having two bowlers who could bowl at 140 Kmph and swing it at that speed. Hence Zaheer Khan's first spell of 6–4–5–1 on the opening day of the Lord's test was heartening but not surprising. Ashish Nehra supported Zaheer Khan to perfection to restrict England's score to 50 for 1 at a run rate of 2.77 per over. Good opening spells from India's fast bowlers allowed Sourav Ganguly to introduce Kumble in 19th over. Kumble relished the rare opportunity to bowl at two English batsmen who had scored virtually nothing in the first hour of play. He reduced England to 75 for 2 which soon became 78 for 3 in the first session. India won the session after losing the toss. That again was very rare.

Nasser Hussain had not yet established himself as a good ODI batsman but he was one hell of a good test batsman. He had scored a very clumsy hundred at the Lord's in the NatWest Final. 12 days later, he returned to his favourite whites and boy did he enjoy it! He had given the first session to Indian bowlers. 2nd was his to take. The patient Hussain brought out some delightful strokes in the second session on a rapidly flattening pitch. The 2nd session went wicket–less and one glaring shortcoming in the Indian fast bowling became apparent – its inexperience.

The inexperience of Indian bowlers resulted in inconsistent bowling spells and hence even after the bright 1st session, India grappled with the age–old daunting task of chasing a big 1st innings score which called upon its openers; another of Indian cricket's long–lasting problems overseas. The history of Indian opening batsmen outside India over the years resembled the history of its fast bowlers if not worse. After Sunil Gavaskar, India had struggled to find an opener worthy of the demands of that position. At Lord's, India featured Wasim Jaffer as one opener and the choice of other was a recipe for disaster. Virender Sehwag's batting theory of 'see the ball–hit the ball' was tailor–made for ODIs. Purists wrote him off for test cricket. When he was selected to make his test debut in South Africa, it was presumed to be the end of his test match career. The man went on to score a debut hundred in the most difficult conditions in South Africa. The captain had now asked him to open the innings which had the potential to end his test career. Sourav Ganguly had taken a gigantic call. Sehwag, a member of Ganguly's young brigade chose Lord's as his stepping stone towards becoming one of the greatest Indian test openers.

One of the openers followed the usual course. Sehwag stuck to his unorthodox technique and an unique approach to test match opening. India, for 33 overs of its first innings cruised like playing at home. If Sehwag prescribed to attacking cricket, Dravid demonstrated textbook defense but the 34th over brought the curtain down on India's short revival. After Sehwag's dismissal, India managed only 93 runs. England chose not to enforce the follow–on. Eden Gardens 2001, it seemed had taught world cricket a lesson. England's decision to bat again nullified India's chance of winning the match, if there was any at all.

It lost the match by 170 runs but not before raising some hope of drawing the match. A brilliant partnership of 126 runs between Laxman and Agarkar produced one of the most iconic moments in Indian Cricket's history. India's two legendary batting heroes, Sunil Gavaskar and Sachin Tendulkar, had two things in common. Both hailed from Mumbai and both had not scored a test match century at cricket's home ground, Lord's. Till the 5th day of the Lord's test, Ajit Agarkar shared both things with them. On the last day of the Lord's test though, Agarkar wrote one thing off that list. No! He did not shift base from Mumbai. He happened to notch up a test hundred at the Lord's.

HEADINGLEY TEST

The rain–affected 2nd test stamped Virender Sehwag's ascent as India's long–term opener. He scored a charming hundred in overcast and seaming conditions. The world already knew Sehwag, the dasher ODI batsman. Tent Bridge established him as a very effective test opener. The Indian batting came into its own in the 2nd innings. Rahul Dravid led the innings with a century. Sachin and Ganguly missed theirs by a whisker. India's batting excelled but the bowling once again not only struggled to pick up wickets but also leaked runs. By now, it was apparent to Sourav Ganguly that the batting presented him a better chance of winning a match. His inexperienced bowling needed the cushion of runs. He had decided to bat first even before reaching Headingley. A greenish pitch and overcast conditions greeted him in Headingley. The Indian bowlers, after the 1st session at Lord's, had found very little to cheer. Headingley settings offered the Indian bowlers a splendid chance to get back in business. They prayed for their Captain to win the toss and bowl so that they could use the conditions. The batsmen prayed for the captain to win the toss and bowl first to avoid batting in such treacherous conditions. No batsman in his right mind would have wished to bat in such difficult conditions. The captain's decision hence put them in a tizzy. Their prayers were answered but the call was not. Sourav Ganguly chose to bat in the most adverse batting conditions possible.

The Indian test team was always considered lame ducks outside the subcontinent. Big names such as Gavaskar, Kapil, Tendulkar, Dravid and Ganguly were part of these teams which faced drubbings abroad. Their individual brilliance always fell short in a team sport. In India's redux, after the match–fixing saga, the new captain wanted to focus on winning abroad. Losses in South Africa and West Indies in its previous overseas tours under Ganguly did not eclipse the quality of cricket and commitment of his young side. At 1–0 down in the series, the captain had taken a brave, in fact a suicidal call to bat first and losing Headingley test guaranteed a demoralizing blow to India's ambition of overseas success. The captain had asked a lot from his young team. There were two ways to respond to the captain's call. The team chose the captain's way– 'Bring–it–on.'

The conditions negated India's big advantage in Sehwag. Sehwag's technique could not survive such dire conditions. With an in–form opener gone in the 7th over, the decision appeared to have backfired. Rahul Dravid had the requisite technique and patience to stay on that pitch but did he have the support? Sanjay Bangar, the latest in the endless list of Indian openers was least likely to offer it; or so everybody thought. The human mind works in mysterious ways. Its control over the body is astonishing. What India witnessed during the next 2 days was the mind's sheer ability to conquer any and every obstacle.

SANJAY BANGAR

236 balls, 296 minutes. That was the duration of Sanjay Bangar's marathon innings. He played 40 overs himself and stayed at the crease for 5 hours. His scoring rate became irrelevant as he wore down the England bowlers with his strenuous defense. He hit only 33 scoring shots. Rest of the 202 were either defended or left alone. The concentration was surreal, sometimes even unnatural. He showed no urge to score runs. India needed him to stay at the wicket and that's all he did. England tried every ploy possible to get him out.

It tried bouncing him out; it tried getting him on the front foot, even tried to get him scoring so that he offered a chance. Bangar accepted nothing, with a straight face and an even straighter bat. It took Flintoff's round the wicket line to get Bangar's glove. Sanjay Bangar defied England bowlers on a grassy pitch under overcast conditions for 75 overs. This was his career best performance, not statistically but for its worth. He had answered his captain's call.

RAHUL DRAVID

The No. 3 position in test cricket is of vital significance. That is the man, who more often than not, anchors the innings. Anchor was the precise word to describe Dravid. Where every batsman from either team was expected to struggle on the Headingley pitch, Rahul Dravid was expected to score. He possessed two of the most fundamental qualities required in such conditions; impeccable technique and abundant patience. His 148 runs were traditional, elegant, breath–taking but not at all unexpected. You need soft hands to prevent the edges carrying to the slips; a decisive front foot to cover–drive a swinging ball; you need the bat close to your pads when you flick a ball cutting in; your head needs to be still when you pull a short ball; you need to get on top of the ball to cut it. Rahul Dravid's technique possessed all these qualities and hence Rahul Dravid's magnificent 148 comprised all these shots.

SACHIN TENDULKAR

Sachin Tendulkar walked in at a delicate moment with the next new ball due in 6 overs. Flintoff had his tail up. There was a hint of cloud cover. Sachin approached the first part of his innings with caution. He got beat quite a few number of times; he edged a few but looked determined to hang in the middle. He had to capitalize on the mammoth efforts of Sanjay Bangar and Rahul Dravid. All his shots in his first 100 runs bore a stamp of class but also of prudence. By controlling himself from playing those booming, free flowing shots, he was respecting the conditions and more so the hard work of Bangar and Dravid.

The country was not used to seeing Sachin bat with so much caution. His next 93 runs though bore a familiar aggressive look. The sound his six to Andrew Caddick made, perhaps, was heard in Manchester too. It was a wake–up call for England literally and figuratively. Unfortunately for England, it came too late in the day as Sachin Tendulkar had decided to cut lose. The rest of Sachin's knock included six magnificent fours and three huge sixes; one of which dented a window of a nearby apartment. The innings of 193 made a decisive dent in England's chances.

SOURAV GANGULY

Three of his batsmen had overcome the challenge thrown by the captain. Sourav Ganguly now himself faced that formidable task. He had been given a wonderful platform; 335 runs and English bowlers at his mercy. While other batsmen started their innings, cautious of the conditions, the Indian captain batted as if he played at Eden Gardens. His opposite number extended a huge favour to him which played a role in his aggression. Any batsman is a bit nervous at the start of his innings. Sourav received a gift in the form of a left arm spinner as Hussain continued with Giles. Christmas arrived early for Ganguly as he milked Ashley Giles for runs. By the time the English captain brought back his pacers, Ganguly was in his elements. Light was deteriorating fast. It was up to the Indian batsmen to accept bad light and end the proceedings of Day two. It had been a fulfilling but mentally exhausting day. India deserved rest. That was the sensible and obvious choice but to win matches abroad, you need to go beyond the obvious. Ganguly had already done it once by batting first. He did it again by not accepting the light and deciding to continue batting. Playing in the murky light entailed a risk as it became difficult to sight the red ball but India held a commanding position and accepting bad light would have cost it precious time. The captain was not thinking of resting. He was focused on winning. And in the gloomy dark afternoon at Headingley, he lit up the sky with humongous strokes. Sourav Ganguly started stepping down the wicket and hitting English seamers over the infield. The counterattack was a` la NatWest Final. The session witnessed 14 fours, 3 sixes, a bloodied spectator with an open skull and a reeling English team, all because of Ganguly's scorching century. On the pitch which was supposed to bury India in the series, India amassed 628 runs, the highest total ever by India in India–England bilateral series.

ANIL KUMBLE & HARBHAJAN SINGH

Sourav Ganguly desired the cushion of a huge total and his batters had obliged. He now could use his inexperienced seamers as a support to the two outstanding spinners at his disposal. To depend on spinners on a green pitch again involved high risk. The captain had gambled for support from his spinners in a similar way in which he had gambled for support from his batsmen. And just like his batsmen, the spinners obliged too. Both of them bowled 51 overs to claim 6 English wickets. Harbhajan extracted decent turn from the pitch and Kumble used the uneven bounce on offer to his advantage. A disciplined and patient bowling attack allowed India to enforce a follow–on. Who could have imagined that! After a faltering 1st innings, England steadied its second innings with a crucial 91 runs partnership between Nasser Hussain and Alec Stewart. Both remained unbeaten overnight on Day 4. Day 5 promised to be fascinating. India needed 6 wickets for a famous win. Kumble helped India take a giant step towards victory by dismissing Hussain in his first over of the day. The ball bounced out of nowhere and took Nasser Hussain's glove. India, within 17 overs after claiming Nasser Hussain, finished England's second innings to cap a memorable win.

All of Ganguly's gambles paid off. The moment Sourav Ganguly decided to bat first on that pitch, he was labeled stupid. The match that was going to embarrass India's captain, resulted in a historic win but more than the win, one fact emerged again and again. Sourav Ganguly trusted his team beyond any doubt, even to the point of being called stupid, and the team was ready to stretch its limits just to prove otherwise.

INDIA'S TOUR OF NEW ZEALAND 2002-03 – THE DEBACLE

India's competing performance in West Indies and an inspired outing in England was rapidly establishing it as a force to reckon with even in overseas conditions. The current Indian side was steadily vanquishing its pushover status. After tasting success in the Caribbean and England, India's ambitions to win a series overseas went a few levels up. New Zealand was perhaps the place where India fancied itself for an overseas series win. It had a perfect bowling line up for the conditions and its batsmen were in the form of their life. India felt confident of picking 20 New Zealand wickets, and its batting harbored ambitions of getting big scores. Amusing emotion ambition is! It takes you to places you had never imagined. But if uncontrolled, it puts you in your place in no time. The dream of winning did not take into account two crucial factors – New Zealand's super–fast bowling spearhead Shane Bond and the amount of grass left on the pitches in New Zealand.

THE TEST DIBACLE

1ST TEST – WELLINGTON

"I just fought and scrapped and poked and pushed." the highest scorer of the match, Mark Richardson was candid while describing his innings. One needed all the fighting, scrapping, poking and pushing to survive on the green pitch in Basin Reserve, Wellington. He missed so many balls that one lost count. He defended so many balls that nobody desired to count. None could stop admiring the determination of the man though. His 89 kept a fired up Zaheer Khan at bay for a large amount of time. His long stay at the crease intensified Sourav Ganguly's worries. After getting blown away for 161 in the 1st innings, New Zealand's score of 181 for 3 entailed only one result, a heavy defeat for India.

On the first morning of the match, it took the Indian team considerable time to tell apart the pitch from the outfield. New Zealand's decision to bowl spoiled India's odds further and to make matters worse, a fit and hungry Shane Bond looked prepared to dismantle the Indian batting. Where the rest of the world was advising USA to adopt a soft approach against Iraq, Indian batsmen took the message quite seriously and dropped their guard in meek surrender. If India's grand trio of Tendulkar, Ganguly and Laxman could not adjust to the swing Shane Bond and Co. derived from the grassy pitch, expecting Sehwag and Sanjay Bangar to put up a fight was unfounded. It was Dravid again who countered the swing and bounce with his flawless technique but even his resolute 76 did not provide any respectability to India's total.

New Zealand's reply of 181 for 3 threatened to take the game away from India. Ajit Agarkar and Ashish Nehra failed to get purchase from the same conditions but Zaheer Khan refused to give in. He assumed the responsibility of getting India back in the reckoning. He was quickly becoming Ganguly's go–to man. His next spell cast light on why he had acquired that distinction from his captain. Nathan Astle, Robbie Hart and Daniel Vettori too discovered the reason for Zaheer's rise in the Indian ranks by paying the ultimate price. A spinner was just expected to support the fast bowlers in England yet Harbhajan Singh had played a pivotal role in the Headingley test match. Conditions in Wellington were even more inimical and still, he put his hand up to pick two critical wickets. In 30 overs, India got 7 wickets and restricted New Zealand's lead to 86 runs.

India called for a strong batting performance in the 2nd innings to make a match out of it. It had the ability, but the conditions outdid the ability once again. Shane Bond tormented the Indian batting with pure pace. His opening spell of 12–5–19–3 kicked India out of the match. He was so at the peak of his prowess that he dismissed Tendulkar twice in the innings in a similar fashion, once of a no ball and once legitimately. The team which had fought back in West Indies and England capitulated for 121 runs in New Zealand. India's ambition of winning a series abroad got severely fractured. Adverse conditions made one fact extremely clear. India was not yet ready to win abroad. It now had to forget its noble desire of winning an overseas series and concentrate on Hamilton as it stared at a whitewash. Its batting had to deliver a better performance to have any kind of chance.

2ND TEST – HAMILTON

99 is a dreaded figure in Cricket. Batsmen always struggle to score that one run even if the previous 99 have been fluent. 99 indeed was a dreaded figure for India after the start of the 2nd test in Hamilton, not because any single one of its batsmen got out on 99. The entire team was bowled out for 99! Just when India thought that it would not get any worse after Wellington, there came a shocker in Hamilton where it failed to even reach a three–figure score in the first innings. The pitch at Hamilton was no doubt greener. The conditions were for sure tougher but to get bowled out for 99 was plain

shameful.

Zaheer Khan resented the humiliation of the Indian batsmen. The names were the icons of the game and to see them ridiculed so much, hurt him. He decided to give some back to the Kiwi batsmen. His 5 for 29 ensured a bizarre scenario in the match. India, after getting bowled out for 99, took a first innings lead of 5 runs. India bundled New Zealand for 94! In the quest for making the conditions unfavourable for India, New Zealand had created a monster which its own batsmen could not handle. For a visiting team, a team total of 99 was shameful. But for a home team, 94 was a sin.

After three disastrous batting outings, India had one final chance to set the records straight and secure a test win. In Wellington, the pitch went from green to brown as the match progressed, making batting a bit easier. There was no such luck in Hamilton. The pitch retained every bit of its greenery, thus providing a herculean task to Indian batsmen one more time. Another failure of the Indian batting order (154 all–out) gave New Zealand a target of 160. Zaheer, Nehra and Yohannan made it as hard as possible for the hosts with their relentless bowling but New Zealand held its nerves to chase the total. Despite four horrendous batting outings, India managed to produce a few sparkling moments in both the matches but the extreme nature of the pitches garnered the talking points. The green pitches hogged the centre stage even though the series involved big stars like Tendulkar, Dravid, Fleming, Astle and Bond. The Indian team had to surmount the nightmare in white colours and prepare to embrace color clothing. It was going into its last ODI tournament before the granddaddy of them all. World Cup 2003 was just two months away. The seven–match series, India's longest ever ODI series in New Zealand, was the ideal curtain raiser.

ODI SERIES

The format changed. The clothing changed. The color of the ball changed. But, the batting woes of both sides continued. In the test series, India did not cross 200 even once. In the 1st ODI at Auckland, it battled hard to go past 100. The Indian batting could not cope with the movement of the white ball. Frustration due to the inability to play for any decent length of time, soon gave way to mindless shots which resulted in India's pathetic score of 108. Astonishingly, by the 19th over of New Zealand's batting, India emerged clear favourites to win the match. India, while defending 108, reduced New

Zealand to 52 for 6. It had been that kind of a series. Even the home team failed to cope up with the conditions. It certainly could not cope up with India's old warhorse who appeared to be at his lethal best in his second stint as India's spearhead.

Javagal Srinath held all the attributes to be one of the best fast bowlers in world cricket but despite his envious tally of 500 plus international wickets, he was tagged an under–achiever, someone who had failed to exploit his full potential. In his 2nd stint as India's leading fast bowler, he had fire in his belly to claim his place in the gallery of legends. It transpired on the ground as his phenomenal pace troubled every Kiwi batsman. Indian blowers made a match out of it but New Zealand prevailed in the end. That was the story of this tour for India, the batting letting the team down and the bowling trying to pick up the pieces of the debacle.

India's highest total on the tour so far was 161. Hence when it was asked to chase 255, it appeared next to impossible. How would Indian batsmen break the shackles of uncertainty in their own ability created by the last five innings? The form of a batsman is driven by his mental state. A composed mind exudes confidence and batting is always about confidence. Indian batsmen seemed to have left theirs in India. Only one man in the Indian dressing room had an uncluttered mind despite five failures. He was not one to be weighed down by any baggage. That was the strength of the man. The man once again, introduced India to himself; to Virender Sehwag.

On a pitch relatively easier to bat on than all previous pitches in the tour so far, Sehwag made a mockery of the conditions. The small boundaries of Napier ground helped him to a large extent. The sound his bat made every time the ball hit it reverberated throughout the ground. Of all the talented batsmen India had in its arsenal, flashy and carefree Sehwag was the least expected to score a century. His first lofted shot came against a spinner which suggested that there was something more to his batting than just careless aggression; that there existed a method to his madness. Sehwag was sublime, but the struggle continued for the rest of the Indian batsmen. Sehwag got no support from any of the other batsmen. A moment came when he realized that he had to do it all by himself and in the clear desperation of that realization, he ran himself out and so did India's chances.

The proceedings went back to usual for the next 2 ODIs. India scored 108 and 122 respectively. Even the bowlers ran out of ideas to defend such low scores. By winning both the matches, New Zealand clinched the series.

In the 5th ODI, India discovered its lost art of winning by chasing 168. Though the game was thrilling, the win heaped more pressure on Ganguly than releasing it as it was Zaheer Khan's 34 that saved the day for India. The batting troubles just refused to depart. Sehwag scored his 2nd century of the tour in the 6th ODI as India bagged the thriller. The last match of the series was a recap of India's disastrous past 30 days. India got bowled out for 122 and New Zealand won the match. In a month–long tour, India managed to win only 2 matches. India's curtain raiser to World Cup 2003 turned out to be a horror show. India was at the peak of its form and abilities one month ago but New Zealand's tour changed it all in no time. The tour pushed the side in the dark of self–doubt. The losing streak took the sting out of its spirit. India's youthful exuberance and energy abandoned it in haste. Efforts of the last two years in building a team appeared to have gone in vain. The team's morale dropped to the lowest point possible and Sourav Ganguly could not afford it to stay that way. He had to bring back the spark. For that, he needed to take some tough decisions. Indian fans were seething. The atmosphere was volatile. Sourav Ganguly and his team had to put on a worthy performance to quiet things down back home. It looked difficult though as India headed to a place it would have wished the least to visit. World Cup 2003 was scheduled in South Africa and India's record in South Africa was not even worth mentioning.

ICC WORLD CUP 2003 – A DREAM RUN

INDIA V/S NETHERLANDS – THE REALITY CHECK

A match against an associate nation usually provides heartening positives but India's opening match against the Netherlands raised many uncomfortable questions. Even after travelling 7200 miles away from New Zealand's green tracks, the batsmen continued their tryst with poor form. Indian fans had somehow digested India's capitulation in New Zealand but the much–famed Indian batting line up's plight to score runs against an associate nation threatened to open the lid on the volcano. Fortunately for the Indian cricket team, three veterans saved the blushes.

Sachin Tendulkar continued his sweet affair with World Cups with a silky 52. India's old fox, Javagal Srinath, returning to International cricket at the persistence of Ganguly bowled with venom and pace to blow away the Dutch top order. India's third veteran was no stranger to demolishing the batting sides. The poor Dutch had no clue how to counter Kumble's quick leg spin.

The margin of the win projected the false image of a comfortable win. The inexperience of the Netherlands gave India chances to recover from early difficulties. The mighty Australians were sure not to give India such respite. India needed to take the reality check given by the minnow in its stride as it prepared to face the world champions.

INDIA V/S AUSTRALIA – THE ROCK BOTTOM

For India to stand a chance against Australia, Ganguly needed to take two bold decisions but for the first time in his captaincy career he looked reluctant. The Indian squad carried a better opener than the under–performing captain. Yet he decided to open the innings again, committing a fatal mistake. The centurion pitch commanded three fast bowlers and a lone spinner, which meant he had to pick between a legend and his favourite off–spinner. He avoided the difficult choice and picked both along with two pacers. The damage caused by his first decision left no space for the second to inflict any. The incompetent Indian batting was pitted against the best bowling attack in the world. It was a no contest as Glen McGrath, Jason Gillespie and Brett Lee raked mayhem on the Indian batsmen. If Ganguly and Sehwag found their feet glued to the ground against Brett Lee's speed, Dravid and Kaif were reintroduced to the Centurion bounce by Jason Gillespie. Yuvraj got a taste of the precision in Glen McGrath's line and length. The star–studded Indian top–order was shredded to pieces in 41.4 overs. After the appalling performance against Netherlands, the Indian batting hit rock bottom against Australia with a team score of 125 runs. The batting woes in New Zealand prior to the World Cup had made India least favourites to win it. Its mediocre show against Australia put them on the verge of an early exit. Ganguly's reluctance to take hard decisions caused an embarrassment to him and his team. Sourav Ganguly was demure in admitting in post–match presentation that India was outplayed. Fans back home were not so humble though.

The Indian fans reacted in the only manner they knew. Effigies of all members of the Indian team were burnt on the roads in several parts of the country. Hostile processions were marched throughout the country. Last rites were performed on the figurines of some of the players. Indian fans reached a new low by stoning the residences of players and setting up large fires in front of the players' houses. Players' families were given police protection. Not even the mighty Sachin Tendulkar could escape people's wrath. Fans who had upraised these players to the status of gods, now hurled shoes and sandals at their dummies. The news flash of Mohammad Kaif's house being painted black from outside marked the most shameful day in Indian cricket. The fans had stooped to the saddest low possible. In addition to the two poor performances, players now stressed over the violent reactions and safety of their families. With such hostile backlash back home, it became uncertain how the team would react to this pressure.

"If putting a fire in front of my house or painting it black is going to help me score runs, then please do it again." Mohammad Kaif was visibly hurt. "We need your support at this point of time to get us through this phase." He appealed to the fans. A few sensible heads identified with Kaif's and the team's pain. They decided to be the twelfth man the Indian team badly needed. 'The Bharat Army', as they called themselves, a group of faithful Indian cricket lovers, travelled to Harare Sports Club to extend their unconditional support to the team. In Harare, the Bharat Army found a determined, focused and wounded Indian team. The intensity in its practice suggested that something special was on the cards.

INDIA V/S ZIMBABWE – THE BEGINNING OF THE STREAK

India never enjoyed playing at Harare. The pitch carried a spongy bounce and the ball came slowly on to the bat. India's free flowing batsmen struggled to time the ball on the pitch. No wonder India held a dreadful record at the ground. The match against Zimbabwe was beyond these petty reasons though. No matter what the conditions were and no matter what the past was, India had to defeat Zimbabwe. To rise above these obstacles of conditions, history and the pressure created by the public back home, India required the old Ganguly who inspired his team irrespective of his personal ups and downs. So far in his captaincy career, he had always discovered something within. This time, he needed to find the courage to make the right decision, in fact two of them. He could not afford to operate with only two fast bowlers anymore. To accommodate the 3rd seamer, he had to pick either Anil Kumble or Harbhajan Singh. With a heavy heart, he asked the legend to sit out. The second choice was more personal. The opening slot is the best place to bat in ODI cricket. It allows you maximum time to score runs and get back in form. How dearly Ganguly desired some form. He would have traded anything for batting form but by the time India landed in Zimbabwe, he realised that his quest for form and obstinacy to open the innings was severely hindering the team's performance. He acknowledged (along with his squad who voted 14:1 in favour of Tendulkar–Sehwag Opening pair in a vote conducted by John Wright)that his squad included two better openers than him. The moment he accepted the truth, the decision became easy. For the betterment of the team, he sacrificed his opening slot which was perhaps his only way to get back into form.

It is said that success demands sacrifices. Ganguly's sacrifice of his opening slot yielded immediate success. For the last three months, India had struggled to stitch a decent opening partnership but in Harare, the new openers in Sachin and Sehwag joined forces to put on 99 runs. Sehwag's ability to score fast enabled Sachin to take it easy. Sehwag's uncluttered mindset negated the conditions and the pressure of the game. A relaxed Sachin at the other end spelled danger for the Zimbabwe bowlers. The maturity and confidence behind each of his shots started transpiring onto the incoming batsmen. Though India lost wickets regularly, the rate of scoring remained high throughout the innings. Sachin's 81, well supported by other batsmen secured a competitive total of 255.

The Indian bowlers needed to respond to the heartening batting display. Srinath was the first to react as he surprised both the Zimbabwean openers with his pace. The actual challenge lay ahead as the Flower brothers joined hands. India had suffered both of them so many times in the past. Indian fans were certainly not in a state to revisit those years anymore. India's first two matches had already reminded them of the Indian teams of yester years known for their jaded batting, uninspiring bowling and lethargic fielding! In the last couple of years, this team had broken the shackles of that image, especially with a sea of change in its fielding. It tried a new concept in this World Cup by appointing Mohammad Kaif as India's fielding captain. The overall poor performance of the team somewhat eclipsed his fielding performance. The match against Zimbabwe provided him an ideal stage. The bowlers were fired up by a competitive total and two early wickets. A good fielding effort and enthusiastic body language in the inner ring increases the intensity. Indian fielders, led by Mohammad Kaif did that to perfection. All of them ran hard, attacked the ball and dived like kids. The extraordinary energy in the circle heaped pressure on the Flower brothers. They were not allowed easy singles. As India stifled them more and more, a mistake seemed just around the corner.

Harbhajan Singh, India's preferred spinner over Kumble caught sight of the window of opportunity and bowled a wonder ball. The ball turned square to knock Andy Flower's leg stump from behind. To dismiss the big fish in such a comprehensive manner lifted the Indian team's spirit a couple of notches higher. When in control, Sourav Ganguly's captaincy was characterized by bowling changes which were difficult to describe but often successful. That one change symbolized his hold over the game. For the first time in the World Cup, he made his peculiar bowling change. He brought himself on.

For Ganguly, the recent criticism felt strange. Not so long ago, India had gleamed with buoyancy. It had drawn a test series in England and dominated every single series at home. Some of its exemplary ODI performances included the famous NatWest series win, reaching the final of the ICC Champions Trophy 2000 and co–winning the ICC Champions Trophy 2002. It had all gone wrong since then and Ganguly's ability to contribute was now placed under the scanner. His batting had no doubt taken a dip but on the Harare pitch, under overcast conditions, he fancied the bowler in him. He hit bull's eye as his gentle medium pace folded the Zimbabwe middle order in no time. His 3 wickets led India to its most crucial win in the World Cup.

Three moments stood out in India's disciplined bowling. First, Sourav

Ganguly ran his lungs out to chase a straight drive from a Zimbabwe batsman. Infamous for his fielding, Ganguly's commitment marked India's determination. Second, after the fall of every Zimbabwean wicket, the team gathered in a circle putting arms around each other's shoulders. It gave goosebumps to fans for no clear reason. It was called 'The Huddle', and it was to become the most powerful symbols in Indian cricket. And third, Andy Flower used to feature prominently in the long list of batsmen who used to walk all over Indian spinners abroad and in India. Every significant turnaround is sparked by an impactful incident. Andy Flower's 'bowled from behind his legs' was a trigger to the greatest streak in Indian cricketing history.

INDIA V/S NAMIBIA – BRUSHED ASIDE

ICC World Cup 2003 featured an extended league phase of six matches. In such a format, momentum is of paramount significance. India played close to its own self against Zimbabwe and a satisfactory outing boosted its morale. To continue its ascendancy, India called for a dominating display. India's next match, against World Cup debutants Namibia, arrived at the right time. The game had so many sub–plots. It offered one more opportunity for Sourav Ganguly to score some runs. It was another chance for the Indian middle–order to perform. Four precious points were also on offer. India had everything to play for against a minnow.

Ganguly avoided the temptation to open but at one down, found his old timing and placement again. He rediscovered his swift feet to dance down the wicket and hit the spinners over the head. His 112 comprised of 6 fours and 4 sixes. Although it was a century against a weak team but those were valuable international runs. His innings shot out a quiet reminder of his capabilities. But even such a dominating knock failed to deflect the focus from the other end where the genius was at work.

Sachin Tendulkar had top scored in all of India's three matches so far and had looked in ominous touch. He continued his rich vein of form to hit Namibia's bowlers to all corners of the field. His 18 boundaries sucked the life out of Namibian bowling, two of which nearly took the life out of one of the umpires and his skipper. Both avoided Sachin's brutal shots by a whisker.

Sachin's belligerent 152 lit up the beautiful Pietermaritzburg. Against India's rapidly improving bowling, Namibia was never in contention to chase 312 runs. India won by a whopping 181 runs and now was in the apt state of mind to play against one of the big guns. And if it lacked any motivation, Andrew Caddick decided to throw in some.

INDIA V/S ENGLAND – ONE NIGHT AT DURBAN

Unlike Football, cricket goes through mundane pre–match and post–match conferences. Every player attending them assumes his diplomatic responsibilities and babbles routine predictable lines but Andrew Caddick decided to have a bit of fun in the pre–match conference before the game against India. He went into lengthy details of Indian team's struggles in the Cup with a vicious jab. His observations were correct to a certain extent but then came the biggest jab. "Even Sachin did not play well despite his century (against Namibia). Sachin's just like another batsman in the Indian team and there are a lot of others in the Indian team." Andrew Caddick had done his homework on the Indian team but sadly for him, he had not done his homework on Sachin Tendulkar. He perhaps was not aware of the response Sachin usually gave to such insinuating comments.

"Oh! That's out of here, may be somewhere in Pietermaritzburg!" The commentator's reaction to the monstrous six Sachin hit to Andrew Caddick conveyed the audacity of the shot to the teeth. The sound of his bat hitting the ball echoed throughout Kingsmead. Sachin, by hitting Andrew Caddick out of the stadium had answered to the criticism, in his characteristic style. The sheer brutality of the shot introduced Caddick to the tough nut behind the baby face. The six transported Indian fans to Sharjah 1998 when an angry Sachin had unleashed on poor Henry Olonga. Sachin's six came in the middle of a devastating attack by Indian openers on the English bowlers.

Sachin commenced the proceedings against Caddick with a glorious flick. He followed it up with a strange pull shot. Then, he played a textbook cut to Anderson, one more trademark flick before exporting Caddick out of Durban. Caddick had said Sachin was just like any other Indian batsman. One of the 'other Indian' batsmen was Virender Sehwag, a Sachin devotee and he also decided to have his say. If Sachin demonstrated pure class, Sehwag applied brute force. James Anderson, the hero against Pakistan in its previous match bore the brunt of Sehwag's power hitting. The Indian batting which had struggled to get bat to ball for the last three months, was transformed into a big hitting unit in a space of 9 overs.

A quick opening stand allows the middle order time to rebuild, in case wickets fall in a cluster. So even though India lost Sehwag, Sachin and

Ganguly within 12 overs, India had plenty of time to rebuild a good score, a task relished by Dravid. Along with Dinesh Mongia and Yuvraj Singh, he went on to do his job. His patient 62 and Yuvraj's quick fire 42 set up a good platform to launch an assault in the last 5 overs but Yuvraj's ill–timed wicket in the 47th over halted India's charge and a gettable score of 300 got reduced to 250. India fell short by at least 50 runs. The target of 251 looked achievable, but one massive element was yet to be considered. Durban had switched on the floodlights and England needed no reminder of what the white ball could do under those lights in South Africa. Jamie Anderson had given England a sneak peek of the swing under the lights' against Pakistan in its previous match. England knew how difficult 251 runs were going to be!

Nick Knight and Marcus Trescothick spent the first over by Zaheer Khan in search of the dreaded Durban swing. Both found no swing and looked extremely tentative. On the first ball of Javagal Srinath's next over, Nick Knight defended the back of a length ball and called for a sharp single. He was deep into his crease but was confident to make it against a fast–approaching Indian fielder. Somewhere 4–5 steps down the line, he realised that the fielder ran much faster than he had anticipated. Still, he backed himself to reach the crease before him. 2–3 steps further, he saw the fielder collecting the ball cleanly at one go. He still had a couple of seconds that fielder required to throw the ball. He then caught sight of him dive full length and release the ball at the same time. Now that was impossible! How did he do that? And one step further, he realised his doom. Mohammad Kaif had hit the stumps directly with a full–length dive to run Nick Knight out. After the fixation about swing bowling, India's fielding captain did the trick.

Where did the god damn swing disappear to? The England openers had prepared a game plan to counter the swing Durban was expected to offer but the Indian bowlers did not extract any swing. Both Zaheer and Srinath bowled back of a length and got bounce instead of swing. The England batsmen kept waiting for the swing. After 6 overs, Marcus Trescothick grew fed up of waiting and decided to take command of the situation. Unfortunately for him, he chose a well–directed bouncer from Zaheer to hit his way out. On the night when it was supposed to swing like never before, India resorted to back of the length bowling and outsmarted England.

After two wickets, Nasser Hussain and Michael Vaughan seized hold of India's game plan and steadied England. Now was the time to hand the killer blow. Now was the time for the Durban swing. Ashish Nehra changed his length altogether from that of India's opening bowlers. He bowled full and the Durban swing made a striking entry. A late out–swinger forced Hussain to poke at it and Dravid held on to a comfortable catch. England's next batsman, an old hand of more than 100 ODIs made up his mind to watch out for an out–swinger before even facing his first ball. As he saw the next ball pitching on middle stump, he pre–empted the ball to swing towards his off stump and took position for a strenuous front–foot defensive block. Before he could realise, the ball swung back and thudded into his pads. The umpire did not hesitate even for a second to judge him leg before.

Michael Vaughan saw both dismissals from the other end. Hussain fell to an out–swinger and Stewart to an in–swinger. He gathered that England required a great amount of fortune to survive the Durban conditions. He met none while trying to cover–drive Nehra's away swinging delivery. India had not seen a spell of fast bowling of such quality before. Every ball was pitched on correct length, had a decisive line and every ball clocked a speed of above 140 kmph. England succumbed to the Durban swing and Ashish Nehra. His funny celebrations added an uncanny charm to his spectacular bowling. India had rarely seen its fast bowler dominate an entire batting line. Ashish Nehra was the toast of the town. Even vomitting after eating a banana could not stop him from claiming his career best performance of 6 for 23. It gave India a commanding win over England.

Andrew Caddick's conclusion, from India's performances so far, of India being a below average team consisting of under–performing batsmen and unimpressive bowlers was accurate to some extent but after England's match, the scenario had changed. All Indian batsmen looked in good touch. The bowling seemed sharp. The fielding looked world class. An all–round performance against England sealed India's berth in the next round. Its remaining group match became a dead rubber having no bearing on its position. India could afford to sit back; even consider resting players. If anyone thought on these lines, he or she for sure had paid no attention to India's next opponent. The day was marked instantly after the ICC had announced the groups and fixtures for the World Cup. 1st March 2003 was a day to revive the old war, to revisit the intensity, emotion and passion of the mightiest cricket match on the planet. Time had come to instill life in Cricket's fiercest rivalry, which had lost its spunk in the past few years. It was time to meet the neighbors after 3 years.

INDIA V/S PAKISTAN – PRESENCE OF PURE GREATNESS

1947 added two sovereign nations to the world. The basic fabric of both the nations was very similar to one another, apart from the majority religion. Both nations vowed to come out of the imperial shadows and for achieving it, they needed to set up institutions to guide and govern the country. Stability in daily life was a principal concern but it was the most difficult thing to achieve for the infant governments of both the countries. India had an advantage of half established systems. Pakistan required starting from scratch. Hence India's road to recovery and self–dependence was quicker than Pakistan's. The general state of the countries also got reflected in the development of its common passion, Cricket.

Indian cricket in the early years of independence was blessed with individual excellence which ensued in good team results every now and then. Pakistan was likewise blessed with stupendous talent but it never got transformed into team success. The lineage of greatness was impossible to ignore though. Fazal Mahmood, an epitome of the word 'fast', inspired several generations to pursue fast bowling. Pakistan's very own 'little master' Hanif Mohammad, was one of Pakistan's finest batsmen ever. They still talk about his technique and concentration. No wonder he became the first Pakistani batsman to score a triple hundred in a test match. Zaheer Abbas was known as the 'Asian Bradman' not for nothing. His capacity to play swing and spin bowling with equal finesse earned him the status of a legend. His flamboyant mannerisms perhaps left a stronger influence on the next generations of Pakistani batsmen.

These names were legends but remained individual talents. Pakistan the team never blossomed till an Oxford graduated fast bowler assumed charge of Pakistan Cricket. Imran Khan infused confidence in the team, of achieving international glory. Under his captaincy, Pakistan won the 1992 World Cup and declared its arrival on the international stage. Pakistan, after the 1992 triumph, never looked back and established itself as one of the leading teams in international cricket.

In all its inconsistent years in international cricket before Imran Khan, Pakistan always compelled India to seek from the farthest corners of its ability but India somehow managed to have an upper hand. Until 18th April

1986! 18th April 1986 changed it all. Chetan Sharma's full toss completely transformed Pakistan's approach of playing against India. Javed Miandad's last ball six handed Pakistan a psychological edge. Pakistan dominated India for the next 14 years.

Pakistan ruled India for the following one and half decade. The horror of those defeats kept resonating in the minds of the fans amidst deteriorating political relations between the two countries which had resulted in zero cricketing ties for the last 3 years. Pakistan's supremacy over India had made a lasting impact. Much had changed since. India had undergone a radical makeover in its approach and mental strength. Nothing had changed in Pakistan Cricket though. It still had those big players who used to rub Indian faces in the ground. It was still marred by internal politics but one point was damn sure; despite its internal politics and miserable World Cup 2003 so far, Pakistan was certain to bring forth its best cricket against India. Pakistan's excellence and the fearless attitude of young India guaranteed an epic, iconic and grandeur cricket match. Little did the cricketing world know that a little fellow named Sachin Ramesh Tendulkar had decided to bestow Super Sports Park, Centurion with his majestic and godly batting.

Centurion was filled to capacity, spawning relentless noise. Both sets of fans had waited 3 long years for the appointment. The wait had added extra spice to the contest. Pakistan's 11 had already made the Indian fans edgy. The first name in the batting order itself did not need any introduction. He had whipped former Indian bowlers for seven years with the ease of playing school cricket. Indian fans were sure that a terrible World Cup so far would not stop him from scoring in this match. He did not disappoint. It seemed nothing had changed for him even though India's bowling had gone under complete overhaul in the last couple of years. Saeed Anwar, the man who had scored 194 against India 6 years ago, reached his first century of World Cup 2003, without breaking a sweat. His elegant 101, ably supported by Mohammad Yousuf, Younis Khan and Rashid Latif guided Pakistan to a commanding score of 273. Despite India's deep transformation, Pakistan's innings resembled any other 1990s match between the two sides. Hell, it even had an 'Inzamam run out.' Indian supporters remembered how those matches used to end in the 1990s and how Pakistani fast bowlers used to rip the Indian batsmen apart! Pakistan still possessed the same lethal bowling of Wasim Akram, Waqar Younis and Shoaib Akhtar! The first half of the match brought back old nightmares. There was all likelihood that the second half would follow suit. In the anxious seconds of anticipation, Indian fans got a huge surprise. Every Indian fan knew Sachin Tendulkar's dislike of facing the first ball of the innings. Stories of him being tricked by his batting partners into taking strike were legendary. To the absolute shock of everyone, Sachin took strike in Centurion, that to against his old nemesis, a fellow called Wasim Akram.

Wasim Akram had mastered the method of setting up Sachin Tendulkar. Step 1 was to bowl two or three balls swinging across, which Sachin would normally leave. Step 2 was to follow it up by an in–swinger, forcing Sachin to play across which more often than not resulted in LBW. Wasim Akram's third ball in Centurion, his first move in the grand plan was implemented to precision. The across–ball pitched on the precise spot but the outcome was quite distinct. Instead of leaving the ball, Sachin rocked back on his back foot, created room and smoothly drove it for four. The confidence in his feet movement indicated that something special was in the offing. Nobody had imagined at that point, the quality of batting that would enthrall world cricket for the next 145 minutes.

For any batsman, a duck is a nightmare. But a golden duck is a rotten feeling. Sachin Tendulkar in his long glorious test career went through it only five times. Amongst those five, the one against Pakistan was perhaps the most embarrassing. A tall, muscled up, longhaired Pakistani bowler, running 40 yards, intense hostility in his eyes, had shattered Tendulkar's stumps all over the pitch. The sight had stunned the packed Eden Gardens into pin drop silence. Four years later, Shoaib Akhtar marked his run–up, 40 yards and gazed around the electric Centurion. At the other end, Sachin marked his guard and glanced around with inexplicable confidence. If Akhtar looked menacing, Sachin seemed determined. On the 4th ball of Shoaib's over, India finally earned its redemption to Javed Miandad's six. A short, wide but very fast ball of Shoaib Akhtar was dispatched by Sachin into the stands with an inhuman calm. How could one consider such a shot to an aggressive fast bowler! Where did he find the time to react to a 150 Kmph ball! It took just a couple of seconds for the ball to soar into the crowd. In those mesmerizing two seconds, India snatched back the leverage Javed Miandad had given Pakistan 17 years ago. Many felt at the time that Sachin's six to Shoaib would go on to define 'India–Pakistan Cricket' for the coming 10 years. The flick and straight drive which succeeded the immortal six, not only flattened Shoaib Akhtar and Pakistani bowling, it also started the long chain of glorious strokes and heavenly batting by India's batting God.

Pakistani bowlers sought to induce the edge of his bat by bowling outside his off stump but he moved his front foot majestically to hit them through the covers. When they bowled at his body, he found all the time in the world to jump on his back foot and flick them through mid–wicket and square–leg. Everything that the Pakistan trio had, they dished out at him and everything that was dished out was met with a divine stroke. Many artists find themselves in the middle of a creative spell where it proceeds organically. A few unhindered brush strokes create a masterpiece for a painter. Vague thoughts transform into wonderful poetry. An unbridled vision becomes the greatest film of all time. Sachin Tendulkar's master class inning of 98 was nothing less than a beautiful piece of art. The artist in him crafted one of the most stunning innings of his life.

Sachin Tendulkar's 98 captivated everyone to such an extent that they overlooked the 21 other individuals taking part in the match. During his 98, the match produced typical India–Pakistan moments. Pakistan's back–to–back strikes to send Sehwag and Ganguly back into the hut threatened a collapse. Sachin Tendulkar's only feeble moment of the match was immediately after those two quick wickets which almost got him out. A dropped catch from Abdul Razzaq was summed up by Wasim Akram in one line– *"Tuze pata hai na tune kiska catch choda hai?"* (I hope you know whose catch you have dropped.) The most critical stage came when Sachin's body began cramping. Throughout his career, Sachin was always reluctant to take a runner. He believed he himself could be the only judge of quick singles and a runner complicated his thinking. But as his body gave in, he had no choice but to take a runner. So, with a runner and a cramped leg, he braced himself to face Shoaib Akhtar again. Sachin had owned him in his first two spells but with restricted feet movement, he was severely handicapped; an opportune moment for a fast bouncer. Shoaib Akhtar finally got it right as it pushed Sachin in an awkward tangle and he could not keep the ball down.

And so, it ended. Sachin Tendulkar chose the grandest and toughest match of India's World Cup campaign to play the greatest ODI innings of his career. He had demolished the Australian bowling in Sharjah before, with similar disregard. But the quality of bowling he faced in Centurion and the quality of every stroke of his elevated the innings to unparalleled heights. His dismissal provided one last twist to the match. India still required 97 more runs. Pakistan in the past had seen India squander the advantage innumerable times after Sachin's dismissal. How many times had Indian fans seen a dramatic collapse after Sachin's wicket! While half the television sets were switched off on one side of the border, Sachin's wicket handed a second lease of life to the other side. The Indian bowling performance in the match did not reflect the transformation it had gone through in the last three years. The Indian middle order got the splendid opportunity to introduce it to the neighbour. An unbeaten partnership of 99 runs between Dravid and Yuvraj hit the final nail. India marvelled at the temperament shown by a 22–year boy playing his first India–Pakistan match, that too in a World Cup. No wonder he found a solid supporter in his captain. Yuvraj's 50 assured India of a future star. Dravid's 44 assured India of a rock–solid middle order anchor. For Pakistan, the loss was hard to take. India scored 97 runs after Sachin's departure, without losing a wicket. With wins only against Namibia and Netherlands, Pakistan crashed out of the World Cup. With its 4th consecutive win, India surged into the Super Six phase.

In 1989, a 16–year–old boy had continued batting with a bloodied nose to defy odds and the ferocious Pakistani bowling. 14 years later, his best one–day inning resulted in Pakistan's lowest point in 4 years. The loss put an end to some of the most illustrious cricketing careers. The magnificent pair of fast bowlers, 'the 2 Ws' decided to bid adieu to cricket. (It was Waqar who had given Sachin that bloodied nose). While one neighbour lost itself into the wilderness, the other celebrated its impressive success. While one mulled over restructuring its team, other braced itself for the second phase of its magnificent streak.

INDIA V/S KENYA – THE CAPTAIN'S KNOCK

If India's heavy plunge into mediocrity and the tremendous surge to rise above it was the story of Pool A, Kenya's entry into the Super–Six stage was certainly the talking point of Pool B. Bombings in Mombasa which had killed 16 people had fueled New Zealand's security concerns over playing in Kenya. ICC rejected New Zealand's plea to shift the venue for the match compelling New Zealand to forfeit the match which gifted 4 valuable points to Kenya. Kenya was a single upset away from its best World Cup achievement. The upset came against Sri Lanka and Kenya marched into the Super–Six phase.

Losing to Kenya at Gwalior five years ago had been haunting India for long. Much water had gone under the bridge since. When a big team plays a minnow, there's always a question mark on its intensity. It requires greater resolve to keep focus in such matches. Kenya's decent score of 225 cast a doubt on India's attitude while bowling. India's batting needed to put in a disciplined display to continue its momentum further into the tournament.

The law of averages has a peculiar trait. It strikes in the hour of utmost need. Sachin had scored runs in every single match so far. The law of averages struck him soon after he struck a wonderful straight drive. Following the early dismissal of Sehwag, Sachin's wicket intensified pressure on the team, more so, on the captain who had only 172 runs to his credit from 6 matches. Considering 112 of them were against Namibia, he stared at a potential career threatening failure. The Kenyan bowlers extracted swing in the air due to overcast conditions which made life further complicated for Ganguly but to his advantage, the ideal foil stood at the other end to absorb the pressure. Rahul Dravid had featured in two of the biggest ODI partnerships in the last four years; 331 runs with Sachin against New Zealand and 318 runs with Sourav Ganguly against Sri Lanka. While Sachin's 186 took the attention away from Dravid's 153, Sourav Ganguly's 183 against Sri Lanka had received all the limelight. Dravid never grumbled. That was the charm of the man. He always sported a supporting role in ODIs without any fuss. In Cape Town, against an on–song Kenyan bowling, he was required to soak the pressure to facilitate stroke making at the other end.

For the next 20 overs, Rahul Dravid looked his defiant best as he played out ball after ball after ball. His 73 balls 32, allowed the under–performing and under fire captain to play his natural strokes. India took it slow till the 30th over and then unleashed the onslaught in the last 20. Dravid's wicket when India still needed 118 runs from 20 overs endangered the plan for a while. The match appeared evenly poised until Yuvraj Singh, fresh from his match winning knock against Pakistan, started bashing the Kenyan spinners. His aggression transpired on Ganguly to do his favourite thing. There was no better sight in world cricket than seeing Ganguly use his feet and hit spinners out of the ground. His big hitting depended more on timing than power and hence it was always comforting to the eyes. A delicate situation was converted in a dominating one–sided victory in 48 overs. Sourav Ganguly scored his 2nd hundred of the tournament. The first ton had given him some assurance. The 2nd, the more valuable one, led India to an important win. India almost had a foot in the semi–finals. In fact, it was just a win away from it.

INDIA V/S SRI LANKA – 23 OVERS, 3 BOLWERS

India traditionally has been a batting country. On placid pitches made for spinners only, India churned out wonderful batsmen but good fast bowlers were a rare species. Centuries were more alluring than 5 wickets hauls. The primary job of an Indian fast bowler was to take the shine off the ball for enabling spinners to prevail. Many times, India went into a test match with only one fast bowler. Indian fast bowling was non–existent, barring two or three exceptions for nearly 5 decades until Ganguly prioritized it. Conscious efforts to make fast bowling equally pertinent had yielded mixed results so far. Indian pacers had lacked consistency in the World Cup thus far. They were unplayable against England but leaked runs against Pakistan. The Super–Six stage was no place for inconsistency or incompetence. Javagal Srinath, India's spearhead grasped the gravity of the situation. A tough challenge awaited him as he was up against a batting lineup which had milked him for runs for years. He had accepted Ganguly's proposition to return to international cricket for exactly these sorts of situations. He required to a set few things right.

So, even after Sachin Tendulkar's sublime 97 against Sri Lanka, Sehwag's dominating 66 and Ganguly's 48 mirroring his old self, Javagal Srinath bagged the man of the match award for his 4 for 35. That was an uncommon occurrence in Indian cricket. The Indian bowling had the cushion of a big score but the opponent batting featured Sanath Jayasuriya, Aravinda de Silva and Marvan Atapattu. These names gave nightmares to Indian bowlers throughout the last decade. It felt surreal when India got rid of Atapattu, Jayawardene and Aravinda De Silva for ducks. It almost felt illusory to see Jayasuriya struggle for 45 minutes against his favourite bowling attack to eventually hold out in covers. The batting line up which used to clobber India black and blue was bundled out for 109 in 23 overs. India required only three fast bowlers to finish off the Lankan batting. Indian cricket had changed beyond doubt.

The match had witnessed Sachin's famous back foot cover drives, his million–dollar straight drive and of course a replica of the Shoaib Akhtar Six. It had witnessed Sehwag's merciless cuts and drives; Ganguly's trademark cover drives and his famous 'shuffle across the crease' to hit Sri Lankan seamers out of the ground. Despite such batting on display, 23 overs bowled by India's three fast bowlers stole the show. With one match to spare, India was through to the Semi–Finals. The next match though was not about points or semi–final places. India's miserable last three months had started on those green pitches in New Zealand. It was time to return the favour.

INDIA V/S NEW ZEALAND – THE RETURN GIFT

"We always knew our bowling had tremendous talent. The New Zealand conditions gave them confidence. I admit our batsmen struggled there, but those were extreme conditions. Even New Zealand's batsmen struggled. I was sure with the quality we had in our batting, all of them will stand up when required. It was our bowlers who required a bit of confidence and thanks to New Zealand's tour, they found it. I always knew any batting line will struggle against our confident bowlers. I was not surprised at all with New Zealand's collapse today."

Ganguly's final poke at New Zealand put a smile on Indian faces. Indian fans had spent hours analysing India's pathetic batting in New Zealand but Indian bowlers had troubled New Zealand batsmen throughout the tour. Zaheer Khan, in particular, had put in stunning performances in the tests and ODIs. In India's last Super–Six match of the World Cup, he took only three balls to remind the Kiwi batsmen of his skills. In those three balls, he picked up two wickets. His first over started another fantastic bowling performance by India.

Zaheer found swing and utilized it to perfection. Ashish Nehra found bounce and used it splendidly. The future of Indian bowling looked richer than ever, as both of them reduced New Zealand to 47 for 4. The young guns dictated the first 15 overs. India's old horse provided a decisive break in the 18th over. Stephen Fleming had already lit up the World Cup 2003 with a devastating 134 against the much–fancied South African attack. He also was one of those batsmen who loved scoring against India. Where other New Zealand batsmen wriggled under the lively Centurion conditions against India, he strolled to 30 runs. His ease of scoring spelt danger for India until Srinath's pace surprised him into playing an awkward shot. With half the side gone within first 18 overs, India was on its route to annihilate one more batting line–up. Three years ago, the pair of Chris Cairns and Chris Harris had snatched the ICC Champions Trophy from India's hands. Harbhajan had not played that match. He made sure that history did not repeat when in the conditions conducive to fast bowling, he extracted extra bounce from the pitch and Cairns could not control his cut shot. The remaining innings was a formality as Zaheer finished it off to end up with 4 for 42. After demolishing Sri Lanka for 109, the Indian bowling shredded New Zealand for 146.

Shane Bond had been a headache for the Indian batsmen throughout its tour to New Zealand. The Indian batsmen just could not handle his pace. Their misery against him continued in South Africa too as he blew away India's top order. India's middle order, especially Mohammad Kaif had not yet gotten an opportunity of any significance with the bat. So far his substantial contributions were 35 runs against Pakistan and an 'a la Jonty Rhodes' run out of Nick Knight against England. The situation was tailor–made for him to shine and he seized it. The partnership between Kaif and Dravid reinforced India's endeavour to end its over–dependence on Sachin. The pair showed exemplary patience after the top order fell for 21 runs. Dravid was renowned for his composure and Kaif had shown his temperament in the NatWest Series Final. Together, both of them scored with pleasing effortlessness. Both looked under no pressure despite hostile bowling spells by Shane Bond. Both showed no signs of the desperate struggle they had been through against the same bowling attack a couple of months ago. India's comfortable 7–wicket win with 56 balls to spare prompted the captain to thank New Zealand. According to him, it was because of the New Zealand tour, that India found itself in the World Cup Semi–Finals. In reality, New Zealand found itself knocked out of the World Cup because of India. It was a fitting return gift for the ordeals endured three months ago. India reached the Semi–Finals of a World Cup for the first time since 1996. It gave goosebumps and shivers to all Indian fans at the same time; goosebumps because India had excelled way above expectations and shivers because of the memories of its previous World Cup Semi–Final appearance. It knew the threat posed, because it faced a double–edged sword of playing Kenya, a minnow in the Semi Final.

INDIA V/S KENYA – THE SEMI FINAL

Sri Lanka was an unknown cricketing entity in 1996. Nobody had heard of Kaluwitharana, Gurusinha, Mahanama and Dharmasena. India knew a little of Muralitharan, Vaas, Aravinda de Silva and Ranatunga. The semi–final at Eden Gardens was deemed a walk over for India despite having lost earlier to Sri Lanka in the group match. Even after Sri Lanka had posted a challenging first innings score in the semi–final; none would bet against India. Till the time Sachin stood at the crease, it looked every bit of a walk over. But Sachin's dismissal caused a rapid collapse. The score of 98 for 1 became a disastrous 120 for 8 in a blink of an eye. Nobody could fathom the inadequacy of India's formidable batting to survive against Sri Lankan Spinners. Indians were supposed to be the best in the world at playing spin. The Indian fans could not digest it. The Eden Gardens crowd certainly did not. It showed its protest by throwing bottles on the ground. It compelled Match officials to award the match to Sri Lanka. 13th March 1996 till date, remains one of the most painful days for many Indian fans.

In the ICC World Cup 2003, India again encountered an identical situation. It was pitted against a minnow, Kenya, who astonished World Cricket by its presence in the top four teams. Long before the match started, the encounter was labelled as a 'full stop' for Kenya. A placard reading 'It ends tonight' precisely articulated the context in which the match was seen. India needed to be careful. It had already suffered the pain of losing a Semi Final to a perceived minnow. More than cricketing abilities, India required mental fortitude to put aside the talk of a dominating win and concentrate on the game at hand. Kenya had nothing to lose and India had everything to gain. India understood well how dangerous the 'nothing to lose attitude' could get. No wonder India felt the pressure.

India's in–form bowling unit licked its fingers at the prospect of bowling in overcast conditions. That was India's best chance to finish the match as early as possible. Sourav Ganguly's decision to bat first hence puzzled one and all. Perhaps, he wanted to avoid the pressure of chasing in a semi–final. Perhaps, he wanted to escape revisiting the memories of that fateful day in 1996. The Indian top–order had its task cut out. In addition to the overcast conditions, India needed to watch out for a potential threat in Aasif Karim, a gentle left–arm orthodox who had given Australia a big scare five days ago. India enjoyed one considerable advantage though, to counter the pressure.

The uncomplicated method of Sehwag's batting provided India with a solid start. That it was the occasion of a Semi–Final or the conditions certainly did not matter much to him. He treated each ball without any baggage which resulted in quick runs and settled early jitters. By the time Sehwag departed, he ensured a good foundation for the rest to build upon. It soon reflected in Tendulkar's straight drive but the other end garnered all the attention. Kenya had strangled Australia in the Super–Six match with its variety of spin bowling. Australia struggled against the combination of an off–spinner, a leg spinner and a left–arm spinner. For Sourav Ganguly, all three were his favourite types.

Ganguly announced his mood by hitting an off–spinner for a six over long–off. It took him no time to dispatch the leg spinner outside the ground with dazzling foot–work. When Sachin got out on 83, Indian fans panicked a bit. India's collapse against Sri Lanka in the 1996 Semi–Final ran through their minds. At that precise juncture, Ganguly chose to underline the difference between the 1996 team and the 2003 team. He went berserk after Sachin's wicket, to hit the Kenyan bowlers all over Kingsmead. To watch him use his feet, come down the track to smack Kenyan fast bowlers out of the stadium was idyllic. He brought up his century by sending another bowler into the stands. He punched the air, looked at the dressing room and showed his bat with an astounding tenacity. His one gesture highlighted the difference between 1996 and 2003. The 2003 team had a captain who stepped up at the right moment to inspire his young team. The 2003 team believed in its ability, courtesy its ever defiant captain. The 2003 team was the first solid 'team' India had had in the last 13 years. The 2003 team was a team, not 11 individuals.

It looked beyond Kenya to chase 271 in Durban under lights against the Indian bowling. Even the Kenyan players accepted the reality but the Indian team refused to acknowledge it. The bowlers came out with an intensity of defending 171! India had never seen such a ruthless attitude from its team before. Zaheer & Srinath started with hostile speeds and exquisite accuracy. Zaheer Khan took the first wicket with a yorker. The sight of the Indian lead pacer bowling a yorker had vanished in the last decade and it felt good to see Zaheer Khan bowl those yorkers on cue. Ashish Nehra's pace and awkward bounce outclassed Kenya's middle order. The performance, as they like to call it, was clinical. Even Ganguly's part–timers claimed 3 wickets and the ticket to destiny was booked. With eight consecutive dominating wins, India entered the final of the World Cup after 20 long years. 20 years ago, Kapil Dev and his team had transformed a sport into a national hysteria. Sourav Ganguly and his players stood one match away to restore the pride and the glory of India's most loved game, its national craze.

INDIA V/S AUSTRALIA – A DREAM THRASHED

"Can we score a boundary each over? It means 200 runs from 50 balls. That leaves us with 160 runs from 250 balls. Let's try to do it!" Sachin Tendulkar rearranged some numbers to inspire his team to chase down a target of 360 runs in 50 overs. The Indian team had gone into a state of shock and distress after it had been subjected to one of the most bullying batting shows one had ever seen in recent history. It had all begun with a contentious decision of the captain four hours ago.

Australia came into the final, unbeaten throughout the tournament. Apart from scares against England and Sri Lanka, its road to the final was smooth as a freeway. It boasted a dominating batting and a fearsome bowling unit. The other finalist, India, tasted defeat only once. A lot had changed since that loss which had turned out to be between the struggling Indian batting and world–class Australian bowling. Australia went ahead dominating each and every opponent in a similar way while India raised its game in each of its matches. The batting had transformed into a formidable unit, amassing 2359 runs in the tournament, 77 runs more than Australia. Its bowling trio of Srinath, Zaheer and Nehra, the surprise package of the tournament shared 49 wickets between them, second to Australia dominating trio of McGrath, Lee and Bichel by 3 wickets. The statistics drew a stark picture. The two best teams of the World Cup featured in the final. Statistics showed that India was not far behind Australia. Considering India's winning streak, some even dared to put India as favourites but the statistics and momentum did not take into account one prominent factor. While Australia featured 5 players who had played in a World Cup final before, there was none in the Indian team. The toughest task for India was to cope with the pressure. The body language and expressions of India's most senior bowler during the national anthem suggested that the Indian team was miles from it. Sourav Ganguly's inexplicable decision to bowl first was indeed a reason to be shaky.

The pitch looked ideal for batting. It contained some moisture due to the overnight rain. Was Ganguly, by choosing to bowl, trying to exploit that moisture or did he simply want to protect his batsmen? After all, Australia had packed the same Indian batting lineup for 125 runs in the group game. Though India was justified in believing in its bowlers to utilize the conditions, there was another crucial piece of statistics. It had almost been three years (71 matches) since Australia last failed to defend a target of 200 or more. A dubious decision by the captain and an edgy senior fast bowler made Indian fans uneasy. India needed a steady start to calm the nerves and then came the catastrophic start to India's outing. The first over by Zaheer started the longest three and a half hours for every Indian fan and of course, the Indian team.

The moment Zaheer gave a long stare to Mathew Hayden and exchanged some heated words with Adam Gilchrist, without any rhyme or reason, Indian fans sensed that every single Indian player was a nervous wreck. The over lasted 10 minutes and consisted of 2 no balls, 2 wide balls, a fumble on the boundary by Srinath and 15 runs! The dreadful first over was followed by the assault of a lifetime. A moment of naïve aggression from Zaheer challenged the most attacking opening pair in the world. Hayden and Gilchrist looked unstoppable as they pounded the loose balls offered by the Indian fast bowlers. Before India could even get the bearings of situation, Australia had scored 74 runs in 9 overs. India's much talked about fast bowling trio was taken to the cleaners. Ganguly now had to turn to his spinner. Harbhajan Singh had been a nemesis for Australia two years ago. Ganguly hoped that he could bring some sanity to the situation.

Harbhajan's first 3 overs calmed some nerves. He found adequate pace and flight. Both the Aussie batsmen displayed utmost caution against him. He finally induced one false shot from each of the openers to claim two quick wickets. Every Indian on the planet hoped for the famous Australian collapse which had been a routine in India 2 years ago in that classic test series. After all, the next two batsmen were Harbhajan's bunnies. India succeeded in stopping the early mayhem and now hoped to consolidate, but India was unaware that the onslaught by Hayden and Gilchrist was a mere breeze; a hurricane was about to blow away the Wanderers.

Ricky Ponting was indeed Harbhajan's bunny, but that was 8250 Kms away on spinning tracks. The Wanderers had completely different conditions and on a completely different pitch, Ponting was a completely different batsman. Sourav Ganguly did him a huge favour by giving Harbhajan just one over after Hayden's dismissal. As Ponting found his feet against the gentle part–timers, he prepared to launch a heavy attack on the Indian fast bowlers. He relished Damien Martyn's company who went ahead with his business almost unnoticed. Each of Martyn's seven boundaries and a six bore his marvellous timing. The first 15 overs demonstrated brutal hitting. The next 15 were consolidation. And the last 20 were carnage in which Ponting hit three fours and eight sixes. Each six landed deep into the stands, one of which was hit with a single hand. A yorker is a very difficult ball to bowl under pressure. It runs a risk of getting converted into a full toss. Indian fans lost count of the number of full tosses bowled by the Indian bowlers. Ponting accepted each of them graciously. Even the fighter in Ganguly looked deflated and resigned to the obvious result. For the last 10 overs, he waited for the assault to finish. When a captain fails to react, it is very difficult for the team to turn things around. At the end of the 50th over, Ponting ended up with a magnificent 140, the highest team total in a World Cup Final and an opponent who had already accepted its fate.

Sachin knew his calculations were only a motivational *jumla* for the team which looked defeated. The calculations looked overtly simple and faced a big hurdle in the first over itself. Glen McGrath rarely conceded any runs in his first spell. Somebody had to attack him to draw him off the line because one miserly spell by McGrath was certain to end all hopes if there were any in the first place. Sachin decided to take it upon himself, only to find that it was not possible. In his efforts to throw McGrath off line, India's best batsman of the tournament, in fact, the best batsman of the tournament perished on the 5th ball of the first over confirming India's defeat. Not even a Sehwag blinder of 82 and twenty minutes of rain could change the inevitable. Australia again proved its supremacy over India. It conquered its 2nd consecutive World Cup and 3rd overall, the most for any team. Steve Waugh's celebrated Australian side was in capable hands.

For India, the tournament was a dream. India's dominance over every single team, apart from Australia of course, was one of a kind. Nobody had given India a chance to progress to the 2nd round after its first two performances' let alone being a finalist. To perform with such high quality in South African conditions was by far the proudest achievement of Ganguly's young team. India had found a new generation, capable of taking Indian cricket forward. India had found its greatest batsman at the peak of his craft. India had found a captain destined to bring more glory to Indian cricket. India had found its lost passion for the game. Though India lost the Cup, it found a team. Sourav Ganguly's team India had matured from a young team to a force to reckon with. Ganguly's objective of building a formidable team was achieved. Now was the time to focus on the second mission – some overseas success.

INDIA'S TOUR OF AUSTRALIA 2003-04 – INDIA'S SUMMER DOWN-UNDER

UEFA Champions League is considered the toughest tournament in World Football. Its knock–out stages are held in 2 legs: home and away. The away goal carries a premium as the team that scores more away goals advances to the next round. (In case number of goals scored by both the teams is equal over the two legs.) Where the challenge in football lies in performing in front of a hostile away crowd, an overseas cricket tour presents an altogether different one – of playing in foreign conditions which puts a player's technique through the sword.

In the early years of its independence, India was predominantly occupied in coping with its domestic socio–economic problems. The socialist inclinations of its leaders kept it a closed economy. It almost seemed unwilling to let the outside world look at it. In 1991, a milestone year in the Indian growth story, India demonstrated its eagerness to be part of the global growth by opening up of its economy. Indian cricket though was not willing to change just as yet.

India had a proud tradition of spin bowling. It always produced legends to carry the lineage of spin to the next generation. Facing the likes of Bishan Singh Bedi, Erapalli Prasanna, B.S. Chandrasekhar and Venkataraghavan on turning pitches in India, terrified every overseas batsman. Spinners were considered to be the best and only weapon available. No dearth of spin bowling in the domestic circuit and turning pitches created a situation where mostly all Indian batsmen could play spin bowling with their eyes shut. World cricket looked in awe at the struggle the great Shane Warne, legendary Muttiah Muralitharan had to go through against Indian batsmen. But superiority against spin bowling came at a cost – vulnerability against fast bowling.

The Indian fast bowling had no glorious history to brag about. Whenever India toured abroad, it included medium pacers who could swing the ball but the pace (or lack of it) allowed the batsmen to adjust to swing. With no genuine fast bowler and batsmen who could not endure serious pace bowling, India was always in a scramble outside home. Though the likes of Sunil Gavaskar & Kapil Dev tried to break this mould, cricket being a team sport, had the better of them most of the time. Hence up to the year 2000, India was 'Team Invincible' at home but a 'dead duck' overseas. It needed one 'out of the skin' performance to revolutionize the age–old mentality, to instill belief in its ability to bat in alien conditions and take twenty wickets with its seamers. As it came to pass, a niggling history of 50 years would be overturned in December of 2003.

Amongst all overseas countries India struggled in, South Africa probably was the worst. Hence India's outstanding 2003 ICC World Cup in South Africa was a welcome surprise but the demands of ODI cricket radically differ from that of test cricket. It was test cricket that was consuming the captain. Ever since Ganguly took over, India had shown stronger willingness to excel overseas but inconsistency hindered its objective. Ball tampering allegations on Sachin Tendulkar had pushed cricket to the back seat in its South Africa tour. In England, the batsmen proved their competence to score huge runs even in the most adverse conditions but the fast bowling looked inconsistent to take twenty wickets. And then the disastrous tour of New Zealand befell where the self–belief given by the England tour vanished in thin air. Batsmen struggled to get bat to ball, let alone scoring runs on those green wickets, though the bowling came into its own.

Before leaving for the Australian summer, India played a home test series against New Zealand. Ordinarily, it used to be a walk over in these home tests. The batsmen used to pile up runs and spinners used to make the opposition look stupid. New Zealand's visit threw up some surprises. Indian bowlers struggled to dismiss the determined and gutsy Kiwi batsmen. The New Zealand batsmen amassed 1242 runs in three innings. India was asked to follow–on in the Mohali Test. India's preparation and psyche were not the best for a tour like Australia. The bowling struggled to pick wickets and the batting line–up had to follow–on in its own den. Australia was the worst place to visit for a team dealing with confidence issues. The team was certain to get reminders of its shortcomings throughout the tour by the Australian team, crowd and the media. The mind games had already begun Down Under even before India reached its shores. India heard three words repeatedly, 'Sweet Chin Music'. The Australian media had found its narrative for the series. It started pointing out Ganguly's poor record Down Under and thus questioned the team's ability to win at a place where its captain had struggled for runs.

One of the many fundamental problems India had experienced in its 1999 tour of Australia when it faced a humiliating white–wash was an underperforming opening pair. In 2003, an opener in Sehwag promised them a start. The other opener, Aakash Chopra though untested, was touted to be an ideal foil. India constituted a formidable middle order of in–form Rahul Dravid, the great Sachin Tendulkar, the maverick captain and a bloke who preferred playing in Australia than in India. Its lower order included a rookie wicket–keeper in Parthiv Patel, two fabulous spinners in Harbhajan Singh and Anil Kumble and then the inexperienced fast bowling attack. None of them had played a single test match in Australia before, apart from Ajit Agarkar. One of them had not even played test cricket before.

Australia, on the other hand, was plagued by injuries. Glen McGrath's ankle surgery comforted India. Brett Lee grappled with his form. Shane Warne was still serving the ban for doping charges. Australia's imposing batting though was sure to pose a clear threat. The newly developing rivalry was ready to begin a new chapter, the last chapter for Steve Waugh. Australia, in Steve Waugh's actual final frontier, wished for a fairytale ending to his glorious career. The man himself never believed in fairy tales in sports. Sourav Ganguly had proven him wrong once before, by scripting a fairytale series win in 2001 in India. This time though, he wanted to prove the otherwise: "There are no fairy tales in sports."

BRISBANE TEST – BRING ON THE SWEET CHIN MUSIC

Brisbane was a tricky venue to start the campaign for India. It always had bounce, pace and swing, a fatal blend for any Indian batsman. India needed to bowl first, more for protecting its batsmen from the pitch and overcast conditions than actually utilizing the conditions. The toss went in India's favour. India chose to bowl with the bowling attack of Agarkar, Zaheer, Nehra and Harbhajan Singh.

For any side in world cricket, survival would have been the priority on the Gabba pitch, but not the mighty Australian side! Instead, Australia counter attacked with stunning pace. The Indian players were bewildered and did not know what hit them. They hoped to utilise the conditions to impose some early pressure. Instead, they witnessed a run feast.

Australia scored 73 runs in the first 15 overs. The giant run machine called Mathew Hayden became the first player in the history of the game to score 1000 runs in three consecutive calendar years. Even when Zaheer Khan got rid of him, there was no relief. Ricky Ponting, who was in the best scoring phase of his life, stepped in next. Langer and Ponting carried the momentum, scoring 89 runs before Zaheer got into the act again by dismissing Ponting. Langer continued scoring at will, not at all troubled by the Indian bowling. Damien Martyn joined the party adding an unbeaten partnership of 100 runs at day end. Langer reached his 16th Test Century and entered the list of the finest openers the game had ever seen. Australia finished the day with 262 for 2 in 62 overs. After all the anticipation and expectation, India had produced a similar kind of day's cricket it had produced over the years in Australia. The next morning, a section of Australian Media suggested – 'Indian summer over.'

The key for India on Day Two was to keep the Australian batsmen quiet for some time. Australia had scored too freely on Day One. The bowlers recognized it. The first over fetched only a run followed by two maiden overs and a single run was scored in the 4th over. 2 runs in 4 overs was just not the Aussie way. So, in the 5th over of the day, Langer tried to force the issue and despite hitting a boundary on the first ball of Agarkar's over, the will to dominate led to his downfall. The next over brought a dramatic shift in the momentum of the match. Damien Martyn's run out was followed by Steve Waugh's bizarre hit wicket dismissal. Those were two of the unlikeliest modes of dismissal but the Indian team was not complaining. Zaheer in his next over removed the ever so dangerous Gilchrist (Laxman held on to a smart catch). All of a sudden, from a commanding position of 262 for 2, Australia stuttered at 276 for 6.

Andy Bichel and Simon Katich tried to hit their way out of trouble. Zaheer had found superb rhythm by then, becoming impossible to play. He along with Agarkar wrapped the innings on 323. Australia lost 8 wickets for 55 runs. It resembled one of those rapid collapses Australia had had in India in 2001. The bowlers had stood firm against the might of Australian batting. Now it was the batsmen's turn to rise to the occasion.

The uncomplicated batting style of Sehwag theoretically suited Indian pitches. Yet he had proved his prowess as an opener in the testing conditions of England. Australia was a bigger challenge though. He needed to come good against short–pitch balling, one of his weaknesses. Nobody knew much about Sehwag's opening partner. He was said to be the traditional opener who derived pleasure in grinding out sessions. With the untested pair of openers, India began its 1st innings.

Sehwag began his innings with caution. His respect for conditions and opposition was a welcome change. It confirmed India's determination to do well. A young man showed willingness to curb his natural aggressive instinct and wait for loose balls. It was a promising sight because for India to have any say in the series, the openers needed to give a solid start. Aakash Chopra struggled in the beginning but started to find his feet moving as he spent more time in the middle. After facing a barrage of short–pitched deliveries and hostile opening spells from Australia's fast bowlers, India posted an encouraging score of 61 runs in 19 overs. The Indian openers continued the good work started by the Indian bowlers. But after all, India stood against Australia. It was the great Australia. Their comeback was inevitable.

Nathan Bracken produced an important break–through for Australia by forcing Sehwag to edge an away swinger. Dravid at one–down was on a career high, scoring runs all over the world in all types of conditions. During this period, he had become more reliable than the great himself. His was the wicket Australia wanted. His was the innings India wanted. Steve Waugh brought in his most experienced bowler in the match. Gillespie steamed in and bowled a fast out–swinger against which even Dravid's technique was found wanting. India lost its best batsman without any contribution. This small spell of time threatened to destroy the hard work of Indian bowlers and openers. All hope now rested on Tendulkar's shoulders. And then the calamity called Steve Bucknor struck.

When a batsman is hit on a pad while leaving a ball, it always looks awful. Your instant reaction is, he is a goner. As a layman, you forget that the primary parameter for adjudging an LBW is that the ball must be going to hit the wickets. When Sachin misjudged a back of a length ball from Gillespie and tried to leave it, Steve Bucknor reacted as a layman. He did not consider the bounce Gillespie had got. His finger went up. Even Sachin Tendulkar could not hide his disbelief. With Bucknor's raised finger, all of India's hopes came crashing down. Gillespie had dismissed Dravid & Tendulkar in the same over, leaving India at 62 for 3.

The captain marched in. He had struggled in the previous test series in Australia. He was vulnerable against the short pitch stuff. Australia had talked about sweet chin music. Ganguly needed to defy the odds. Sourav Ganguly needed to prove himself by rising above his perceived limitations. He decided to go a step further. The Indian captain decided to change the nature of India's approach to cricket in overseas conditions forever.

The game of cricket is played as much on the pitch as in the mind. Ganguly assessed the state of the match and conditions in Brisbane. The most likely mode of dismissal on that pitch in those overcast conditions would be edging the ball behind the wickets. A batsman required a clear and assertive judgment in his footwork. Ganguly needed to forget about the short pitch stuff. And he exactly did that.

A clearer thought process allowed him to duck under the short balls comfortably. It enabled his front foot to move effortlessly, going to the pitch of the ball, allowing him to play his favourite cover drives. He nudged the ball around for quick runs, played delightful drives and cuts on the off side in between. He kept the scoreboard moving which took the scoring pressure off Aakash Chopra who preferred to dig in. Both of them started to build a partnership with Ganguly contributing most of the runs. The moment he treated each ball on its merit and avoided pre–empting bouncers, he rediscovered his great eye for gaps and his silken timing. It seemed India was making a comeback in the contest.

As Ganguly grew in confidence with each passing minute, his footwork became a pleasure to watch and no matter how many fielders Steve Waugh stationed on the off side, he managed to find the gaps. However, just when India started believing in its comeback, another brute of a delivery by Gillespie forced Aakash Chopra to hold out to Hayden. The long stoic toil of Aakash Chopra ultimately came to an end. He played at the strike rate of 26, but it was the innings of heart and not statistics. His ill–timed wicket meant India had to rebuild and the last pair of pure batsmen stood at the crease. V.V.S. Laxman joined the captain at 127 for 4. His last innings on Australian soil was a breath–taking combination of stroke making and timing and his last outing against Australia did not call for a reminder. Ganguly was striking the ball at almost 80. Laxman also, by nature was a fast scoring player but he curbed his instinct. He followed the old maxim – give the bowlers the first one hour and then take the rest.

As the ball got older and softer, swing began to disappear which allowed Laxman to use his wrists and play his trademark front foot drives and back foot punches. He and Ganguly took a special liking to Stuart McGill, Australia's lone spinner as they milked him on both sides of the pitch. Their blossoming partnership began to take India closer to Australia's first innings score inch by inch. Each stroke was a statement of assertion.

At the end of the 70th over, India reached 249 for the loss of 4 wickets with Laxman on 60 but Ganguly's 98 garnered all the attention. McGill, perhaps the only bowler Ganguly would have preferred at that stage, bowled on his pads. Ganguly paddled swept it. He ran hard and returned for a tricky second. He kept running beyond his crease. Then the awkward jump in the air came. The captain had made the announcement. We are here to compete.

It was his first Test Hundred in Australia but personal landmarks mattered less. It was more a captain's hundred than Sourav Ganguly, the batsman's hundred. The one player, who was considered to be the most vulnerable in the Australian conditions, crafted his most brilliant century there. The man in charge of Indian cricket took a giant step in shaping its future. His jump was mistimed but the occasion of the innings and its impact was not.

As it happens in team sport, the confidence of Ganguly's innings rubbed on to other teammates. How else, could one explain a novice 19–year–old Parthiv Patel staying at the crease for more than 2 hours, especially after losing Laxman (75 runs) at a crucial stage? His partnership with Ganguly not only added 56 runs and gave India a lead but it also wore out the 2nd new ball. The last time India had taken a 1st innings lead in Australia was way back in 1992. Ganguly's young warriors were responding to the call of their master. Hence, even after the captain got out on 144 to a standing ovation from the sporting Brisbane crowd, India was not willing to budge.

Ajit Agarkar walked into tremendous applause and cheers, not because he was an Aussie favourite. He had 5 consecutive ducks to his credit in India's last tour of Australia, 4 of which were golden ones. The match headed towards a draw but India had to keep its nose ahead. Agarkar needed to save his. India was required to play out another 10 overs in the day. But Agarkar did not surrender. He scored his first run Down Under in 6 innings. He received a standing ovation for his run to which he merrily reciprocated by raising his bat. India again put forth its mission statement: we will not be sitting ducks and who better to say it than Agarkar himself. Along with Parthiv Patel, he added 33 runs to close the day at 362 for 6, 39 runs in front. Another 41 runs stand between Harbhajan & Zaheer on Day Five ensured it crossed 400 in Australia for the first time in 12 years.

Both captains eventually agreed to be equal. For India, Brisbane signified more than a draw. Sourav Ganguly, the man of the match said, "We are looking forward to Adelaide." No previous Indian captain had ever said so because no previous captain had such an incredible performance in his bag. Adelaide Oval was waiting. India geared itself to dish out one more performance. It felt confident of a good show. What transpired in Adelaide was beyond imagination. The Indian team and its captain were about to write a golden page in the history of Indian Cricket.

ADELAIDE TEST – INDIA'S GOLDEN PAGE

Though overwhelming and euphoric, India needed to put Brisbane behind it. As an underdog, sometimes it's easy to play without pressure when you have nothing to lose but by the time India reached Adelaide Oval, expectations had reached a higher level. India could harbor a thought of upsetting the giants at Adelaide as the pitch usually turned. But then India received two body blows. Zaheer's fiery spell in Brisbane had ignited India's comeback and hence losing him to an injury dealt a hefty blow to its aspirations of taking twenty Australian wickets. India lost its seam spearhead with no experienced replacement. One man's loss is other's gain. Irfan Pathan was selected to make his test match debut. The second injury blow hurt more considering Adelaide's spinning tendencies. Harbhajan Singh had made a habit of picking Australian wickets in a bundle. On a fast Brisbane pitch, he played a supporting role but Adelaide was certain to assist him. The pre–match setbacks did not help but India desired to move pass them and concentrate on the game. For one thing was sure, Australia was going to come hard at them. After all, India had challenged them in their backyard.

The primary reason for Australia's dominance in the test arena was its ability to score at over four runs per over. An aggressive opener in Hayden always provided Australia a quick start. When Irfan Pathan, on his debut claimed the ever–so–dangerous Hayden, India discovered a new star. Irfan Pathan had grabbed limelight with his 9 for 16 against Bangladesh in the Asian U–19 tournament. To get Hayden out in the 3rd over of one's international career and that too in Australia suggested that he belonged to international cricket. His spell displayed glimpses of his talent. India was over the moon. But Ricky Ponting, coming at number three was ready to bring India back to earth.

The last three years had seen the tremendous rise of Ponting to the pedestal of being one of the greats in world cricket. He was in scoring form of his life, making runs for breakfast. After Hayden's wicket, India attempted to exert more pressure. Australia reacted to the pressure in a manner only Australia could, with a sudden counter attack which wiped out India's enthusiasm in no time. There was India hoping to take more wickets, and then there was Australia that responded with 135 runs in 27 overs. The post lunch session saw Australia at its dominant best, handing India a beating of a lifetime. By the time the fourth wicket fell, India had surrendered the day. It looked drained and appeared to be waiting for play to end. It was a perfect time for any batsman to help himself. Simon Katich did not need an invitation. He creamed his way to a meticulously crafted 75, adding 138 runs for the fifth wicket. End of day's play had Ponting on 176, Australia on 400 for 5 and India on its knees.

After leaking 400 runs on Day One, India hoped for a disciplined bowling performance on Day Two. Though it avoided an Adam Gilchrist onslaught, it could not prevent Ponting from scoring his second double hundred. Ponting's 200 was effortless, fluid and his ease in scoring those runs left the spectators speechless. The Australian tail added to India's misery by scoring another 130 runs to take Australia to 556. It marked an uphill task from that point onwards. As Australia scored the runs in just 127 overs, India had to bat almost two sessions on Day Two itself after fielding for 127 overs. The time left by Australia by scoring quickly was perhaps an opportunity in disguise. India had ample time to chase down the Australian score. But did it have the patience?

Sehwag started in complete contrast to his cautious outing in Brisbane. He returned to his original self. His hitting ensured a good start of 61 in 11 overs. But then came thirty minutes of inexplicable panic and madness. Aakash Chopra hit the ball straight back to Bichel when the Indian score was 66. Sehwag flashed hard at a ball outside his off stump only to get a thick edge to Hayden. At 81 for 2, India now expected stability. Sachin Tendulkar was teased outside his off stump for six balls and eventually nicked the widest of them to Gilchrist reducing India to 83 for 3. And horrendous running between the wickets took out the captain leaving India stuttering at 85 for 4.

It's curious how the mind takes command over actual conditions. India's precarious position in the match made the pitch that resembled a batting beauty at 66 for no loss a few minutes ago, bring out its evil face. The bounce made the batsmen hustle. India had played out of its skin in Brisbane but to sustain the similar standard of quality and consistency for an entire test series was perhaps asking for too much. The 2nd day in Adelaide appeared to bring Indians down to reality. The Indian team looked under–prepared for consistent overseas success. The captain required a spectacular performance from his team to get out of the hole. It had already produced a miracle once at Eden Gardens and it, happening again would be a curious case of destiny. But if it was not for destiny, then why was the 'Eden Gardens pair' at the crease at India's precarious score of 85 for 4?

India lost its 4th wicket in the 21st over. The next wicket fell in the

115th over. Rahul Dravid and V.V.S. Laxman had done it again. For those 94 overs, it was Eden Gardens all over again. If Dravid exemplified solidity in defense and held the one end up, Laxman was at his magnificent best. If Dravid defined precision with his footwork, Laxman's timing was heavenly. The partnership included 34 sizzling boundaries but more importantly an extraordinary resilience. Both the batsmen looked equally comfortable and elegant on front foot and back foot, a rare combination for an Indian batsman. Both had magical strokes to every delivery Australian bowlers threw at them. Both played every shot in the book. Above all, both looked in complete command.

Dravid brought his century first with an uncharacteristic pull shot that went into the crowd. It was his 1st century in Australia and perhaps the one he would be remembered for. Laxman soon followed with his trademark boundary to score his 6th Century, his 3rd against Australia. Both pulled India out of deep trouble with a partnership of 303 runs. The pair had done it once again against the mighty champions. The last time, it had resulted in a famous win but when Laxman got out this time, India still trailed by 168 runs and its tail was exposed. Young Parthiv Patel indicated again that his temperament was beyond his age. His 65 minutes stay at the crease added another 59 runs. Agarkar confirmed that his 'duck tales' were a story of the past. But the day belonged to one man alone. Rahul Dravid, the backbone of Indian batting, India's best test batsman at that time finished the day agonizingly close to a landmark; on 199.

It took him just one ball on Day Four to reach his 4th double hundred. Rahul Dravid, India's anchor, India's savior had done it one more time. He had once again taken India from an inevitable loss to a possible win; and that too in Australia, the hardest place to score. With his double ton and India's fightback, there was a strong realization that India's 'willingness to fight' was not just a bunch of words. It indeed was its attitude. India conceded a lead of only 33 runs. The batsmen put on another good total but the bowling without Zaheer Khan posed a serious shortcoming. India needed one of its bowlers to rise to the occasion to translate the batting effort into bowling effort, to continue the momentum shift in the match. The unlikeliest fellow put his hand up to take up the responsibility.

To analyse Ajit Agarkar's career would be a hell of a task. He burst on to the scene with the record of being the fastest to 50 ODI wickets (23 matches). He is India's 3rd highest wicket taker in ODI cricket (288 wickets) and the quickest to get 200 ODI wickets and 1000 ODI runs. He scored a test match century at the Lord's which even Sachin Tendulkar did not manage. Yet, he always bore a tag of an underachiever. He chose Adelaide Oval to be a 'must–mention' in the history of Indian cricket.

33 runs behind and Langer, Hayden and Ponting as Australia's top order meant that even after the resolute retaliation from India, Ganguly had his headaches. With 2 more days of play left, he somehow had to get rid of the Australian top order for very few runs. To dismiss these 3 batsmen without conceding any runs was India's only outside chance of getting a favourable result. Then he saw an opening. Ajit Agarkar got the new ball to swing in a beautiful arc in his first two overs. Langer looked evidently in discomfort. In the 3rd over, he found the ideal line, perfect length to support his swing. With Langer's wicket, one third of Ganguly's problem was solved but the bigger problem took guard to face his first ball.

The game of cricket is the noblest leveler. Ponting had scored an effortless double hundred with 31 fours in the first innings but couldn't score a run from the 16 balls he faced in the second innings. Ganguly had played his master stroke. India put a lid on Australia's scoring rate. It scored only 18 runs in 7 overs. After facing 16 balls without scoring a run, the urge to dictate, drew Ponting into playing a flashy shot to the worst ball Agarkar bowled in that spell. The man, who had got a chanceless 242 in the 1st innings, was out for a duck to an average ball. The Indian opening bowlers had executed the captain's plan to virtue by picking up two wickets without conceding too many runs. The captain now expected his 3rd seamer to continue the good work. He did a little better.

The Australian batsmen were kept under pressure for 15 overs. Something had to give. Hayden tried to take control, only to find surprising agility in Sehwag's fielding. A 'diving forward' catch by him ended Ganguly's major worries. The Australian top order had been a thorn. His team reduced Australia to 44 for 3. Now began another test. The Indian bowlers had stifled the free–flowing Australian top order to induce errors from them. At 44 for 3, Australia went into rebuilding mode and hence the on–field pair did not face the pressure of scoring. For the next 15 overs, India missed the trick by allowing easy singles to Martyn and Steve Waugh. Australia slowly inched towards taking the hold of the match. A special move was needed from the Indian captain as the partnership was threatening to take the initiative away from India. And at this delicate moment, Ganguly turned to an improbable bowler, a player who was yet to contribute anything on this Australian tour.

The Dravid–Laxman partnership had already taken India back in time to Eden Gardens. In that match, due to the prodigious nature of Laxman and Harbhajan's performances, one man's bowling contribution went unnoticed. Sachin had the lion's share in Australia's dramatic collapse in the second innings as he had picked 3 crucial wickets of Hayden, Gilchrist and Warne. That had happened on a fifth day turner in Kolkata. Even though the Adelaide track offered a bit of help to spinners, Kumble was yet to extract any turn from it. With India's lead spinner struggling, fast bowlers tiring and tea only 8 overs away, bringing a part timer seemed sensible. The choice of the part timer baffled many. When the lead leg spinner struggled; what good could a part–time leg spinner do; especially when India possessed a more than handy off spinner in Sehwag? The answer perhaps was destiny, again.

Sachin could always turn the ball big. The problem was that he by default bowled at least two horror balls per over. When Steve Waugh smashed him for two consecutive boundaries, the move seemed to have back–fired. The critical part for any wrist spinner is the release. Sachin released it to precision in his 3rd over. Martyn went for a booming drive and if the delivery was an exceptional piece of cricket, Rahul Dravid's one handed reflex catch was a stunner. The part timer had done his job. It was time to unleash the seam bowlers on to the new batsman but Ganguly did not subscribe to cricketing reasoning. He fancied one more wicket from Sachin. The 35th over of the innings, the extra over Sachin got from his captain revealed the captain's specialty. It is not always about reasoning. Sometimes, it is about the instinct. Another enticing tossed up leg spinner got the edge of Steve Waugh's bat. Dravid had a simpler catch this time. Sachin Tendulkar, India's leading run scorer in Australia turned the contest around with his part–time leg spin. His double strike reduced Australia to 112 for 5 at tea on day 4. India, for the first time in the match, emerged clear favourites.

Anybody who had followed Indian cricket for the last decade prayed for one thing. 'Please do not let the tail to wag.' The Indian team needed to seize the moment. India's liveliness on the field in the third session demonstrated its awareness of the situation. Though a partnership of 71 between Katich and Gilchrist endangered India's position for a brief while, it never lost focus. Agarkar, who started the collapse, bowled an excellent 2nd spell. The Indian bowlers did not give the Australian tail a chance to wag. (Australia was all out for 196.) The Indian opening pair in its second innings absorbed the pressure to keep the fierce Australian bowling at bay and ended the day on 37 without losing a wicket. India was 193 runs away from creating history. India was 193 runs away from a prestigious win. India was 193 runs away from beating Australia in Australia, the toughest feat to conquer in world cricket. Sourav Ganguly was just 193 runs away from realizing his long pending dream. 11 individuals required 193 runs to witness the proudest day of their lives. With lots of anticipation and even more anxiety, India awaited Tuesday, 16th December 2003.

It was nervy, tense and jittery. Both openers could not hide their nervousness. India knew that Australia would make those 193 runs a lot more difficult to chase. Australia stepped up the pressure by disciplined bowling and outstanding fielding. Aakash Chopra succumbed to the pressure first. Rahul Dravid, the man who led India from a defeat to this position, was required once again to anchor the ship. Sehwag at the other end was battling himself. He curbed his instincts and tried to play for the situation. While he handled the seamers well, as the overs went by, he grew impatient. Steve Waugh sensed the fragility and brought his spinner into the attack. The move worked to perfection. Sehwag's eyes lit up as soon as he saw the spinner. His attempt to hit McGill out of the ground handed Gilchrist a simple stumping.

Sachin Tendulkar had scored a single run so far in the series. India needed him the most as it found itself at an extremely delicate position. Sachin's wicket was sure to put heaps of pressure on the rest of the batting. He knew it well. His determined face said it all. India survived the remainder of the session. A well contested session in which Australia picked up 2 wickets and India scored 71 runs set up a tense and fascinating 2nd session. Sachin began the post lunch session with positive intent. He still struggled outside his off stump but looked determined not to throw his wicket away. Dravid was solid as ever. Together, two of India's greatest knights started taking India closer to its dream. The pair added 70 runs and looked comfortable to take India past the finishing line but two quick wickets (Tendulkar and Ganguly) brought Laxman to the crease. Australia was sick of seeing them together. They continued tormenting Australia with a decisive 51 run partnership. The partnership of 303 in the first innings had brought India out of the dark hole, a partnership of 51 in the 2nd innings ensured India's brightest achievement.

The game of cricket, they say, has a remarkable sense of glory. It was fitting that the winning boundary was hit by Rahul Dravid and Ajit Agarkar stood at the non–striker's end (His score was 0). The two had handed a gigantic moment to the country. Sourav Ganguly's embrace to both of them spoke a thousand words. He had fulfilled his dream, and he knew exactly whom to thank. The team that used to get a whimpering overseas, won a test in the toughest country to play cricket in. The team that was slated to go down like bunch of bunnies rocked the cricketing giants. One of the newspapers ran the headline – India goes 1–0 up in 4 test match series.

MELBOURNE TEST – ONE MAD SESSION AND THE GAME WAS GONE

Since ages, Cricket has been said to be a game of technique, particularly batting. One sphere which requires immaculate technique is the opening position. The legendary opening batsmen such as Sir Jack Hobbs, Len Hutton, Herbert Sutcliffe, Sunil Gavaskar had three features in common – text book technique, an ability to concentrate for hours and hours and loads of patience. Virender Sehwag's batting possessed none of these qualities. Yet, Sourav Ganguly had promoted Sehwag to open the innings. More suited for flat Indian pitches, Sehwag's technique to counter swinging and bouncy overseas conditions was still doubtful. He had shown his ability to handle swing in Nottingham. He chose a grandeur stage to cast aside any doubts on his ability to handle bounce; the Boxing Day Test Match at Melbourne Cricket Ground.

After Adelaide, India felt assured of its batting. Apart from Sachin, all batsmen had scored in the first two test matches. To India's advantage, Australia struggled to find its bowling combination. Nathan Bracken was new to test cricket. Brett Lee was making a comeback. Stuart McGill was just not Shane Warne. It formed an ideal bowling attack for Sehwag to feast on, and a feast it was! Sehwag followed an uncomplicated technique. He stood still at the crease with minimal footwork, relying heavily upon his hand–eye coordination. His philosophy was even simpler–hit the ball if it is there to be hit. It took time for the openers to adjust to the intimidating MCG crowd which vociferously backed its team to get back in the series. 42 runs in 21 overs with Sehwag at the crease seemed a little hard to believe. India after two fantastic batting performances showed its maturity by offering respect to Melbourne conditions. Both of them succeeded in implementing the plan of not giving wickets to fast bowlers. Steve Waugh tried all possible combinations of his fast bowlers but could not get a wicket. So almost reluctantly, he introduced spin. Sehwag knew his moment had arrived. He welcomed McGill with a six that travelled to MCG stands. Followed next was the onslaught of extra–ordinary caliber which elevated Sehwag to the league of greatest openers the game has ever seen.

He stood still and smashed. It did not matter who the bowler was. It did not matter how good the ball was, and it certainly did not matter what the field setting was. The brutal attack saw even the mighty Steve Waugh lost for answers. When was the last time India had scored over 200 runs at tea on the first day of an away test? Sehwag was rewriting Indian history books. Sehwag's score of 137 at tea included Nineteen boundaries and three sixes. India's score of 219 for 1 at tea on Day One felt surreal to every Indian fan. That used to be the entire team's score a few years ago. Wow! Indian cricket was transforming.

Australia was put under some serious pressure. It was not used to such pressure but still managed to have a backup plan for it in the last session on Day One. Steve Waugh held one end up and rotated his fast bowlers from the other end. After all the noise over India's incapacity to play serious fast bowling, Steve Waugh's gentle pace gave Australia its most crucial breakthrough of the series. After five days of Adelaide and two sessions of Melbourne, Australia finally saw the back of Rahul Dravid. Dravid's wicket allowed Australia to get a foot in the door. Sachin's struggle outside his off stump had become the talking point of the tour. In Melbourne, a delivery sliding down his leg side claimed him. Apart from the line of the ball which got him, nothing changed. His struggle continued. The low scores continued. It was another duck for him.

At 286 for 3 with Ganguly and Laxman still to bat, Boxing Day belonged to India. To be precise, it belonged to Sehwag. He was on 178 when Sachin fell and he took only 8 balls to reach 195. Then came the flip side of being Sehwag. At 195, he faced a part timer Simon Katich. The field was spread on the boundaries allowing Sehwag ample gaps to score the remaining five runs. A rational batsman would have milked Katich for singles to score his double century but Sehwag's urge to get to a double century in one ball defeated him. A typical Sehwag innings finished in typical Sehwag style. The crowd quickly recovered from the disappointment and gave him a roaring ovation. A standing ovation from a packed MCG crowd! That's what dreams are made of. But the roaring applause had an undercurrent of a question. Was the big shot needed? There lay the answer to Sehwag's success; he never asked that question to himself. He just batted without any care in the world.

After recovering from Sehwag's brilliance, India realized that they had lost three wickets for 33 runs. It ended the day on 329 for 4, still comprehensively winning the day but the last 3 wickets made Australia feel good about themselves. It sensed a hint of an opportunity of a comeback. You never give Australia any chance. The glimmer of hope that Steve Waugh saw at the end of Day One was turned into a session that changed the course of the match entirely.

The first hour of the 2nd day was critical. A good session from India would have bagged the match. For Australia, it was make–or–break. Australia rarely got pushed to such an extreme corner but Australia was most dangerous in such situations. Nathan Bracken & Brett Lee put their heart and soul into their spells. The 2nd new ball was 8 overs old, and it always swings early at MCG. Ganguly, who had been meticulous in pacing his innings till then, chased a wide ball from Brett Lee and perished in the 5th over of the day. The captain exposed his tail to the new ball. Parthiv Patel was tenacious in Brisbane and Adelaide but could not cope with Melbourne surroundings and fired up Australian bowlers. Ajit Agarkar had ended his long series of consecutive ducks in Brisbane. He looked in a hurry to start a new one. His reckless running cost India its 3rd wicket of the session for only 24 runs and with Laxman's first failure of the tour, India threw away the fabulous advantage it had gained on Day One. In a bizarre 8 overs of play, India lost 6 wickets for 16 runs. It was bowled out in an hour. After playing ten days of incredible cricket, the India of old resurfaced and gifted Australia the upper hand by asking it to bat in the best possible conditions for batting. 40 minutes of madness meant India had to chase the game from that point on.

Hayden had failed in both innings in Adelaide. Ponting had scored a duck in his last innings. That did not happen often. Both had to correct it and they both obliged in stupendous style. If India's senseless batting in the first hour of Day Two did not bury it completely, Hayden and Ponting's belligerence certainly did. So many batsmen would be happy to score back–to–back centuries. But Ponting belonged to a higher class of batsmen. He scored back to back double centuries and when Mathew Hayden scored a century, he obliterated the opposition. It was annihilation for the Indian bowlers. Hayden and Ponting smashed all of them all over the MCG. Australia's heavy knock–out punch did not give any chance to India to recover. After Australia's mammoth total in the first innings (558), India gave up its hope with a timid batting performance in the 2nd innings (286). After losing in its own backyard, Australia cruised to a 9–wicket victory and restored the parity. India was given a reality check. It was thrashed to the ground.

India paid a heavy price for those careless 40 minutes. Australia's brutal attack on Indian bowlers not only took the match away from India, it also snatched the belief Adelaide had given them. All of a sudden, the win at Adelaide was touted as Australia's bad performance rather than India's good performance. India required mental strength to regroup. It required motivation to bounce back. India needed determination to give a fight. Sachin Tendulkar chose the Sydney Cricket Ground to extend a whole new meaning to the words motivation and determination.

SYDNEY TEST – OFF SIDE.... I DON'T SEE IT

One of the key strengths of Sachin Tendulkar was his ability to score without restraint. He played every shot possible, even invented a few. The front foot strokes came naturally to him but his height or lack of it never hindered his back–foot play. His cover drives, cuts and off drives were always an ecstasy to witness but when he braced Sydney Cricket Ground with his captivating 241, the cricketing world marveled at the power of his mind. He had produced another master class, powered by his mind and not his strokes.

He walked in to bat at India's commanding score of 128 for 2. Sehwag had continued his good scoring form. Aakash Chopra had accomplished his duty once again. Dravid had looked in ominous touch. But Melbourne had taught India a lesson. India could not afford to relax, even for a moment. Sachin had not put on a decent score in this trip yet. His struggles on his off stumps were discussed at length. The sudden dip in his form had raised quite a few questions. His age and reflexes were scrutinized. Some even dared to put his ability under the scanner. Nobody questioned his attitude though. Everyone wanted him to succeed but nobody knew the road to success. Nobody but Sachin Tendulkar himself; it was on his leg side. For the next ten hours, he astonished one and all with robotic command over his mind. Out of his 241 runs, 186 runs came on the leg side and only 55 on the off side. He hit only 35 scoring shots on the off side which included only 3 boundaries out of his 33. The man blatantly refused to play on the off side even though it implied not playing half of his natural scoring shots. He patiently waited for the balls on his pads. He played 317 dot balls. Whenever Sachin Tendulkar scored runs, everyone talked about his strokes. After Sydney, everyone talked about his appetite to score runs. It was as important a factor to his success as his strokes. Sachin Tendulkar showed the world how desperate he was to score runs. His desperation showed in his celebration. His desperation had brought his form back.

V.V.S. Laxman on the other hand continued his dream run. His innings of 178 at SCG was poles apart from Sachin's leg side affair. He played all around the scenic SCG. His 30 boundaries embodied divine grace. God had gifted him delicate wrists, and he used them to the fullest. Two contrasting innings in nature achieved one common objective. Melbourne did not repeat. In fact, India scored its highest total on Australian soil. The Australian bowling attack and fielders surrendered to the large run appetite of Indian batsmen. Justin Langer said it eloquently, "The reality of this series is the extraordinary Indian batting. I can't remember being under pressure in this manner– the pressure to bowl against them, field against them and to chase a huge score." 705 was indeed huge. India assured itself of not losing the Sydney test. It now stared at a golden opportunity to win the test match and the series.

A cushion of 705 runs allowed the Indian bowlers some breathing space. They were required to be patient. The pitch suited stroke making and India knew from the word go it was going to be hard for the bowlers to bowl to the in–form Australian top order. India needed to forget the amount of time it would require to dismiss Australia. It needed to forget the match situation itself and just bowl over after over. Fortunately for India, it had a perfect man for the job. Anil Kumble bowled a staggering 31 overs in an entire day to grab 4 wickets to keep India in the test. On the morning of the 4th day's play, Australia was 350 for 7, courtesy Kumble's 5 wickets and Irfan Pathan's yorker that claimed Gilchrist. The yorker had got Wasim Akram in the commentary box more excited than Pathan himself. India smelt a win. They had put Australia under such severe pressure on numerous occasions in this series. And as a champion team, Australia had crawled its way back out on almost every single occasion. It had found a saviour every time. In Sydney, it was Simon Katich and a stubborn Jason Gillespie. Gillespie stayed at the crease for 2 hours 22 minutes, played 113 balls and supported Katich to his well–made hundred. The partnership of 117 runs pushed the match out of India's grasp. Despite Kumble's valiant effort (he bowled 47 overs in total for 8 wickets), India's perpetual inability to finish off the tail haunted it again. The pair of Katich and Gillespie ate out a very significant amount of time. Ganguly was faced with a dilemma no previous Indian captain ever came upon; a decision whether to enforce a follow–on or to bat again. Indian bowlers had toiled in the field for 118 overs and deserved rest for sure. He decided to bat again to set a target of 443.

Only two results looked feasible on Day Five. India was content with either. Apart from the second innings in Adelaide, India had failed to take Australian wickets in quick succession. The 2nd innings at SCG was no exception. Every Australian batsman got runs and the match headed towards the inevitable result. Day Five on SCG was not about a drawn test though. The occasion was focused on celebrating a wonderful career. At 170 for 3, Steve Waugh, Australia's most successful captain, set foot on a cricket ground wearing his Baggy Green for the last time. He had 50 overs to get a good score. He had not scored in the entire series and Sydney presented an appropriate occasion for the great man to have his final word. It was as if he had waited for the occasion. His ever so effective cut shots and back foot cover drives came out of box one last time to grace SCG to the joy and cheers of a packed SCG. His 80 saved the day for Australia much to his relief. He now could afford a smile and look back on his glorious career.

And hence concluded the toughest home series Australia had played in recent times. After 20 days of test match cricket, it was difficult to separate the two sides which displayed the richest quality cricket. The result was fitting 1–1. As Australia said good bye to one of its greatest captains of all times, India welcomed its greatest captain. The tour had begun on 4th December 2003 in the gloomy and overcast Brisbane with a placard – Indian Summer Over. It ended on 6th January 2004 with the placard – 'don't let it end this way Steve'. After an outstanding summer Down Under, it was time for India to prepare for its next venture. The fellow sub–continent giant was waiting to welcome its traditional rival. History beckoned, as India arrived in Pakistan after 16 long years.

INDIA'S TOUR OF PAKISTAN 2004 – A RIVALRY REINCARNATED

There are many parameters to judge the significance of any tour; the tournament for example. Nothing can be more important than the World Cup. One parameter might be the country you are visiting. A tour of Australia is more important than a tour of Zimbabwe. One more aspect might be your past record in that country. One always desires to better the previous performance. But the Indian Prime Minister's visit to the airport to bid farewell to the team redefined the word 'important' for Team India. The Indian team boarded the flight to Lahore in honorable Atal Bihari Vajpayee's presence and with his message; "khel bhee jitiye, dil bhee jitiye" (Win matches as well as hearts). That is how significant India's next assignment was.

India had played exceptional cricket in Australia, outperforming Australia on many occasions, casting aside the tag of being 'the chokers' in the overseas test matches. Such tags carried zero significance for India's tour of Pakistan. The contest surpassed the game itself. Such was the history of two nations. A gap of 15 years after India's last tour to Pakistan provided an additional spice to the tour. Both countries had undergone a severe demographic change which meant the spectators from both countries knew little about each other. Both set of people judged each other through the prism of political opinions. The interactions between the common man on either side of the border had always been scanty. This tour was about to achieve a rare feat of bringing them face to face. Given the history of animosity between the two nations, it was a substantial feat. Pakistan's last tour to India in 1999 was pleasantly surprising for Pakistan due to the hospitality of Indian public. The Indian players themselves wondered whether Pakistani people would reciprocate. The only certain fact about the tour was the pressure it carried. "We always travel as ambassadors of our country. People are looking at this tour differently because we are going to Pakistan," Ganguly tried to calm nerves. But he, of all the people, understood the magnitude of the tour to him and his team.

The political tensions between the two countries never hampered the quality of cricket the tie always produced. It was a full tour this time and Indian players had no clue about the Pakistani conditions. The entire cricketing world admired the lineage of fast bowling in Pakistan. The obvious assumption was that the conditions must offer a good deal of assistance to fast bowlers. When India landed in Karachi to play the first of the 5 ODI series, it was shocked to see a flat pitch which could give any Indian pitch a complex. How the hell did these fast bowlers emerge from these flat pitches? India asked. None the less, on the flattest Karachi pitch, India began its quest to conquer the territory of its arch rivals.

For India, the Pakistani team looked familiar. It had endured so many big innings from its middle order of Inzamam–Ul–Haq, Mohammad Yousuf and Younis Khan. How could India forget Abdul Razzaq who kept getting Sachin out again and again throughout the 90's? The bowling featured the usual suspects barring Naved–Ul–Hassan. For Pakistan, except the grand trio of Sachin–Ganguly–Dravid, the entire Indian team bore a new look. Some of them had played in that epic World Cup 2003 match. But the two bowling sensations of the Australia ODI Tri–Series, Irfan Pathan and Lakshmipathy Balaji were not known. Why was India not continuing with the great opening pair of Ganguly and Sachin? Who is Virender Sehwag? Pakistan embarked on the series with such questions in mind.

THE ODI SERIES

1ST ODI – WHAT A START

Sehwag introduced himself to the Pakistani bowlers in regal fashion by smashing Naved for 24 runs in his 1st over, continuing the absolute slaughter of Pakistani bowling initiated by Sachin in the previous ten overs. Sachin's miserable Australian ODI series looked like a thing of the past as he smashed four boundaries and a massive six. His score of 28 looked below par but its impact was anything but below par. Ganguly also left his batting worries behind and continued Sachin's good work. He had made the 'shuffling across the crease' technique his own. He got the requisite pace from Pakistani bowlers to hit 3 fours and 2 sixes.

Sehwag at the other end was his usual self with an innings of 79 in 57 balls, which comprised 14 boundaries and a six. By the time India lost Yuvraj, it had scored 220 in 28 overs. Till that point, India seemed less worried about wickets in hand but after Yuvraj's wicket, sanity returned to the proceedings; needless to say Dravid took command of the situation. He supervised the next 20 overs with his 99. At the end of 50 overs, India reached 349, which was way below par considering the start it received. It was still a huge score to chase, almost impossible; although one thing was sure – India–Pakistan matches always challenged the word impossible.

The Indian bowlers knew nothing about Pakistani openers (Yasir Hameed & Imran Farhat). They also did not bother introducing themselves in the match but at 34 for 2, it was business as usual for Inzamam and

Mohammad Yousuf. Both appeared to be at an alarming ease as if time had rolled back to 1990's where they used to score against India for fun. Indian cricket had gone through such a profound change but for the Pakistani pair, it was all very much the same. Yousuf scored a classy 73, Inzamam scored a brilliant 122. Pakistan was on its course to draw first blood. Then at that exact moment, India introduced its transformation of last four years to Pakistan.

Inzamam always used to finish these matches, but he offered one tough chance to Dravid, and Dravid the keeper held on to a sharp catch. So many times in the past, India had squandered such chances. But not this team! Ganguly persisted with Murali Karthik despite him leaking runs, showcasing another change in Indian cricket: a captain trusting his bowlers to the end. Karthik delivered by ending a threatening partnership between Razzaq and Younis Khan (27 off 16). Zaheer Khan at the age of 26 had already become India's lead bowler. He revalidated his claim with a superbly disguised slower ball to get rid of dangerous Razzaq. Next was India's latest talent on show. Shoaib Malik skied a ball and Badani ran straight under it. Kaif came out of nowhere, dived over Badani and took an absolute blinder of a catch. Pakistan had not seen India take such catches earlier. The brilliant catch accounted for a more than capable batsman in the situation.

After all the twists and turns, Pakistan needed 9 runs from the last over. Javed Miandad, the Pakistan coach watched over from the dressing room balcony. How India sighed with relief to see him on the balcony instead of in the middle! There was no Miandad on the ground. Nehra had to ensure that he would not become the next Chetan Sharma. And boy did he do that! His absolute cracker of an over gave India a narrow win by 5 runs. The India–Pakistan tie had produced another gem. Though the nail–biter match was as good a start as one would have hoped for, 100 overs of cricket was rendered inconsequential by the reception & ovation the Indian team received after winning the match. The people of Pakistan had reciprocated with even more warmth and love. After 100 overs of the typical India–Pakistan drama, the Pakistani crowd was the ultimate winner.

2ND ODI – OH PLEASE! NOT AGAIN

It was Pakistan's turn to score 300 this time. Prior to this match, Rahul Dravid had met Yasir Hameed in his hotel lobby and mistaken him for a bowler he had faced in the nets. Yasir Hameed made sure Dravid would remember him forever by scoring a fluent 86. India had historically faltered while chasing, especially against Pakistan. Sachin Tendulkar's 37th ODI century hinted to end the trend for a while but he lacked support. Late hitting by Balaji and Ramesh Powar brought India closer, but the match was never within reach. Another close finish gave Pakistan the series leveling win. After 200 overs and 1339 runs, the series was at par.

4TH ODI – A MUST WIN – ALRIGHT

Pakistan clinched the 3rd ODI on a bowler friendly Peshawar pitch and hence India, after a promising start to the series faced the usual score line against Pakistan. It trailed by 2 games to 1. The 4th ODI followed the historical route of an India–Pakistan match for the first 75 overs of the match. Inzamam scored a century. Pakistan put up another near 300 score. At exactly the halfway stage of the Indian innings, India, at 162 for 5 stared at a defeat. The scoring rate was way above needed but the wickets lost were also way above acceptable. In the 1st ODI, Pakistan was introduced to India's young bowling brigade and its comfort in handling pressure. The 4th game brought Pakistan face to face with India's two new finishers, one rediscovering his ODI cricket and the other discovering his potential. For the remaining half of India's innings, it was calmness personified. Dravid and Kaif did not panic for a single moment and a single ball. Both kept taking singles at will and both shifted gears at opportune moments with utmost ease. The team, which at one point of time was on the verge of losing the series, won the match with 5 overs and 5 wickets in hand. Pakistan had seen this side of India once before in the World Cup 2003 encounter and believed it to be a fluke. It was used to seeing India panic, stutter and surrender. From almost losing the game, the transformed Indian team came back to level the series at 2–2.

5TH ODI – THE UNPRECEDENTED HAPPENED

In the 5th ODI, Laxman who still felt bewildered over his exclusion from India's World Cup 2003 squad, led the innings with a 107 (India scored 293 for 7). An in–cutter from Balaji, an in swinger from Pathan, an exposed leg stump from Taufeeq Umar and a brilliant catch from Yuvraj cost Pakistan four wickets and heaped tremendous pressure on it. The presence of one fellow though, was enough to make India jittery even after being in a commanding position. Inzamam obliged as he toyed with India's bowling for the next 8 overs.

The series so far had provided some special knocks and special spells. The series deserved something more than special. Sachin had contributed little in the series apart from his century in the 2nd match. What he did on the 4th ball of the 21st over made up for his lack of runs! Inzamam's fiercely hit flat shot, headed for a six over long on, was caught out of thin air by the shortest man in the team (He also managed to avoid any contact with the boundary rope with a spectacular balancing act). Sachin's spectacular high jump catch handed Pakistan a body blow as India's old adversary fell short this time. Moin Khan's and Shoaib Malik's late fightback did justice to India–Pakistan tense finishes, but India's dream was realised earlier with Inzamam's wicket in the 21st over. Moin Khan's wicket in the 48th over made it official. Sourav Ganguly and his team had created history. 5 enthralling ODIs had resulted into one of the closest ODI series in recent times. India won a series on Pakistani soil for the first time. 'On Pakistani soil' felt strange after the support Indian team received from travelling Indians and local Pakistani fans. Political tension between the two nations was pushed to the back burner by the common passion of both the nations. After all the drama, excitement, anxiety and joy, it was easy to judge who actually won. It was the common man from both sides of the most dreaded border in the world.

THE TEST SERIES

The Indian team had a good hard look at the Pakistan team for the test series. For the first time in eighteen long years, Pakistani bowling looked weak. For the first time in eighteen long years, Pakistani batting seemed fragile. After almost two decades, India genuinely believed it could win against Pakistan. Such was the past of India–Pakistan clashes that India never stood a chance to win against Pakistan but winning an ODI series in Pakistan changed the mindset to a considerable extent, not to mention India came into Pakistan test series on the back of a fantastic test series in Australia. For the first time, Shoaib Akhtar was not looking menacing. Saqlain Mushtaq was not looking threatening. For the first time, India went in to a Pakistan Test series as favourites. And then, Virender Sehwag decided to take Multan and the world of cricket by storm.

1ST TEST MULTAN

A STEP TOWARDS GREATNESS

Virender Sehwag had scored five test match centuries before taking to field in Multan. Astonishingly, three of them were in unfamiliar and demanding conditions of South Africa, England and Australia. Astonishing because his technique was suited for flat batting conditions of the sub–continent. After his success in overseas conditions, no bowler wanted to imagine how devastating he could be in the conditions that suited his batting. The Pakistani bowlers were to find out in the first two days of the Multan Test as they were forced to go through living hell. That's right, the first two days. The guy scored his first triple hundred in just 364 balls and he did it in only 9 hours! What he failed to do in Melbourne, he accomplished in Multan. In Melbourne, his attempt to hit a six fell a few yards short. In Multan, it went a few yards beyond the boundary. He was on 195 in Melbourne. In Multan, he was on 295. The mindset of thinking of hitting a six on 295 was beyond reasoning, especially when he had already done it in the same innings when he was on 99 (that too to Shoaib Akhtar.) The highlight of this massacre was the destruction of one of the great off–spinners of all time. Saqlain Mushtaq, who used to pick Indian wickets like plucking flowers from the garden, was taken for 204 runs. Virender Sehwag with his unique attitude entered the world of greats as he became the first Indian to score a triple hundred.

THE DECLARATION SAGA

At Sydney, Sachin had chosen to avoid half the side of the field. In Multan, initially, he gave the feeling he had forgotten it exists. While Sehwag went ballistic at the other end, Sachin took time to find his fluency but once he did, the innings transformed into an usual treat. His cover drives were back. The off drives with his trademark straight–bat were back. The forceful cuts were back. He rediscovered his off–side in a grand manner. Sehwag's arrogance in batting rubbed on to Sachin as well. The master was feeding off his protégé. The efficiency with which Sachin batted against his old adversaries, Saqlain and Abdul Razzaq raised hopes of a special score. His 33rd test century validated his return to form and what a return it was! He was about to score his 2nd double hundred in three innings. Yes. He was about to.... but alas!

India was in a commanding position at tea on Day Two. The calculations were simple. Sachin had to get to his 200 quickly. Yuvraj had to ensure India reaches 700 even quicker. 15–20 overs at the tired Pakistani openers and one or two wickets before the end of 2nd day's play would have secured the match. Everything went according to plan except Sachin's part. He struggled to get any flow to his innings. Post the drinks interval the slow progress (he scored 29 runs in 36 balls with only 2 boundaries) by Sachin put the stand–in captain in an uncomfortable situation. As Sachin took more time than required to score runs, Dravid started realizing that sooner than later, he would be required to take the toughest and perhaps the most controversial decision of his life. Yuvraj Singh's wicket on the 5th ball of the 162nd over put Dravid right on the spot. He had two options – wait for Sachin's double hundred or stick to the plan. Allowing Sachin to get the personal milestone required precious time which was allocated to bowling. Dravid followed the new mindset of Team India: team first. At the risk of facing the wrath of millions of Indians, the innings was declared on 675. More importantly, India declared with Sachin not out on 194. That was a confirmed headline in next day's newspapers.

THE NEW BOYS AND THE GATEWAY OF PAKISTAN

Indian fans and media were fuming. India had declared on Day Two so that bowlers could take a couple of wickets but the failure to do so fuelled the anger of not allowing Sachin to score his double hundred. Sachin's evident disappointment while leaving the field after the declaration and his admittance of it in the press conference did not help either. Even after scoring 675 runs, India felt the heat. The bowlers needed to step up on a flat Multan pitch to calm the storm in waiting. The job looked difficult as the Pakistani middle order comprised of Inzamam, Mohammad Yousuf and Razzaq and the love they shared for Indian bowling was no secret. Patience was the code for India and it showed plenty of it on Day Three. The bowlers kept at it for the entire day. The partnership of 160 runs between Inzamam and Hameed did not dampen their spirits. Anil Kumble led the pack and hence 'never drop the shoulders' attitude was a given. It was Kumble who gave India its decisive breakthrough in the form of Inzamam. Even after Inzamam's wicket, Pakistan continued scoring runs but India chipped in with a wicket or two. Before the last over on Day Three, India had picked up 5 wickets for 361 runs. It had been a long day and India looked forward to some much–deserved rest. Ganguly asked Sachin to continue his spell for one more over. It was time for Indian bowlers and fielders to put their feet up. The captain himself appeared disconnected and switched off. However, Sachin's first three balls woke him up. For some strange reason, Moin Khan looked quite uncomfortable against Sachin's leg spinners. Ganguly noticed it and moved the slip a bit wider, encouraging Sachin to turn the ball more. Moin Khan noticed the change in the slip position and prepared himself for a big turning leg break, forgetting that Sachin possessed a fabulous googly in his arsenal. The ball pitched perfectly on middle stump and by the time Moin Khan moved his front foot to play the leg spinner, he realized it was a googly. He had planted his front–foot across to cover the spin which left a huge gap between his legs. Sachin's googly found that gap as well as Moin's leg stump to perfection. Moin Khan went through the same fate as the great Shane Warne had gone through in Kolkata in 2001. Sachin who looked dejected a night before because of a controversial declaration celebrated the priceless wicket like a school–boy. Any talk of a rift within the team was put to an end. Through the legs of Moin Khan, India found its gateway to victory. One of the journalists aptly called it – The Gateway of Pakistan.

IT WAS DESTINY

Day Four had a sense of inevitability. It felt like it was destiny. What else could explain Abdul Razzaq, the overnight set batsman, nicking the first ball of Day Four or Sachin Tendulkar taking a wicket on a rank loose ball or Kumble's delivery somehow finding a passage through Mohammad Sami's legs to hit the stumps. Pakistan's first innings ended in a blink of an eye and there was more to follow.

Things fell into place for India in Pakistan's second innings as well. Parthiv Patel who so far went through a torrid time behind the stumps took a reflex catch of Anil Kumble's bowling to get the first Pakistani wicket. Perhaps it was one more sign that India was destined to win. Anil Kumble's biggest strength, his accuracy enabled him to bowl wicket to wicket for hours and hours. Hence, when Taufeeq Umar offered his pads to Anil Kumble, the umpire did not hesitate for a second to judge him out and when Yuvraj Singh's direct hit ran Inzamam out on zero, India believed it was destined to write history. There was no other explanation for Inzamam's duck against India. Even Yuvraj Singh chipped in with his first test wicket. After the eventful two sessions, Anil Kumble was left to do his favourite job of finishing the tail. He did it with his customary ruthless efficiency. Though Pakistan frustrated India with a 70 runs partnership for the 9th wicket, the outcome was worth waiting for. When Mohammad Yousuf's mistimed pull shot landed in Dravid's bucket hands, the Indian team accomplished what no previous Indian teams had achieved. It registered its first ever test match win in Pakistan. India had watched so many abject surrenders against Pakistan in the past that the Multan win felt surreal. Multan was a huge win, worthy of a special page in the history books of Indian cricket. The Indian batting had outclassed and outperformed Pakistani Bowling. The contest had turned out to be one–sided, and being an India–Pakistan match it surprised all. Pakistan required bouncing back hard and considering the track record of India–Pakistan encounters, Pakistan's fightback was inevitable.

2ND TEST – TAKE THAT!

The 1st test clearly outlined that Pakistan had to somehow catch hold of Indian batting. It was made to toil hard by the Indian batsmen in Multan. Another big batting performance by India threatened to put the series to rest. Pakistan invested in Umar Gul to restrict India and he fetched returns in 2 overs. First, he got rid of Sehwag who started as if he was continuing his Multan innings (His 39 included 6 boundaries and 1 six). No wonder the wicket brought a big celebration even from otherwise subdued Inzamam. Then in his next over, he trapped Sachin in front of the wickets with an exquisite in swinger. After dismissing two centurions of the Multan test, came Laxman's dismissal who poked at a wide delivery. The next scalp was the biggest of them all. Dravid had seen every ball swinging in. Thus, he failed to react within time to the one that went away and nicked it. It had taken Pakistan 162 overs and 675 runs to get 5 Indian wickets in Multan. In Lahore, it achieved the same feat in only 27 overs and 125 runs. India lost the match there and then itself.

Yuvraj Singh's first test century and Pathan's gutsy 49 took India to a respectable total of 287 in the first innings, but it was far from enough. India had dismissed Inzamam for two low scores in Multan. Third consecutive failure against his favourite bowling side would have been miraculous, but it wasn't to be as Inzamam got to business with a century. Mohammad Yousuf too enjoyed his favourite attack to the fullest with 72. Imran Farhat scored a ton, Asim Kamal registered 73. Sehwag and Parthiv Patel steadied India's second innings after Pakistan had scored 489 and India had lost its top order. At one point of time, both of them even entertained a thought of crawling out of the rabbit hole but Pakistan never permitted them to take charge. Sehwag's 90 and Parthiv Patel's 62 could not save India from a loss.

Only Pakistan was capable of such a turnaround. The side that conceded 675 runs in the 1st test, bowled out the same batting line for less than 300 in both the innings of the 2nd test and like every other India–Pakistan series, this series too went to the last match. The city of Rawalpindi was the final venue for this historic tour. Best known for Shoaib Akhtar, the city was set to add the concluding chapter to the most enchanting Test Series between the two rivals.

3RD TEST

THE SMILING ASSASSIN

Did he actually smile so much or was it his face–cut? Regardless of the answer to that question, Lakshmipathy Balaji became an instant hit with the Pakistani crowd. He had charmed the Pakistanis with his huge six to one of the fastest bowlers in the world in one of the ODIs. His shy request of change of bat when Shoaib Akhtar broke his willow to half the next ball, was even more amiable. His skills were visible, his fighting spirit unmistakable and his ever so gleaming smile or the face–cut was reassuring. Despite consecutive good ODI series in Australia and Pakistan, he had struggled in the first two test matches against Pakistan. In the 3rd test, he found his captain desperately missing a performance out of him, to justify his decision to include him. The fighter in Lakshmipathy Balaji was itching to take the field and do the job.

On a green top and in the overcast conditions in Headingley, Ganguly had taken the boldest decision of his life. In Rawalpindi on a greenish pitch, when he returned to his favourite role of captaincy after a lay off due to injury, everybody wondered whether he would take a similar risk again. He did it in Headingley to give a push to his young team. In Rawalpindi, he knew his team was prepared to make the best use of the conditions. He chose his 'smart hat' over his 'risk hat'. His batsmen had backed him up in Headingley. His bowlers repaid his trust in Rawalpindi, Balaji in particular, who extracted extra help from the Rawalpindi pitch. There is always a chance of a bowler getting overexcited to see grass on the pitch and forget the basics of bowling. It had happened to Indian bowlers on innumerable accounts in the past. Indian bowlers often used to sacrifice accuracy in trying to go for the glory balls. Same thing went on with India in the initial part of the innings as all three Indian pacers bowled erratic lines. Balaji was the first to find his head. He also found a full length and the late swing did the rest. His late out swingers decimated the Pakistan middle order. The smiling assassin had done his job.

WHERE ART THOU?

6, 33 and 0 were Dravid's scores in the first 2 tests. He had become the mainstay of Indian batting in the last 3 years. India was not used to seeing him fail. The anchor–man had been troubled by Pakistani bowlers so far but how long could they hold India's run machine back? By the time both the teams reached Rawalpindi, Dravid's patience was over which was a menacing sign for Pakistan. One thing was for sure – if Rahul Dravid lost his patience outside the cricket field, he was more than certain to find it on the field and when Rahul Dravid found his patience on the field, he usually scored a big, match–winning knock. He bestowed the Rawalpindi Cricket Stadium with majestic 270 runs. He withstood some initial scares by surviving two close LBW shouts. Then he flicked the third ball to perfection, followed it up with a splendid cover drive on one knee. He never looked back from then. The feet moved, the bat flourished, and the scoreboard started getting a familiar look. On the most bowling friendly pitch in the series, Dravid got his fifth test match double hundred. It was his 3rd double hundred in the last 7 months, first against Pakistan, 17th overall and 11th away from home. After Lahore, India had cried where art thou? Dravid in his trademark quiet style said– I had never left.

At 261 for 4 and 21 overs still to play on Day Two, Ganguly took guard in a delicate situation. India led by mere 37 runs. India wanted one good partnership to get a firm grip on the match. He was coming back from an injury and he never was fond of brisk pace. All odds were stacked against him but he had established in the last four years that he thrived in such circumstances. He faced a bombardment of short balls. He negotiated some with comfort and looked out of place while defending others. He also survived a close run out but he did the most important thing: staying in the middle to fight it out. His was the vintage Ganguly innings, filled with class, timing and crisp boundaries through the off side. His decisive 77, and a partnership of 131, put the Indian team on the verge of immortality. Where art thou captain, the country had asked. He replied with a series defining inning – I am here now.

THE LAST HUDDLE

India began Day Four with ludicrous catching and sloppy bowling. They dropped 2 sitters in the first 3 overs of the day after having already conceded runs through bad fielding. The team, it seemed, did not turn up to play. Balaji's accurately pitched in–swinger made Kamran Akmal's off stump fly away and the sight shook the Indian team out of its lassitude. India's fielding for the first fifteen minutes was pathetic to be kind but Parthiv Patel's diving catch to the leg side more than made up for it. Pakistan was reduced to 94 for 5 and the result became a foregone conclusion. Mohammad Yousuf and Asim Kamal built a partnership to irritate India for some time. Ganguly had the luxury of going to Kumble and asking him to do his thing. In a spell of 6 overs, Anil Kumble took care of Pakistani lower order and brought India closer to the historic win.

Ganguly had brought on board four like–minded and like–hearted seniors who were as desperate as him, to get Indian cricket back on course. Four years later, Sourav Ganguly's pillars, Rahul Dravid, V.V.S. Laxman, Anil Kumble and Sachin Tendulkar, laid the foundation on which India orchestrated its tremendous surge from the ugly depths of match–fixing. India rebuilt its team on these four magnificent cornerstones. Ganguly had also picked a few talented young players. Together with these four legends, he turned them into stars. With a genius support staff, headed by the ever so calm John Wright, the future looked bright in the hands of Virender Sehwag, Yuvraj Singh, Harbhajan Singh, Zaheer Khan and others. India now was a team with brilliant batsmen, superb bowlers and outstanding fielders. It was now a team capable to win overseas. India was now a team which understood a thing or two about success. It had been a finalist of ICC Champions Trophy 2000, joint winner of ICC Champions Trophy 2002, and a World Cup Runner up. It had conjured some amazing ODI wins like the NatWest Final, a bilateral series win in Pakistan. Its awe–inspiring home dominance included an epic test series win over Australia. It had drawn a test series in England and Australia. When Sourav Ganguly took Danish Kaneria's catch on Day Four of the Rawalpindi test, he added another feather to his cap. He became the most successful Indian test captain ever. India for the first time in its long cricketing history won a test series in Pakistan. It was time to reminisce on India's extraordinary adventure of the last 3 years, time to draw curtains on the most glorious season in Indian cricket. It was time for one last huddle.

PART II

THE DOWNFALL

THE SEASON STARTS ON A WRONG FOOT – ASIA CUP 2004

India's 2003–04 season transformed the way cricket was played in India for many decades. Long gone were the worries the turn of the millennium had brought with it. Another monumental season awaited Team India. Yes, Team India – that was the new name assigned to this team by the fans. Going into the next season, India possessed two factors it never had before: a captain who never faced an issue of self–belief and a bunch of incredible fast bowlers, a luxury no previous Indian captain enjoyed. After a healthy break of 3 months, India braced itself for Asian glory.

In the decade of 1980, many of the Asian Countries strived for only one objective – survival. These countries were riddled with problems underdeveloped countries usually face. Cricket though, was never affected by any other socio–economic or political factor. India, after winning the 1983 World Cup, had slowly begun to get a sense of belonging to the international arena. Pakistan strove to convert its blessed talent into consistent results at the highest platform. Sri Lanka, at the time, was still considered a minnow. The popularity of cricket among other Asian countries like Hong Kong, Malaysia, and Singapore was limited to local Indian communities. All these nations desired to strengthen their ties and there prevailed no better means to achieve it than cricket.

And hence, India, Pakistan, Sri Lanka, Bangladesh, Malaysia and Singapore formed the Asian Cricket Council and the idea of Asia Cup was floated. The first ever Asia Cup was held in Sharjah in 1984, which India won. The second edition was hosted by Sri Lanka. However, India withdrew from it due to its troubled cricketing relationship with Sri Lanka. ACC saw India's withdrawal as an opportunity to take the game to new countries and hence Bangladesh was inducted. Pakistan pulled out of the 4th edition (hosted by India) as the political relations between the two countries deteriorated further. The Asia Cup throughout the 1990s remained marred with political prejudices but after the seventh edition in 2000, political leverage over it began to fade.

India, after its initial success in the tournament never delivered noteworthy results in the Asia Cups. In the 2000th edition, it won a solitary match against a weaker Bangladesh before its humiliating exit from the tournament. After that, the Asia Cup seemed to disappear from India's radar. The next Asia cup was scheduled for 2004. By then, India had attained a redefined mindset towards International cricket. India's new mindset, coupled with its last season, made them favourites to win the Asia Cup 2004.

India's opening match against UAE, a supposedly walk in the park was anything but easy. Indian batsmen scrabbled to score against the medium pacers of UAE on a slow Dambulla pitch. The captain himself crawled his way to 56 off 102 balls. Where India was expected to score in excess of 300, it required Dravid's rescue act of 104 to put a face–saving total of 260. It turned out to be a steep target for the inexperienced UAE batting. "The boys are a bit rusty. That is understandable after a long break." The captain's explanation rang serious alarm bells as he never hid behind such excuses. Maybe he was telling the truth, India consoled itself.

After a 'rusty' performance against the UAE, India needed to be at the top of its game against the hosts. India of late had enjoyed a good run against them but it came mostly in overseas conditions where it was always a struggle for Sri Lanka. Every cricketing nation dreamt of beating Sri Lanka in Sri Lanka. Dismissing Sri Lankan batsmen on Sri Lankan pitches was always a tough row to hoe. The Indian bowling too faced the same predicament, as all Sri Lankan batsmen put them to sword. Adding to India's agony was its batting which looked jaded throughout its innings. Another of Dravid's 'back against wall knock' was not enough as India lost by 12 runs. By now, it was clear to even a 10–year–old that the problem was much deeper than 'rustiness'. The spark of the previous season was nowhere to be seen. The team that did so well the preceding season scraped to the next round largely due to UAE's inability to win any of its matches.

For a World Cup finalist, advancing to the second round due to UAE's poor performance was embarrassing. India's next match against Bangladesh presented an appropriate opportunity to get back to business. And it was business indeed. The new boy–wonder Irfan Pathan rediscovered his swing. Other fast bowlers discovered some spite in the pitch. The fielding rediscovered its sharpness. Spinners rediscovered their line and Sachin Tendulkar revisited his bowling days by claiming 3. He then along with Ganguly guided India past the finishing line. Both of them looked far from their best. Both played subdued innings which many times sprang from one side to other of that thin line between a matured innings and hustle for runs. India's lackluster batting resulted in a 8–wicket win. Though it did nothing for India's confidence, it earned them a bonus point. A new addition to International Cricket Rules. Nobody quite understood the significance of a tiny bonus point. However, Pakistan was about to learn it the hard way in its next match, which happened to be against India.

It was time for the big–ticket extravaganza, the much–glorified clash between the two squabbling nations. However, this time, it was without the glamour, the fuss and strangely, with a certain sense of boredom. After all, India and Pakistan had been at each other's throats for the last 2 months. The real charm of an India–Pakistan match lay in its scarcity. The match was not a must–win for India but losing it would have made its next match, a knock–out. Hence, the target of 301 had to be approached cautiously. Caution was particularly not Sehwag's virtue and he paid the price for it with another low score. Rest of the batting continued its grind for form except Ganguly who, for the first time in the series looked fluent. Sadly, he could not carry on for long. None of the batsmen stayed at the crease to support Sachin who played with composure but just when Sachin seemed poised to take India home, he got out. India needed 87 runs from 7 overs.

The winning target was impossible but there was a sub–target, the bonus point target (240 runs). India needed only 26 runs to get the bonus point and with two more than handy batsmen in Pathan and Harbhajan at the crease, it looked doable. It was evident from the next two overs that India tried to earn the bonus point. Every single cricket follower in India realized it. Every single cricket follower in Pakistan realized it but 11 individuals who mattered the most for Pakistan, failed to acknowledge it. Either Pakistan did not catch on the plan or just did not care. The pair of Pathan and Harbhajan added 9 runs in 3 overs before Harbhajan fell. Pathan got out on the fifth ball of 49th over after adding another 10 runs with Balaji. Balaji scampered for 2 more runs to take India's score to 235 for 8, only 5 runs away from the bonus point.

India's quest for the bonus point converted the otherwise boring match into a typical India–Pakistan finish. Before Pakistan could fathom the worth of the bonus point, India's number 10 and 11 sneaked in 2 byes on the last 2 balls, courtesy Pakistan's lethargic fielding. Pakistan won by 59 runs but India grinned. The one crucial bonus point it earned on the day kept it above Pakistan in the points table. India had one final chance to salvage its pride and get the campaign back on track.

The writing was on the wall and it was bold and clear. India had to win against Sri Lanka to reach the final of the Asia Cup 2004. The pitch at Premadasa was slow and low or as they say a 'win the toss and bat first' pitch. Sehwag for the first time in the tournament started flowing, and he usually flowed at a strike rate of near 100. His 81, Ganguly's patient 79 and Yuvraj Singh's 50 ensured a challenging score of 271. It was a do or die situation for India whereas Sri Lanka's place in the final was already booked. India's desperation turned out to be the difference between the two sides in the early parts of the Sri Lankan batting as it lost half its side for 134 runs.

Though India took a firm grip on the match by dismissing Sri Lankan top order, it constantly felt distressed due to the presence of one man at the crease. India's old nemesis, Sanath Jayasuriya stood solid between India and a place in the final. The contest soon began to shape up like one of those horrifying games in the 1990's, where Jayasuriya used to decimate Indian bowling. So far in the tournament, India had missed the one element responsible for the stark contrast between the Indian team of the 1990's and the current team. India hoped for its captain to do his thing, make that special move, which more often than not turned the game on its head.

Bringing a part–time spinner when Sri Lanka needed only 37 runs from 42 balls with 2 set batsmen ran a tremendous risk. India stood on the verge of an exit from the cup and hence at that stage, the risk appeared worthwhile. Sehwag in his first spell had pocketed the priced wicket of Sangakkara. The ball was gripping the pitch and an off–spinner with a traditional action would extract additional help from the pitch, the captain thought.

Sehwag did not disappoint. He dismissed Dilshan with a brute of a delivery in his first over of the second spell and then went on to claim the big fish, Jayasuriya. Within 3 overs, the game swung completely towards India. Ganguly's captaincy for the first time in this series showed itself, and it was about time! The Sri Lankan tail could not handle the tension and succumbed. India miraculously won by 4 runs and booked its place in yet another final. The tournament was a struggle for India and hence reaching the final felt like a triumph in itself. India had reached many finals in the previous season but had won very few. It was expected to make the transition from runners–up to winners in this season but the early hardships had wiped out that expectation. Perhaps it called for a grander stage to fulfil it. The occasion of the final would probably turn it around, or so India thought.

India's consistent bowling was one of the reasons for India's achievements in the previous season. The same bowling had shown no teeth in the tournament so far. It chose the final to make a grand re–entry. Irfan Pathan took care of swing and wickets. Zaheer and Nehra adhered to line and length restricting the run flow and India's part–timers restricted Sri Lankan middle order and its score to finish off a solid bowling display.

India's batting debacles so far in the tournament, coupled with its inability to win the finals throughout the last season, made the target of 229 very tricky. India's temperament to win big matches faced some serious doubts. India desired a strong opening partnership to settle its nerves. Instead, it was reduced to 26 for 2. An inconsistent V.V.S. Laxman failed to prove that not selecting him for the World Cup 2003 was a mistake as he got out for 12 and the law of averages eventually caught up with Dravid, reducing India to 96 for 4.

The match was done and dusted. India extended its failures in the finals. But suffering yet another defeat in the final was not its sole concern. India had played poorly throughout the series which suggested that there was something wrong deep inside somewhere. It often tried to surface but did not show itself up completely. The beginning of the season was not exactly ideal. Little did the Indian fans know that things were about to get worse.

TENNIS ELBOW AND THE NEW LOWS – VIDEOCON CUP AND NATWEST SERIES

'Sachin Tendulkar cannot hold or lift a bat.' The breaking news headline sent quivers down the spines of Indian fans. Was it the end of the legend? Would he play again? What the hell is a tennis elbow? All these questions clustered their minds. The injury itself was never heard of. Something so uncommon always seems incurable. Each day brought fresh updates on the status of Sachin's elbow. It ranged from his superfast recovery to his retirement, bringing the nation to a standstill. The notion that India had seen the last of its batting god refused to sink in. The ambiguity and suspense over it made it worse for the country and for the out–of–form Indian batting, especially after its dismal show in Sri Lanka. Its batting icon was injured and nobody knew for how long! He had previously survived a career–threatening back injury. The whole of India prayed for another comeback from its idol. He was gone for now though and India needed to look ahead. The Indian batsmen needed good batting conditions to boost their morale. A new cricketing venue where India was scheduled for its next series seemed very unlikely for any such thing to happen. The slow and low Sri Lankan pitches had made life miserable for India's stroke–making batsmen. The new ground looked every bit of the same.

Since its inception, cricket was confined to 8 to 10 British colonies. Even after evolving over a century, cricket failed to find an audience in other countries largely due to the lengthy duration of the game. For a football fan, a five–day sport with the possibility of a draw was baffling. In the globalised new millennium, revenues dictated terms and hence cricket had to pierce new markets which prompted ICC to bring three giants of world cricket – Australia, Pakistan and India to the Netherlands to play a tri–series. ICC viewed it as an opportunity to promote cricket beyond the regular territories. For India, the event provided a platform to gain some much needed salvation. For that, it wanted good solid pitches and conditions on which it's batting could blossom. In the oceanic town of Amstelveen, India found neither.

The tournament was marred by bad weather and a poor pitch. India failed to even reach the final. The tri–series held little significance to Indian patrons who kept asking one question– 'How was Sachin's elbow?' and just like the past month, there was zero clarity on it. India now travelled to England to play an important 3 match series as the series presented a chance to get acclimatized for the ICC Champions Trophy 2004 to be held in England.

INDIA IN ENGLAND – 3 ODI SERIES

The under–performing Indian batting came up against the resurgent and refreshingly aggressive England bowling attack. It was a no contest at all. England dominated the first two ODIs to win the series 2–1. Indian team's confidence of the last season was all but gone by now. Nobody had anticipated such a downslide from a team that dreamt of ruling the cricketing roaster. The bowling seemed scattered, batting weak and for the first time in his tenure as the captain, Sourav Ganguly looked out of ideas and bereft of his regular zeal. The manner in which India was outplayed and outclassed so far in the new season rendered it least likely to have any impact on the upcoming ICC Champions Trophy. The Champions Trophy symbolised the culmination of champions and the current Indian team looked far from being one.

THE DISASTROUS ICC CHAMPIONS TROPHY 2004

The Indian captain had converted Rahul Dravid the batsman into Rahul Dravid the wicket–keeper batsman. The move was the most astute of all Ganguly's decisions. It offered India the flexibility to play with seven batsmen. More so, it provided impetus to Dravid's ODI career. Dravid, the ODI batsman, had struggled till that point to keep up with the pace and fitness of the physically demanding ODI cricket. Physical requirements of being a wicket keeper fostered a brilliant ODI player in him which in turn translated in India's success in ODI cricket.

The new season, however, was a contrasting story. India, the semifinalist of ICC Champions Trophy 1998, runners up of 2000 and co–winners of 2002, did not even feature amongst the favourites to win it in 2004. Some drastic measures were necessitated to shake the team up and hence India decided to go into the match with a regular wicket–keeper batsman, relieving Dravid of his wicket keeping duties.

A Score of 290 against Kenya was a sign of much–desired form. The Indian batsmen faced the monumental task of negotiating the Pakistani bowling in the next match. On a grassy pitch and in overcast conditions, India came across a Pakistani bowling unit, true to its glorious past. Shoaib Akhtar ripped apart the Indian middle order with his lethal pace. Only Rahul Dravid stood thick with his 67. He along with Agarkar (47) took India to 200, which was not much but something to fight with.

Although the match provided the usual India–Pakistan moments (at one point of time, India even entertained a thought of winning the contest by reducing Pakistan to 152 for 6), the target was never out of reach for Pakistan, given India's continual incapacity to dismiss Inzamam–ul–Haq & Mohammad Yousuf for a low score. The consistent poor performances by the Indian batting meant that India was knocked out of its favourite tournament at the group stage itself.

India had lost its fourth series in a row now. The joy of last season dissipated in five months. The team looked a pale shadow of its last year's outfit. Sourav Ganguly, the fierce motivator, had his task cut out. India threw in the towel without putting up a fight in each of the four tournaments. The team could not afford such an attitude as its reputation was at stake. It tried to earn some sympathy from the fact that so far, it played outside India. The fortress of India was yet to be breached. Team India exemplified the word invincible when it came to playing test matches on home soil. But Australia was coming to put that sentiment to test.

THE ULTMATE INSULT, THE ULTIMATE LOSS – AUSTRALIA IN INDIA – OCTOBER 2004

Australia's previous tour of India in 2001 served as the stepping stone of self–belief on which India had structured its rebuilding process. Australia's vulnerability against spin was exposed by a young Harbhajan. Much had changed in these three years. Australia had dominated the test arena, conquering every obstacle put before them. But beating India in India remained elusive.

The epic series had denied Steve Waugh his ultimate dream of winning in India. Australia had craved for it since then. The news of Australia's strenuous preparations for this tour reached India before Australia did. Even after five months of catastrophic international cricket, there was a certain sense of assurance in India. India knew it possessed a destructive option in Harbhajan to exploit Australia's weakness against the spin. And of course, India had the legendary Kumble by its side this time. It also enjoyed a pair of dangerous seam bowlers in Zaheer and Irfan Pathan. The bowling looked solid but it was Indian batting which needed some attending to and hence, BCCI appointed Sunil Gavaskar as the consultant of the Indian team for the series. It did not sit well with John Wright. The rumour of a rift between Ganguly and Wright complicated the equation further. On the eve of the Bangalore test, Adam Gilchrist, captaining Australia in Ricky Ponting's absence, played his first card. He spoke to the media about a specific plan for India's batsmen. Everyone guessed what it would be. Short pitch bowling always posed a menace to Indian batsmen but the sweet–chin–music tactic had been a total failure in India's previous tour to Australia. How would a strategy that did not work in Australia, succeed in India? The mistake was apparent. So why was Australia committing it again?

BANGALORE – 1ST TEST

DAY ONE – DON'T YOU KNOW WHO WE ARE?

The scene was set for the stars in both sides. India had discovered two gems in Harbhajan and Laxman in the last tour but Australia had found a giant. Mathew Hayden had scored 549 runs in 3 tests in the 2001 tour. Australia also featured Langer, Martyn, and Gilchrist. The Indian middle order included Dravid, Laxman and Ganguly. The Australian bowling attack consisted of two legends, Glen McGrath and Shane Warne. India flaunted its own in Kumble. Amongst such big names, two players went unnoticed, in fact, neglected – a bloke playing in India for the first time, and a debutant.

The first 47 overs of the Australian innings were a quick recap to Australia's previous tours to India. It comprised of a big partnership followed by a mini–collapse (3 wickets for 25 runs). Nostalgia gripped the Bangalore crowd. At 149 for 4, India saw a debutant walking in. India smelled another wicket and a firm grip on the match. It had no idea it was looking at the future of Australian Cricket. Bangalore was about to witness the birth of a new star in international cricket.

If Katich dazzled all with his quick feet, Michael Clarke astonished everyone with his. It is a quality essential for playing in the sub–continent, especially in India. The comfort, with which both young boys countered Harbhajan and Kumble, left Ganguly haphazard. India was supposed to run away with the rest of the Australian batting. Instead, the pair added 107 runs. But when the day seemed like belonging to Australia, Kumble produced a twist in the tale by claiming the 5th Australian wicket. At 256 for 5 in 80 overs, the remaining 10 overs were poised for a fascinating contest. Another wicket and the day was India's. Australia had to ensure that the initiative given by its top order was not lost. Adam Gilchrist walked in and where any other team would have tried to play out the remaining overs, Australia scored 60. The score at the end of the day's play bore a radically different look in Australia's favour at 316 for 5.

DAY TWO – WE WERE NOT THERE THE LAST TIME

If Day One frustrated India, Day Two brought utter agony. Clarke scored his first hundred. Gilchrist scored an attacking hundred. Australia scored 474, a near perfect 1st innings total in Indian conditions. Day Two generally brought the best batting conditions in India and hence Australia needed accurate and tight bowling to not let India get away with a flier, like the ones Sehwag was known for.

India had done exceptionally well in Australia in 2003–04. One of the reasons for it was the consistent scores of the opening pair. Aakash Chopra's traditional style complimented Virender Sehwag's audacity. There happened to be another reason though; the absence of Glen McGrath. Aakash

Chopra faced the mighty McGrath for the first time in this series and it took McGrath just 4 balls to stamp his authority. Three good length balls were followed by an unplayable in–cutter. Rahul Dravid, since 2001, had become more dependable than Sachin himself. His was the prized wicket. It took McGrath another 5 balls to break the ever so sturdy defence of India's best test batsman. McGrath announced his arrival by breaking the back of Indian batting.

India called for some stable heads. Sehwag was not going to offer one. So, the captain assumed the responsibility. McGrath bowled at his accurate best. Gillespie adhered to immaculate line and length, not offering any room outside the off stump and stifling Indian batsmen for runs. Australia's special plan started coming out in the open. Australia did not commit the 'sweet–chin–music' blunder again. It came out with a masterstroke instead. The Indian batsmen preferred scoring in boundaries. A boundary was always a pressure–releasing shot. Many of them seemed to give the feeling that they did not believe in running singles and twos. Australia choked Indian batsmen by not giving them easy boundaries. Stifling Indian batsmen was just the first move of the master plan. It had another ace up its sleeve. It was the real masterstroke, the sucker punch.

Michael Kasprowicz's inclusion in the Australian side had amazed one and sundry. Why would a world champion team include a bowler, best remembered by India for the beating he suffered at the hands of Sachin in Sharjah? He was chosen for a special reason. In all these years, he had developed an art. He prepared himself to unleash his new arsenal of moves. He was ready to erase the Sharjah memory. A delivery on the middle leg stump would normally be flicked by Sehwag to the boundary. Virender Sehwag however, ended up flicking it straight into the hands of the mid–wicket. That was the impact of Kasprowicz's new weapon. That was the impact of the dreaded reverse swing.

Left–handed batsmen always struggled against the reverse swing. Ganguly was not an exception, whose wicket left India in tatters. At 98 for 4, Indian fans were tensed but not as much. Laxman stood at the other end and he was almost guaranteed to score big against Australia. The great Shane Warne had tasted very little success in India. The contest between him and Laxman had been heavily one–sided so far. Legends always find ways to conquer their failures. Shane Warne produced a fast version of the 'Mike Gatting dismissal'. The ball pitched outside leg and took the off stump. To the horror of Indian fans, the off stump belonged to V.V.S. Laxman. India was stunned to even react to Laxman's wicket. After toiling in the field for 130 overs, it ended the 2nd day's play at 150 for 6. Australia had won 6 sessions in a row. By the time the 6th session finished, India knew it had lost the match.

DAY THREE & FOUR – NOT AGAIN...DEFINITELY

India's performance so far in the test was not worth talking about. Perhaps a total below 274 and a follow–on would have added some spice to the game. A repeat of the classic Kolkata match would be destiny's call, fans hoped. But Australia was not in the mood to gift India any chance of a comeback. When it bundled India out for 246, Australia disappointed the gathered crowd by not enforcing the follow on. "Oh, they are scared," was the expected reaction from the Indian crowd. It was a well thought–of decision as it wiped out the possibility of India winning, if there was any in the first place. Harbhajan sent a slight warning to Australians of the difficulty to counter him on a 4th day pitch. His '6–for' restricted Australia to 228. India's second innings score of 105 for 6 at the end of 4th day's play while chasing 456, only validated the eventual outcome.

DAY FIVE – JUST LIKE 2001... AUSTRALIA 1–0 UP

Day Five pertained to formalities. Dravid and Pathan postponed the impending to some extent. Australia thrashed India at home by winning the test by 217 runs. Anybody who had tried to cover up India's terrible last 5 months under the garb of overseas conditions, got a crude wakeup call after the Bangalore test and for those who found comfort in the fact that Australia had been 1–0 up in 2001 series too, Chennai was the last chance to make the comparison between the current series with the epic series true. For India, Chennai served as the road to rescue, and it required to take it head on.

CHENNAI – 2ND TEST

DAY ONE – TURBINATOR PART II RELEASED, ALSO STARRING ANIL KUMBLE

India prayed for a miracle in Chennai. Instead, it received a thumping in the 1st session of the match (111 for 0). Australia raced to 136 runs for no wicket in 33 overs. The patient Australian side of Bangalore swiftly transformed into its original aggressive self which caught India off guard. Now was the time for something special. Harbhajan sensed it and delivered. His enticingly flighted deliveries were too tempting for Hayden and Langer. They both fell to their temptation. And then Anil Kumble took over. The sequence of 'batsman trying to defend on the front foot – ball bouncing a bit too much – batsman fending and departing' was repeated seven times in his next 18 overs. Each one resulted in a wicket to Kumble who finished the innings with 7 for 48 runs. Australia lost 8 wickets for 46 runs. At last the prayers were answered. At last the famous Australian collapse in India came about. For the first time in last 5 months, India dominated its opponent. With 28 for 1 at the end of Day One's play, India heaved a sigh of relief.

DAY TWO – NOBODY DOES IT BETTER THAN HIM

With only 235 runs to defend, Australia knew one big innings was enough to take the game away from it. Unfortunately for Australia, that one good knock came from the most destructive batsman in world cricket. Sehwag's 155 (21 boundaries) not only put India in a commanding position, it did it in no time. Mohammad Kaif and Parthiv Patel ended India's day on a high by negotiating tricky 21 overs at the end to give India a lead of 56 precious runs.

DAY THREE – A GUTSY EFFORT

The humidity in Chennai was so high that even the Indian batsmen struggled to cope with it. Parthiv Patel and a cramping Kaif pushed India towards safety by adding 102 runs. The Indian tail supported Kaif but his body ultimately gave in. He could not move his cramped–up body by even an inch to get back in his crease. Never the less, his gallant effort awarded India a healthy lead of 141 runs.

DAY FOUR – AUSTRALIA FIGHT BACK

Playing on a Day Four Indian pitch had always been a nightmare for Australia. Though it ate into India's lead, it lost four valuable wickets in the process. The only remaining Australian top–order batsman, to guide its tail, had an abysmal record in India. Damien Martyn's game possessed every quality required to score runs in the sub–continent. He was light on his feet, had fine wrists and the Indian gift of timing. In the humidity of Chennai and on a deteriorating pitch, he rediscovered all the ingredients needed to be successful in India. His majestic 104 showcased all his attributes – class, elegance and patience. But even after his innings, Australia could set a target of only 229. Sehwag made India's intentions of 'going for the kill' clear by scoring 19 runs in 3 overs. India was going to chase the target. India was going to level the series. India was back in business. But while making such statements, India did not look upwards to the sky. The rain gods were not listening to India's wishes. They were preparing for a busy day ahead.

DAY FIVE – IT RAINED THE WHOLE DAY IN OCTOBER

It took a day's rain to wash away all the efforts India put in for 4 days. Day Five was supposed to bring India the joy of a rare win in the extremely miserable five months of cricket. It was the day to set the series in motion. The entire day got washed out which resulted in a drawn match. India now had to win both remaining matches to keep the Border–Gavaskar Trophy in India. The series was living up to its reputation. The Chennai test made it obvious that spinning the Aussie batsmen out for low scores made life much easier for Indian batsmen. India did not require a rank turner. A pitch with a bit of invariable bounce and a bit of turn was enough to have a hold on the Australian batting. India felt confident that now on it would be very difficult for Australia to cope with the Indian spin–twins on spinning tracks. With this confidence, India landed in Nagpur. And to its horror and utter shock, India saw a pitch which had ample grass, plenty of bounce and big smiles on the Australian faces.

NAGPUR – 3RD TEST

Power concedes nothing without a demand. It never did and it never will –
Frederick Douglass

THE GAME OF POLITICS

A visionary leader often requires to be bold, vocal and willing to exercise his position of power. Sourav Ganguly imbibed these qualities in him because he took over Indian captaincy in turbulent times. Indian cricket at that time necessitated comprehensive restructuring of its team and set up. For that, the captain demanded supreme power in decision making. The structure of BCCI gave supreme power to only one, its president. Fortunately for Ganguly, his captaincy coincided with another Bengali at the helm of BCCI. Jagmohan Dalmiya, a veteran BCCI official and an exceptional administrator was the face of BCCI at the time. He was the ultimate boss, the final authority. Ganguly desired the same degree of power for bringing his vision for Indian cricket to reality. Dalmiya understood Ganguly's demands and let him have his say. Together, Ganguly and Dalmiya formed an alliance nobody could challenge.

The President and the captain had dictated all decisions for 4 years. The more they exercised their power, the more enemies they gave rise to. Jagmohan Dalmiya had made BCCI into a one man show but in the last five years; a strong camp was formed with one objective – to end the reign of the talismanic Bengali. India played good cricket till this season and no one could touch Dalmiya and Ganguly while the team was doing well. The ongoing season was a debacle and in this moment of weakness, the anti–Dalmiya camp caught sight of a little opening. A home series loss to Australia would raise troubling and unavoidable questions. India had always taken pride in the magnificent Australian side's failure to surmount India. The pride was at stake and a green top threatened to destroy it.

"We are playing at home, where our main strength is spin. But this kind of wicket takes the advantage away from us. I asked the grounds–man a few days ago for the grass to be removed but he has not done much. The curator here is the man in charge and he has his own ideas." Ganguly's press conference remarks threw the debate of the Nagpur pitch in the open. The build–up to the most important match of the season for India was surrounded by many questions. Isn't it a normal practice to provide favourable conditions to the home team? Why is the curator reluctant to do so then? It is one thing to not provide spinning conditions but what was this adamancy to provide an Australian pitch. Yes, an Australian Pitch! That's what Adam Gilchrist had called that pitch. The political gambit overshadowed the game itself but the bigger shock was yet to come.

Ganguly declared himself unfit on the eve of the match. His decision, at the back of a debate over the Nagpur pitch, raised many obvious doubts. Some believed that his decision was in protest of the politically influenced stance by the VCA. The decision changed Sourav Ganguly's captaincy career forever. In one moment, he was tagged as a whimpering loser who could not stand disagreements. The Indian team though had no time to react or digest the developments as under Rahul Dravid, it began its toughest home test match.

THE GAME OF CRICKET

India faced extreme adverse conditions. The team was not in the mental frame to conquer the conditions, despite the much–awaited comeback of Sachin Tendulkar. Zaheer tried his best with 4 wickets but lacked the help he required. Poor Anil Kumble and Murali Karthik did not even come into the picture on the VCA pitch. On that green pitch and against McGrath, Gillespie & Co., Australia's 1st innings total of 398 looked like 698. India could only muster 185 in 1st innings. Australia restrained from enforcing the follow on again. India lollygagged its way to 200 in the 2nd innings. With Zaheer Khan's wicket in India's second innings, Australia fulfilled its long overdue dream. It won a test series in India after 35 long years. It played outstanding cricket in Bangalore, got lucky in Chennai, got a surprise in Nagpur and the Final Frontier was at last conquered. The Indian team faced utter humiliation and embarrassment of getting beaten in its own backyard. The result forced John Wright to step down as the Indian coach after Pakistan's tour of India. The partnership of Wright and Ganguly had a lion's share in the team's resurgence. He left India with the love of millions who appreciated his immense contributions in bringing Indian cricket's glory and charm back. Losing a coach like him in such a manner was a real shame. For Jagmohan Dalmiya, it was the beginning of the end to his reign over the Indian Cricket Administration. He was the first victim of India's dismal show against Australia. The small group had managed to pin a tough nut like him with the help of a little grass on the Nagpur pitch. For Ganguly, it was an eye–opener. He realized that things would not be as easy as they were for the last four years. He had no choice but to get acquainted with the changing reality of a shift in the power centres in BCCI. He had responded wonderfully to the challenge of reviving Indian cricket. Now, he needed to be ready to fight a personal battle. The team lost its coach, its 'invincible at home' tag and it appeared to be on the verge of losing its charismatic captain to internal politics. The team that rose to new heights in the last five years completed its downfall within a year.

BATTLE FOR CONTROL

Harsha Bhogle: You have just come back from the press conference. There was some suggestion that there was talk of may be stepping down from the captaincy. Was there too much to that?

Sourav Ganguly: At least not from my point of view; not from me personally, no.

Harsha Bhogle: Was it suggested to you then?

Sourav Ganguly: Yes. It was.

Harsha Bhogle: It could not be very easy. I mean you are going out there, there is someone suggesting that maybe you are not the right man (to lead a side.) Was that the reason for a lot of pressure on you? Or are we reading too much into it?

Sourav Ganguly: Well, I don't want to elaborate the issue, don't want to go into it much more but probably it gave me the kick to fight on for 6 Hours.

Sourav Ganguly's candid confessions to Harsha Bhogle threw the nation into hysteria and disbelief. The interview came at the back of his 262–ball century against Zimbabwe. It came at the back of a disastrous one year in which India won only 3 series. (2 of them against Bangladesh) Greg Chappell in his first test series as the coach of the Indian Cricket team had asked Ganguly to resign. Even though Indian fans fumed at India's wretched last year, they had not held Captain Marvelous responsible directly, not yet. There was always the baggage of emotions associated with Sourav Ganguly and hence the issue required immediate attention. The public display of emotions threatened to blow the situation out of control. Here was a coach in his infant days of international coaching, asking an established captain to step down. Then there was a captain who chose to speak about it in a day–end interview with the casualness of perhaps discussing his dinner menu. Was it necessary to bring the rift out in the open? Was the casual attitude in his interview correct? One thing was sure though. The interview marked the beginning of the bitterest rivalry in Indian Cricket.

New Zealand had required 6 runs off the last ball to tie a match against Australia. Greg Chappell, Australian captain at the time ordered his bowler to bowl underarm, to prevent a very unlikely tie. The underarm ball became the lasting image of Greg Chappell in world cricket, somewhat unfair to a guy with 7000 test runs at an average of 54! India was introduced to his views in his brief commentary stint in India's Tour of Australia in 2004.

He impressed many Indians by his frank opinions and his approach to the game. Sourav Ganguly was one of them. He had consulted him for playing on bouncy pitches in Australia in 2004. His help had worked wonders for Ganguly. So, when Chappell's name entered the fray for appointment as Indian head coach, it became obvious that the committee comprising Gavaskar and Shastri who had worked with him as commentators, would go with him. He also had a big nod from Ganguly himself. He won over the committee with his excellent presentation in which he laid before it his vision for progress of Indian cricket. After a miserable start to the season, the Indian team desperately needed inspiration and fighting spirit and who better than an Australian to instill it! An Australian had never been a coach of Indian Cricket Team. His immediate task was to familiarize with the ecosystem in which Indian cricket functioned. He did not have the time though as he walked into his first assignment straightaway.

THE ALTERNATE LEADER – TRI SERIES IN SRILANKA

Apart from his own batting woes and his team's miserable form, Sourav Ganguly faced another problem. An inexplicable slow over rate in the previous series had handed him a four–match ban. The Ganguly–Chappell partnership at the helm had to wait for a while. Instead, India went into the Sri Lankan Tri–series with a new captain and a new coach.

The causes for India's rapid slide were not yet fully analysed. Some attributed it to complacency, some to rifts in the camp. Greg Chappell had his own philosophy. He related it to the age of the team. Selection of young players like Suresh Raina and Venugopal Rao and axing of V.V.S. Laxman explicitly outlined his mode of thinking. Ganguly had also followed the similar theory when he took over the captaincy. Inclusion of Yuvraj, Kaif, Sehwag, Zaheer and Harbhajan had yielded wondrous results back then but the real reason for Ganguly's success was the method in which the youngsters were groomed; how they were allowed time to adjust to international cricket. Greg Chappell looked in a hurry. Here started the long chain of Greg Chappell's experiments.

After decades, India seemed to have ended its long–lasting wait for a wicket–keeper who could bat. And straight away, Dhoni was promoted to open the innings with Sehwag. Mohammad Kaif became Sehwag's opening partner for the second match. The tweak resulted in a very inexperienced middle order. Dravid's matured 54 was not enough against Sri Lanka in the first match but his 52 against West Indies in the second game gave Greg Chappell his maiden win. After all the infusion of young blood and some absurd batting order changes, the oldest man in the team saved India from an early exit.

Dravid was named captain for the series. Hence, Ganguly, even after returning from the ban, had to play under Dravid. However, inclusion of Laxman in the team and the tried and tested batting order hinted that Ganguly assumed his powers once again. His own conflict continued as he labored to a Fifty at strike rate of 46. He appeared preoccupied with something other than cricket. Cricket was not the first thing on his mind and his tussle with his thoughts showed on the field. India managed to beat West Indies both times, to reach and lose yet another final. Nothing changed for India. But a few knew that everything was about to change. They had sensed the storm coming.

The Tri–series in Sri Lanka brought to fore many glaring problems. India changed its batting order in every game of the series. How long would these changes continue? Was India searching for the right combination or a floating batting lineup was the road forward? A sense of uncertainty had crept in the team. "Thank god we at least have certainty in our captain," India thought. But Greg Chappell had some other ideas about that notion. He had identified an alternate leader, a leader who perhaps suited his modus–operandi. In such volatile atmosphere, India geared up for its tour to Zimbabwe where India was yet to win a test series.

THE TIPPING POINT – INDIA'S TOUR OF ZIMBABWE – 2005

After another loss in a tri–series final in Zimbabwe, pressure mounted on Ganguly. He was named captain for the entire tour and hence; he was about to stand in his 48th test as Indian captain, the most by any Indian captain. A disturbing statistic stared at him though. He had last seen a three–digit score way back in December 2003, in Brisbane due to the valuable inputs from Greg Chappell. The 49th test as a captain looked certain but future beyond appeared bleak. There was a convincing possibility that the 49th test could be his last as a captain unless something happened. He had to do something. He needed to somehow score a century to buy some more time. The thought had taken hold of his mind. A century......yes, a century.

In the first test against Zimbabwe, Gautam Gambhir scored at a strike rate of 78. Sehwag scored at a strike rate of 92; Dravid at 66 and V.V.S. Laxman at 63. Sourav Ganguly however, appeared to be batting on a different pitch and in a different match. He took a staggering 261 balls to score his century. His innings was laborious, slow, many times boring and painful throughout, for diehard fans but he achieved his goal of scoring a century. He was relieved of pain, he thought. He had answered those who gunned for his head, he thought. He now could be at peace, he thought. A casual confession in an interview after the end of that day's play devastated every single notion he had presumed. Not only that, it threatened to tear apart what he had built in the last 5 years. That, he had not thought of.

THE E-MAIL THAT SHOOK THE NATION

Ganguly's interview brought the friction out in the open. BCCI had to intervene and take charge of such an unprecedented situation. Instead, it decided to have a farce. Sourav Ganguly and Greg Chappell were made to appear before camera, playing snooker together to display their unity. Apart from destroying hopes for any future in acting for them, the snooker episode achieved nothing. Both tried their best to camouflage the discomfort they felt in each other's company but failed. No soul in India bothered about the 2nd test win for India. India won a test series in Zimbabwe for the first time. Who cared? What was Greg Chappell's response to Ganguly's interview going to be? That was the million–dollar question.

Being an Australian, Greg Chappell had instinctively decided to respond but decided to adhere to the proper channel of communication – an email to the appropriate authority clarifying his stand on the whole controversy. He took one point at a time and presented his take on it in detail. He knew the higher power was willing to listen. He thought he had done his job. The next morning brought his first awakening of how Indian bureaucracy functioned as he saw his explosive and confidential E–mail being read on almost every news channel in India. At that moment, while contemplating his responses to the situation at hand, Greg Chappell understood the gravity of his actions. He embroiled himself in a direct fight that promised to be fierce. After all, he was pitted against Indian cricket's mightiest warrior. He realized that he had a long battle on his hand. But deep down inside, he also knew he held a trump card. This was not merely a case of 'difference of opinion' between a captain and a coach. Greg Chappell had the backing of the political undercurrent to the issue.

THE E-MAIL & THE COVER-UP EFFORTS

Due to comments made by Mr. Sourav Ganguly during the press conference following his innings in the recently completed Test match in Bulawayo and the subsequent media speculation I would like to make my position clear on two points.

1. At no stage did I ask Mr. Ganguly to step down from the captaincy of the Indian team and;

2. At no stage have I threatened to resign my position as Indian team coach.

Mr. Ganguly came to me following the recently completed tri–series of one–day matches here in Zimbabwe and asked me to tell him honestly where he stood as a player in my view. I told him that I thought he was struggling as a player and that it was affecting his ability to lead the team effectively and that the pressure of captaincy was affecting his ability to play to his potential. I also told him that his state of mind was fragile and it showed in the way that he made decisions on and off the field in relation to the team, especially team selection. A number of times during the tri–series the tour selectors had chosen a team and announced it to the group only for Sourav to change his mind on the morning of the game and want to change the team.

On at least one occasion he did change the team and on the morning of the final I had to talk him out of making another last–minute change that I believe would have destroyed team morale and damaged the mental state of the individuals concerned. I also told Sourav that his nervous state was affecting the team in other ways as he was prone to panic during pressure situations in games and that his nervous demeanor was putting undue pressure on the rest of the team. His nervous pacing of the rooms during our batting in the final plus his desire to change the batting order during our innings in the final had also contributed to nervousness in the players waiting to go in to bat. His reluctance to bat first in games I suggested was also giving wrong signals to the team and the opposition and his nervousness at the crease facing bowlers like Shane Bond from NZ was also affecting morale in the dressing room.

On the basis of this and other observations and comments from players in the squad about the unsettling effect Sourav was having on the group I suggested to Sourav that he should consider stepping down from the captaincy at the end of the tour in the interests of the team and in his own best interests if he wanted to prolong his playing career. I told him of my own experiences toward the end of my career and cited other players such as Border, Taylor and Steve Waugh, all of whom struggled with batting form toward the end of their tenure as Australian captain.

I also raised the matter of selection for the first Test with Sourav and asked him where he thought he should bat. He said 'number 5'. I told him that he might like to consider opening in the Test as the middle order was going to be a tight battle with Kaif and Yuvraj demanding selection. Sourav asked me if I was serious. I said it was something to be considered, but it had to be his decision.

The following day Sourav batted in the match against Zimbabwe 'A' team in the game in Mutare. I am not sure of the exact timing of events because I was in the nets with other players when Sourav went in to bat, but the new ball had either just been taken or was imminent when I saw Sourav walking from the field holding his right arm. I assumed he had been hit and made my way to the players' area where Sourav was receiving treatment from the team physiotherapist, John Gloster.

When I enquired as to what had happened Sourav said he had felt a click in his elbow as he played a ball through the leg side and that he thought he should have it investigated. Sourav had complained of pain to his elbow at various stages of the one–day series, but he had resisted having any comprehensive investigation done and, from my observation, had been spasmodic in his treatment habits, often not using ice–packs for the arm that had been prepared for him by John Gloster. I suggested, as had John Gloster, that we get some further tests done immediately. Sourav rejected these suggestions and said he would be 'fine'. When I queried what he meant by 'fine' he said he would be fit for the Test match. I then queried why then was it necessary to be off the field now. He said that he was just taking 'precautions'.

Rather than make a scene with other players and officials in the vicinity I decided to leave the matter and observe what Sourav would do from that point on. After the loss of Kaif, Yuvraj and Karthik to the new ball, Sourav returned to the crease with the ball now around 20 overs old. He struggled for runs against a modest attack and eventually threw his wicket away trying to hit one of the spinners over the leg side.

The next day I enquired with a number of the players as to what they had thought of Sourav's retirement. The universal response was that it was 'just Sourav' as they recounted a list of times when Sourav had suffered from mystery injuries that usually disappeared as quickly as they had come. This disturbed me because it confirmed for me that he was in a fragile state of mind and it was affecting the mental state of other members of the squad.

I was so concerned about the effect that Sourav's actions were having on the team that I decided I could not wait until selection meeting that evening to inform him that I had serious doubts about picking him for the first test.

I explained that, in my view, I felt we had to pick Kaif and Yuvraj following their good form in the one–day series and that Sehwag, Gambhir, Laxman and Dravid had to play. He said that his record was better than Kaif and Yuvraj and that they had not proved themselves in Test cricket. I countered with the argument that they had to be given a chance to prove themselves on a consistent basis or we would never know.

Sourav asked me whether I thought he should be captain of the team. I said that I had serious doubts that he was in the right frame of mind to do it. He asked me if I thought he should step down. I said that it was not my decision to make, that only he could make that decision, but if he did make that decision, he had to do it in the right manner or it would have even more detrimental effects than if he didn't stand down. I said that now was not the time to make the decision but that we should discuss it at the selection meeting to be held later in the day.

Sourav then said that if I didn't want him to be captain that he would inform Rahul that he was going to stand down. I reiterated that it was not my decision to make but he should give it due consideration under the circumstances but not to do it hastily. At that point Sourav went to Rahul and the two of them conferred briefly and then Sourav left the field and entered the dressing room. At that stage I joined the start of the training session.

A short time later Mr. Chowdhary came on to the field and informed me that Sourav had told him that I did not want him as captain and that Sourav wanted to leave Zimbabwe immediately if he wasn't playing. I then joined Mr. Chowdhary and Rahul in the dressing room where we agreed that this was not the outcome that any of us wanted and that the ramifications would not be in the best interests of the team.

We then spent some time with Sourav and eventually convinced him that he should stay on as captain for the two Tests and then consider his future. In my view it was not an ideal solution but it was better than the alternative of him leaving on a bad note. I believe he has earned the right to leave in a fitting manner. We all agreed that this was a matter that should stay between us and should not, under any circumstances, be discussed with the media.

The matter remained quiet until the press conference after the game when a journalist asked Sourav if he had been asked to step down before the Test. Sourav replied that he had but he did not want to elaborate and make an issue of it. I was then called to the press conference where I was asked if I knew anything of Sourav being asked to step down before the game. I replied that a number of issues had been raised regarding selection but as they were selection matters, I did not wish to make any further comment.

Since then various reports have surfaced that I had threatened to resign. I do not know where that rumor has come from because I have spoken to no one in regard to this because I have no intention of resigning. I assume that some sections of the media, being starved of information, have made up their own stories.

At the completion of the Test match I was approached by VVS Laxman with a complaint that Sourav had approached him on the eve of the Test saying that I had told Sourav that I did not want Laxman in the team for Test matches. I denied that I had made such a remark to Sourav, or anybody else for that matter, as, on the contrary, I saw Laxman as an integral part of the team. He asked how Sourav could have said what he did. I said that the only way we could go to the bottom of the matter was to speak to Sourav and have him repeat the allegation in front of me.

I arranged for a meeting with the two of them that afternoon. The meeting took place just after 6pm in my room at the Rainbow Hotel in Bulawayo. I told Sourav that Laxman had come to me complaining that Sourav had made some comments to Laxman prior to the Test. I asked Sourav if he would care to repeat the comment in my presence. Sourav then rambled on about how I had told him that I did not see a place for Laxman in one–day cricket, something that I had discussed with Sourav and the selection panel and about which I had spoken to Laxman at the end of the Sri Lankan tour.

Sourav mentioned nothing about the alleged conversation regarding Laxman and Test cricket even when I pushed him on it later in the discussion. As we had to leave for a team function, we ended the conversation without Sourav adequately explaining his comments to Laxman.

Again, this is not an isolated incident because I have had other players come to me regarding comments that Sourav had made to them that purports to be comments from me to Sourav about the particular player. In each case the comments that Sourav has passed on to the individual are figments of Sourav's imagination. One can only assume that he does it to unnerve the individual who, in each case, has been a middle order batsman.

Sourav has missed the point of my discussions with him on this matter. It has less to do with his form than it does with his attitude toward the team. Everything he does is designed to maximise his chance of success and is usually detrimental to someone else's chances.

Despite meeting with him in Mumbai after his appointment as captain and speaking with him about these matters and his reluctance to do the preparation and training that is expected of everyone else in the squad, he continues to set a bad example.

Greg King's training reports continue to show Sourav as the person who does the least fitness and training work based on the criterion that has been developed by the support staff to monitor the work load of all the players.

We have also developed parameters of batting, bowling, fielding and captaincy that we believe embodies the 'Commitment to Excellence' theme that I espoused at my interview and Sourav falls well below the acceptable level in all areas. I will be pleased to present this documentation when I meet with the special committee in Mumbai later this month.

As I said to you during our meeting in Colombo, I have serious reservations about the attitude of some players and about Sourav and his ability to take this team to a new high, and none of the things he has done since his reappointment has caused me to change my view. In fact, it has only served to confirm that it is time for him to move on and let someone else build their team toward the 2007 World Cup.

This team has been made to be fearful and distrusting by the rumour mongering and deceit that is Sourav's modus operandi of divide and rule. Certain players have been treated with favour, all of them bowlers, while others have been shunted up and down the order or left out of the team to suit Sourav's whims.

John Wright obviously allowed this to go on to the detriment of the team. I am not prepared to sit back and allow this to continue or we will get the same results we have been seeing for some time now.

It is time that all players were treated with fairness and equity and that good behaviors and attitudes are rewarded at the selection table rather than punished.

I can assure you of my very best intentions.

Yours sincerely,

Greg Chappell MBE

It was unmistakable from Chappell's email that the issue pertained more to egos than the composition of the team. Chappell had accused Ganguly of every sin a professional sportsman would never commit. He had accused

Ganguly of lying, creating distrust in team members and avoiding fitness regimes. The email showed his bias and many times desperation to get Ganguly out of the team. It was naïve of him to think one email would suffice. He failed to envisage the Indian fans' passion in supporting their leader. Greg Chappell was up against an individual who had showed direction to Indian cricket in the last five years. He was up against a man who proudly backed his players to death. He was up against a man who rekindled hope in Indian cricket. His real task began now as he had to establish his accusations. For Sourav Ganguly, it was business as usual. He had to overpower one more person to justify himself. He was ready as always.

Ganguly and Chappell prepared themselves to go at each other's throats. The BCCI had to bring order back to the situation which was threatening to get out of control at any moment. It chose the proven situation–defusing route of 'setting up a committee'. Chappell and Ganguly appeared before it, sans snooker off course, to put forward their points. The outcome of such committee hearings is a pre–known eventuality. BCCI attempted to bury the issue by issuing a statement –

"Indian cricket has to move forward and for that, both the captain and coach have to work together and a professional working relationship has to be maintained. Both Chappell and Ganguly have told the committee they will work together."

BCCI sought a happy ending. By now everybody knew how aggressive Greg Chappell's stand would be. There was no second guessing Sourav Ganguly's aggression. Anyone who hoped for a happy ending was delusional. What transpired during the next seven months was a fierce battle for power, and more agony for Indian Cricket fans.

THUMPING SERIES WIN WAS NOT ENOUGH – SRI LANKA IN INDIA – OCT-NOV 2005

Amidst the Ganguly–Chappell saga, India prepared to play a seven–match ODI series against Sri Lanka at home. Only one man seemed capable of steering Indian cricket through the controversy surrounding it. Sachin Tendulkar had introduced tennis elbow to the nation. Nobody understood the nature of his injury but everybody knew its severity. It had forced India's batting god to sit out for almost a year (except for his brief outing against Australia in 2004). It was official though. He was slated to make his comeback in the Sri Lanka series but even his comeback story failed to counter the Ganguly issue. It was another eye opener for Greg Chappell as he came across the level of emotion Ganguly stirred in Indian fans. An injury to Sourav Ganguly forced him out for the first two ODIs. Under the leadership of Rahul Dravid, India tried to begin afresh.

Greg Chappell resumed his experiments. He had noticed a bit of batting skill in Irfan Pathan hence he was promoted to the top–order to exploit his batting potential. With Sachin Tendulkar in supreme form, a new found all–rounder in Pathan, an explosive wicket keeper batsman in M.S. Dhoni who smashed 183 runs in the 3rd ODI to register the highest Wicket Keeper score, India brushed Sri Lanka aside with a 6–1 win. Ganguly's exclusion from the rest of the series, even after his availability, raised a question without any adequate answer. In fact, nobody even bothered to answer.

THE FINGER THAT GAVE HIM A LIFELINE – SOUTH AFRICA IN INDIA – NOVEMBER 2005

South Africa arrived next to play an ODI series. The question on Ganguly's omission was asked again and brushed aside like before. Slowly but surely, Greg Chappell was getting it done. India's dominating victories helped him ignoring questions on Ganguly's exclusion. But just when he thought that the Ganguly chapter approached its end, BCCI announced the venues for the South Africa series. Unfortunately for Chappell, Eden Gardens, Ganguly's very own den featured in the list.

The series commenced with bizarre changes in the Indian batting line up. Kaif was promoted to No.3 in Hyderabad. Gambhir, a pure opener, batted at No.6. Pathan moved ahead of Dhoni. The game at Banglore was even weirder. India dropped Sehwag to No.4 and Gambhir got a chance to open. Irfan Pathan batted at 3. South Africa won in Hyderabad and India won in Bangalore, courtesy a good bowling performance but both the results hardly mattered. Every single soul in the country awaited Kolkata.

The day arrived at last and it brought with it the sternest test for Greg Chappell and his temperament. Eden Garden was packed to capacity as always. A faithful crowd of one hundred thousand people gathered for the sole purpose of showing Greg Chappell what precisely they thought of him. The scene was unprecedented as the vociferous Eden crowd booed every member of the Indian team. Every single South African run was cheered. Not even Sachin Tendulkar could escape public wrath. Special mentions to Chappell echoed throughout the match. The crowd behaviour rattled India as it capitulated for 188 and South Africa won by 10 wickets. Mark Boucher's remarks in the post–match press conference summed the atmosphere. "We felt like playing in Cape Town."

The proceedings infuriated Chappell. His experiments were not fetching the desired results in the series and now he had a hostile crowd in his ears. He hoped the protests would stay inside the stadium. But he was in Kolkata for god's sake. Kolkata had reserved the day for protests and booing. Bengali fans, Ganguly's fans, continued booing the Indian team to their team bus. And there, Greg Chappell snapped and stuck out his middle finger from the bus towards the crowd.

Sympathy is a strange phenomenon. It unfolds in confounding ways. One never knows its trigger and its impact! Greg Chappell's finger resulted in a massive wave of sympathy for Sourav Ganguly. All the negative impressions of him swiftly disappeared. He came out as the victim of a bigger power battle. That finger showed the world how unreceptive Chappell was to criticism. It reminded the world of his unsporting past. The tables turned a bit but Sourav Ganguly of all people knew the unrelenting truth about the benefits of sympathy. They tend to vanish in haste.

India managed to level the series in Mumbai where an outstanding crowd showed the nation that respect for country comes first. Rahul Dravid was visibly annoyed by the conduct of the crowd in Kolkata but in Mumbai, he was overwhelmed by it. The frailty shown by the coach and the stupendous pressure created by the media worked in favour of Ganguly. His inclusion in the test team against Sri Lanka emerged as almost certain although Sourav Ganguly recognized the mammoth challenge that lay ahead. Here on, began the 2nd chapter of the Sourav–Greg Saga.

THE PICK AND DROP GAME

Sourav Ganguly earned the sympathy of the nation but the place in the team was not earned but gifted. The team management did not want him but he had to be included. More often than not, such situations result in weird strategies for including the player. The batting order changes by the Indian coach so far had prepared Indian fans for 'the weird' but the justification for Ganguly's inclusion for the 1st test against Sri Lanka was plain ludicrous. Sourav Ganguly, the stylish left–handed batsman all of sudden was being portrayed as India's new batting all–rounder.

Ganguly was not the only player on Greg Chappell's radar. There were some others termed by him as detrimental to 'team spirit'. Zaheer Khan, a Ganguly loyalist, topped the list. The batting all–rounder Ganguly with a bowling average of above 50, replaced India's leading pacer. The change projected that to accommodate Ganguly, India's future was being sacrificed which heaped more pressure on Ganguly. A rain affected match did not help his cause. After scoring 5 runs and bowling just 2 overs, Ganguly sensed his departure. This time, Virender Sehwag, another Ganguly loyalist helped him out, albeit unknowingly, as his injury gave Sourav Ganguly another and perhaps the last chance to hold his place in the team. He scored only 40 and 39 and was not given a single over in the match. With Sehwag fit again, Ganguly's exclusion from the 3rd test looked inevitable. His appearances in both the tests, though sluggish, did not tantamount to sacking. The Indian think tank conjured another mind–boggling excuse, this time for dropping him. The chairman of Selectors, Mr. Kiran More said, "It's not done to have Sourav in the squad and not have him in the playing eleven. We are also keeping the future in mind."

These illogical reasons for excluding Sourav Ganguly did not do Greg Chappell any good. Ganguly's portrayal as a victim got stronger due to such ambiguous reasons for picking and dropping him. It made his efforts to do away with Ganguly appear desperate rather than warranted. The Indian team management and selection committee needed a permanent solution to the problem. There was none available immediately and hence Ganguly was selected for the tour of Pakistan. Sourav Ganguly had to ensure that he did not give them one and for that, he needed runs. Time was running out. As he boarded the team bus to Lahore, he very much knew; it was now or never.

Leaving Ganguly on the bench was not an option. It would have been a terrible insult to the man, Mr. Kiran More had said earlier. Yuvraj Singh sat on back–to–back half centuries against Sri Lanka which made it difficult to accommodate Ganguly in the middle order against Pakistan and hence Gambhir was sacrificed. Dravid became the makeshift opener and Ganguly got 'adjusted'. The arrangement pleased none but there was no other alternative. Cameras in those days constantly followed Ganguly. One of the cameras caught another public display of emotion by the usual suspects. The pre–match show captured an emotional and stormy discussion between Sourav Ganguly, Rahul Dravid and Greg Chappell. Ganguly did all the talking. Dravid seemed irritated while Chappell maintained his distance. Ganguly looked quite excited during the course of the conversation. The fans certainly did not want to go through another dispute. Absence of any official statement kept the matter up for speculations. When the match ensued, Pakistan piled up 679 runs. India replied with 410 for 1 as Sehwag again enjoyed the Pakistani bowling scoring 254 and Dravid, the opener, got 128. Sourav Ganguly did not get the chance to bat and with only 6 overs of bowling, he no longer held the 'title' of India's batting all–rounder. After bowling 6 overs and getting no opportunity to bat, Sourav Ganguly was dropped again. The Indian think tank bettered its previous explanation for dropping him." We need to take twenty wickets. Our batting is in top form. Our openers added 410 runs in Lahore. There may be no need for 6th batsman." Sourav Ganguly, picked in the previous series for his bowling exploits, was dropped for the second test against Pakistan for want of a bowler. The reasons for his inclusion and exclusion were becoming more and more absurd with each passing match. The game had reached its tipping point. Something had to give. The green pitch at Nagpur had started Ganguly's downfall as a captain. The green pitch at Karachi for the 3rd test looked set to end the 2nd chapter in the Ganguly– Chappell story.

The 3rd test contained every ingredient of a blockbuster – a first over hat–trick from Irfan Pathan, a grand fightback century from Kamran Akmal, a display of devastating fast bowling, worthy of its illustrious past, by Pakistan, and a spirited rear–guard century from Yuvraj in the 2nd innings. For Sourav Ganguly, it was a tale of two misjudgments. He looked fluent in his stay at the crease but the scores of 34 and 37 were simply not good enough to fight the odds stacked against him. After all the irrational reasons for dropping him, Sourav Ganguly himself gifted a logical reason to the team management. The battle for control which began with an interview, ended with 2 reckless dismissals. Sourav Ganguly with his 'who cares attitude' and disregard to authority, had made many foes. They latched onto the chance to pin him down forever. He had been dropped from the side 4 times in the last 4 months. He had been ridiculed. His attitude and passion for the game had been doubted. He no longer enjoyed the faith of the authority. Players like Harbhajan Singh who tried to speak out were summoned to offices. All the entries were sealed. It was seen as the inevitable end of India's most dynamic, influential and controversial captain of all time. But a bunch of faithful Ganguly fanatics remembered the popular dialogue from an *Arnold Schwarzenegger Movie – I'LL BE BACK.*

AN INDIFFERENT SEASON

The initial nine months of Greg Chappell's stint involved controversies, committee hearings and accusations. With the Ganguly chapter closed in Pakistan, he could now focus on cricket. England was visiting India and for an Australian, beating England topped the 'to–do list'. In the context of India's reign at home and England's miserable record in the sub–continent, Greg Chappell was certain of a thumping win. However, even at the back of a disastrous Pakistan tour, England was a team to beat. It had notched up some outstanding wins in the recent past including a home Ashes win, perhaps the best test series ever in the game's history. India meanwhile was still recovering from the Ganguly episode as well as its dwindling test form. Though injuries to Captain Michael Vaughan, pacer Simon Jones and Ashley Giles hampered England's odds, the tour still offered a good chance to upset India in India; all of this was despite stand–in Captain Marcus Trescothick's unexpected withdrawal from the series citing personal reasons. Greg Chappell had announced his strategy– "Aggression is the key". He could not have asked for a better opponent than an injury–ridden England for his 2nd home test series after an easy win over Sri Lanka (2–0).

ENGLAND IN INDIA – 2006

CLASH OF IDEOLOGIES – 1ST TEST – NAGPUR

England astonished many, by countering its biggest hurdle, spin bowling. Paul Collingwood took command of England's batting with a skillfully crafted century. Though England played above expectations, India missed the trick by playing the waiting game. It expected England to falter instead of taking initiative at key moments. The first two days of Chappell's grand home test against England did not go according to plan. He still had India's much famed batting to rely upon which more than often used to put massive scores on placid Indian pitches. He was certain that the Indian batting would give him a big lead and therefore when Anil Kumble's resilient 58 lent some respectability to India's mediocre score of 190 for 7, Greg Chappell looked forlorn. A day on which India was supposed to take a massive lead, India conceded a lead of 70. Andrew Flintoff's brave overnight declaration gave Greg Chappell one more chance to redeem himself. A successful chase of 367 runs on a Day Five Indian pitch, was sure to win over Indian public and establish him as a fine coach.

India's asking rate was 4 runs per over but it managed 63 runs in the 1st session and 68 in the 2nd session. After all the talks about aggression from Guru Greg, India was settling for a draw in its home. Irfan Pathan's promotion to No. 4 hinted for a fleeting moment that India considered chasing the target in the last session but it was too late. India had fallen behind in the game from Day One. India's confusion whether to chase the target or play–safe reflected the clash of ideologies between the coach and the team. India, who used to dominate these home test matches from the word go, was pushed against the wall throughout the match. Whispers on Greg Chappell's coaching had begun. After a 1–0 loss in Pakistan and an uncharacteristic draw against England, the pressure mounted on Chappell. He had to deliver and do it quickly.

THE FAMILIAR SETTINGS – 2ND TEST – MOHALI

Every necessary ingredient was put in place in Mohali for the usual recipe; a turning pitch and invariable bounce. Kumble used it to perfection by picking 5 wickets. The legendary Indian spinner became the 5th bowler in World cricket to bag 500 test wickets. Kumble's monumental feat failed to inspire India's batting though, as it continued its hardships with another poor batting performance on the 3rd day. Dravid's gritty 95 ensured India took a slender lead. Indian batting had started giving serious trepidations to Indian fans by now. India won the match by 9 wickets, to a large extent due to the terrible 2nd innings by England. The result overshadowed India's lackluster batting. Greg Chappell also ignored it. A 9–wicket win was dominating enough for him to forget his worries. It was time to smile. It was time to put England in its place. Red soil and a rank turner at Mumbai screamed for an Indian win. Chappell smelled a 2–0 series victory. Instead, he got the shock of his life.

THAT SINKING FEELING – 3RD TEST – MUMBAI

"God save the team batting last on this pitch." said one exasperated English commentator! The red soil at Mumbai meant spin and some more spin but then came the massive first shock of the match. Perhaps, believing that it would not be required to bat in the 2nd innings, India elected to bowl first. The theory contradicted Rahul Dravid's usual approach. Perhaps, it was another of Chappell's infamous experiments. India's call brought England straight back on equal footing. The Indian swing bowlers failed to elicit anything from the pitch which made Dravid's decision even more dubious. The English batsmen batted and batted and batted. Andrew Strauss scored a century supplemented by fifties from Owais Shah and Flintoff. England scored 400 in the 1st innings. The mighty plan of batting just once on that pitch fizzled out briskly. India now required scoring huge to avoid batting last on the pitch. Considering the current form of the Indian batting, that goal looked like a distant dream. An insipid batting performance from India in the 1st innings (279 all–out) handed a decisive advantage to England. Though Anil Kumble restricted England to 191 in the 2nd innings, India was not out of the dock. It had two targets. One was chasing 312 which was out of question. The other was playing out Day Five on the Mumbai pitch which also stood next to impossible.

To survive on the Mumbai pitch, the likelier of the two targets, India needed to stick to cricketing senses and logic. Considering Greg Chappell was at the helm, sticking to the obvious was a difficult task. When India demanded sensible heads taking sensible decisions, Irfan Pathan replaced injured Sehwag as an opener in the 2nd innings. Greg's brother, Ian Chappell, always opposed the idea of a night watchman. He felt sending a night watchman was like gifting a wicket to the opposition and putting unnecessary pressure on the batting. Though the argument carried weight, Greg Chappell disagreed as usual. India's night watchman on Day Four, Anil Kumble fell early on Day Five which put India under scoreboard pressure. The pair of Sachin and Dravid took India to lunch without further casualties. All hopes now rested on India's most experienced duo and all hopes tumbled down in the first over of the second session. Flintoff handed a decisive blow to India's chances with Dravid's wicket. To the surprise of all, England had claimed all the scalps with good old–fashioned fast bowling. Till then, the spin was nowhere to be seen when everybody expected it to be the main threat. But in Mumbai, spin never needed an invitation to join the party.

In the 35th over, spin made a sensational entry through Shaun Udal, a name unheard of before who claimed the most prized wicket of Sachin Tendulkar. Losing Dravid and Sachin in consecutive overs dealt a killer blow to India. The score which looked stable at 75 for 3 was turned into 75 for 5 in 7 balls. It soon became 77 for 6. Sehwag, battling with a stiff back could not hang on. 5 overs later, M.S. Dhoni tried to hit his way out and lost his wicket. India lost its entire middle–order in a space of 10 overs. The rest of the innings became a mere formality. The series was supposed to be Greg Chappell's glorious victory. India was supposed to thrash England the Aussie style. Instead, India was bowled out for a humbling 100 runs in Mumbai. Rarely had India gotten that sinking feeling of humiliation on its own turf. Rarely had India been bowled out so cheaply on Indian pitches. It took extreme pride in its spin bowling as well as Indian batsmen's panache in playing spin. India failed miserably on both fronts in the series. England drew the series 1–1 which for England was as significant as an Ashes win. For India, it was time for some serious introspection.

India needed to ponder over its strategies. Some of the decisions of the think tank defied cricketing logic. Overcome with humiliation, it had to prepare for a 7 match ODI series against England. India continued its experiments with the batting order in the ODIs, regardless of the warnings from the test series. However, the Indian batting line up on placid batting tracks and fast outfields, outmuscled English bowlers. India demolished England 5–1, getting its tally to 17 wins out of its last 22 ODIs. It registered 16 consecutive successful chases under Greg Chappell. But despite these accomplishments there was a randomness to India's wins. 14 of those chases had come on flat Indian pitches. Ganguly had built a phenomenal test team over the last 5 years which had performed well even outside India. Greg Chappell had so far delivered fantastic success in ODIs in India. It was the test arena where he had to prove himself. After all, test cricket was the legacy of his arch adversary and he knew what it would mean to destroy that legacy.

INDIA IN WEST INDIES – 2006

THE THIN LINE BETWEEN CONFIDENCE AND ARROGANCE – WEST INDIES ODI SERIES

If one begins to list down the lasting memories of Indian cricket in the 1990's, apart from Sachin Tendulkar's batting dominance, the inability to handle the pressure of chasing would definitely take the cake. India had lost countless matches after being in a winning position. These were no mere losses. These were astonishing collapses, be it the Semi Final of World Cup 1996 where India lost 7 wickets for 22 runs or the World Cup 1999 match against Zimbabwe. For the team which was a sucker at chasing, the record of 17 consecutive successful chases felt consoling. Its 17th chase came in the 1st ODI against West Indies in Kingston. The match that should have been won comfortably was stretched by India to the last over. It reminded the Indian fans of the 1990's. Lots of edges from India and lots of missfield and dropped catches from the West Indies helped India achieve its record–equaling feat. The win did not deserve to be bragged about but the coach chose to pay no heed to the quality of win. There is a thin line between confidence and arrogance. Greg Chappell crossed it after winning the 1st ODI. "West Indies have forgotten what it is to win" – He remarked.

The West Indian sides of yester years were probably the greatest sides ever to take to the cricketing field. Their immortality lay in the manner in which they played cricket and the respect every member of those teams commanded from the opposition. Over the years, West Indies Cricket had fallen from its throne but the respect for those teams and their legacy remained the same. Hence, Greg Chappell's arrogant comment was not at all well received by the entire cricketing fraternity. But what mattered most was the response of the current West Indies team.

The expectation of replying to Greg Chappell increased pressure on the West Indies as it could manage only 198 in the 2nd ODI. West Indies needed a big–hearted effort to get back at India's coach. His remark shot a direct insult to the magnificent lineage the West Indies carried. West Indies used to be synonymous to lethal fast bowling. That was its inheritance. Fittingly, West Indian bowling stepped up to the challenge. Every bowler stuck to the highest level of discipline. The great Indian chasing side faced a certain defeat at 134 for 7. West Indies had a motivation to win the match but so did India. It stood a win away from a record number of consecutive chases. India desired that record badly to cleanse itself of its pedestrian chasing past. Yuvraj Singh and Ramesh Powar added a crucial 43 run partnership to take India within 20 runs of the record. But with only one wicket to take and the No. 11 batsman on strike (Indian score was 187 for 8 in 48.1 Overs), West Indies had a better chance. On the first ball of the 50th over, Munaf managed to sneak a single to bring Yuvraj on strike. It was Yuvraj's match to finish. The next two balls went for two consecutive boundaries and West Indies' plan of proving Greg Chappell wrong came down like a house of cards. West Indies had dug deep within to make a match out of it but unfortunately, Greg Chappell required just 2 runs to prove himself right. But sport always re–enforces a telling motivational line– it is not over until it's over. Dwayne Bravo had missed his previous two Yorkers by a whisker and had gotten punished. The third, delivered to perfection, was a tribute to all his legendary predecessors. The sprint across Sabina Park, Jamaica was for the amazing Caribbean fans. It was to assure them their team still knew how to win. India's dream of creating a record of 18 consecutive chases was crushed by the West Indies but it was not yet done with India.

Brian Lara and his team knew that a solitary victory would not heal the wounds inflicted by Chappell. The realisation was apparent in its determined and composed chase (245 runs) in the 3rd ODI. India, the favourites to win the series now trailed 2–1. Losing the 4th ODI by 6 wickets brought India face to face with the potential horrors of a 4–1 thumping. For Greg Chappell, that was an ultimate nightmare. His nightmares turned into reality after another dull batting performance from India in the 5th ODI. West Indies whipped India 4–1. The series so far was focused on Greg Chappell's statement. After winning the last ODI, Brian Lara finally retaliated. He thanked Greg Chappell for reminding them how to win.

RAHUL DRAVID'S PROUDEST MOMENT – TEST SERIES

The West Indies ODI series was touted as Greg Chappell's road to glory but it had gone horribly wrong. India's test match form so far this season ranged from pathetic to average. The ODI series served as a reminder to Chappell that he needed to worry more about his team than the winning patterns of his opponents. India had sported 3 different top–orders in 5 matches and it had a different member to its bowling unit in each match. The experiments, which succeeded in the sub–continent, were not working overseas. The bigger question though, was whether Greg Chappell was willing to accept and listen. To the surprise of many, he accepted one indisputable fact. India lacked experience in the middle order of its test team. V.V.S Laxman returned to boost the middle order and straight away, the Indian batting order, for the first time in 6 months, put on a score worth mentioning. India's mammoth 521 in the 2nd innings of the first test included a double ton from Wasim Jaffer and solid scores from all other batsmen. It was heartening and somewhat calming.

India scored 588 runs in 2 days in the 2nd test. There was only one batsman capable of pulling off that kind of scoring rate. Virender Sehwag's 180, ably supported by Rahul Dravid's 146 and Mohammad Kaif's 148 offered India a tremendous chance as it had 3 days to get West Indies out twice. It began the task methodically by dismissing West Indies for 215 in the first innings but West Indies played out 85 overs. With rain looming large on the test, 85 overs accounted for two and a half precious sessions. India frantically tried to finish off West Indies but the rain gods won in the end. Another flat pitch at St. Kitts resulted in a drawn test and hence after 3 matches, the score still read 0–0. Both the teams now headed to Sabina Park, Jamaica where India had never won a test match and had put up a decent score 35 years back. Those were big odds to counter.

On a slow pitch at Sabina Park, Dravid fancied his chances. The wounds of Mumbai test against England were still fresh. By winning the toss and batting first, he avoided committing the same mistake but what he failed to take account of was the pace of Jerome Taylor. India did not expect a bowler to generate the kind of speed Taylor did on the slow Sabina Park pitch. Apart from Dravid, every other Indian batsman failed to cope with his speed. Kumble's innings of 45 assured India a score of 200, a score way below expectations.

If Jerome Taylor's speed blew away the Indian batsmen, lack of it came to the rescue of Indian bowlers. India, because of a dismal total of 200, just could not afford to let Chris Gayle score anything significant. Low bounce in the pitch did the trick as Gayle got out on the 4th ball of the innings. The collapse that followed did not surprise many as West Indies had produced such collapses numerous times in the recent past. The architect of the collapse was a complete surprise for sure. On foreign soil, selecting 2 spinners in the playing eleven was a sin. The slowness of the pitch had prompted India to include both Harbhajan and Kumble. Some saw it as another of Greg Chappell's notorious experiments. But more than Chappell, Harbhajan felt the weight of justifying his selection.

It took Harbhajan only 5 overs to turn the game on its head. In those 5 overs, he found vicious turn and unplayable bounce in the pitch. His 5 for 13 handed India a lead of 97 runs. On a pitch which was crumbling like a cookie, Kumble posed a herculean challenge for the West Indies in the second innings. For Kumble, it was an everyday chore. His 6–wicket haul in the 2nd innings gave Rahul Dravid the proudest moment of his captaincy career. India won a test series in the Caribbean after 35 years and fulfilled a long pending desire of Dravid's generation to beat West Indies in West Indies. For Greg Chappell, the result brought redemption. He achieved something even Sourav Ganguly had not managed. It was Greg Chappell's first big accomplishment in tests. The qualms on the suitability of his techniques in test matches were haunting him since his appointment. His smile suggested that all questions had been erased forever. His demeanor suggested – forget the past. The confidence in him said that this was the beginning of glory days.

THE DRESS REHEARSAL FOR WORLD CUP 2007

By registering an overseas Test Series win, Greg Chappell got the monkey off his back. He now could focus on the remaining season. India stared at

5 months of very important cricket ahead including the ICC Champions Trophy 2006, scheduled to be held in India. India's amazing home record made it an instant favourite to win the tournament. It had not won an ICC title since the World Cup in 1983. An ICC event in India presented Greg Chappell the biggest opportunity to prove his superiority over his nemesis. No matter what he did and how hard he tried, his every move, his every strategy was always looked at with a bit of skepticism and with the backdrop of the Ganguly episode. The issue resurfaced every now and then and did not let him be. The Indian team under Ganguly boasted a good record in pervious Champions Trophies, being a finalist in 2000 and co–winner in 2002. This was the chance for Chappell to stamp his worth and put the curtain over the Ganguly chapter once and for all. After all, winning an ICC tournament would elevate him to a special pedestal altogether. It would make him the greatest coach in Indian cricket history. He fancied that crown so dearly. He had been waiting for the moment. He developed a master plan, assigning a specific role to each of the team member, to emerge victorious in the ICC Champions Trophy 2006. He planned and strategized every aspect to the smallest detail possible. He mechanized every single move of his master–plan. Emotions were the bane of any tactic according to him. But in reality, emotional attachment to the team marks a great leader. Greg Chappell was about to know that planning and robotic thinking cannot substitute the human nature of sport.

India was slated to play 2 Tri–series' in Sri Lanka and Malaysia before the Champions Trophy. The Sri Lankan series featured India, Sri Lanka and South Africa. South Africa had cited issues pertaining to its security throughout its stay in Sri Lanka. A series of bomb explosions had gripped the island. South Africa eventually backed out of the tournament as a report by an independent Security Consultant assessed security measures in Sri Lanka as unacceptable. This put the Sri Lankan Cricket board in a fix. The series was already announced and after South Africa opted out, it needed a face saver. BCCI came to the rescue and the Tri series was converted into a bilateral series of 3 ODIs. Heavy rains washed all three matches but India's gesture resulted in the beginning of a long friendship between the cricketing boards of the two Asian giants.

The next series in Malaysia held a lot of significance for India. Sachin Tendulkar was making his comeback from yet another injury and the Tri–series comprised of the same teams that were drawn in India's Champions Trophy group, Australia and West Indies. Sachin's dominating 141 in the first group game overshadowed some worrying signs which sneaked up time and again. Irfan Pathan's bowling figures of 22 runs in 2 overs was not at all discussed. The second match against Australia made Pathan's decline as a bowler even more glaring. He conceded plenty and did not complete his quota of overs. The Indian top order's collapse exposed its inability to face a strong, quality bowling attack. All problems were brushed aside one more time by citing poor quality of the pitch and ground. India's stupid experiment of having 4 different middle order combinations in 4 matches got lost somewhere. Greg Chappell's adamant emphasis on Irfan Pathan's batting which cost India a genuine swing bowler was never discussed. The fact that the Indian new–ball bowlers not only leaked runs but also failed to give early breakthroughs was overlooked. The Malaysian series highlighted some inherent problems in the Indian team but Greg Chappell turned a blind eye & deaf ear to them. Under the illusion of India's breathtaking form on home soil, India prepared for the ICC Champions Trophy 2006.

ICC CHAMPIONS TROPHY – 2006

India was buzzing with excitement for the ICC Champions trophy. The Indian team had won 13 of its last 19 ODIs in India. These wins were dominating one sided results. The home form of the team had taken expectation levels to a new high. The charm of the Champions Trophy is in its format. There are no easy games. Each game is a must win. So, when you get a chance to smack your opponent in such a tournament, you take it with both hands. The history of the tournament clearly reflected that the Net Run Rate (NRR) calculations were as important as a win. England's perpetual lack of understanding of how to play ODIs in Indian conditions handed India a wonderful chance to register a fantastic Net Run Rate. But India countered England's confused batting approach with its own inability to understand the format of the tournament. First, it resorted to some senseless hitting and then produced a terrible crawl to eventually reach the target of 126. India took 30 overs and lost 6 wickets to win the match. A healthy NRR was hardly possible after such a jaded performance but a healthy NRR was the least of its worries after the England game. It had some serious issues to deal with. West Indies, being reminded by Greg Chappell of winning four months ago, seemed eager to humiliate the home giants once again.

The ghosts of the Malaysian series resurfaced to haunt India. The Indian batting played at a stagnant run rate throughout its innings. To defend its ordinary target of 224, India needed early wickets but the inadequacy of its bowlers to take early wickets frustrated the fans. A late mini collapse of the West Indies middle order ensured good television drama but India was never in control of the match. It lost eventually by 3 wickets. Greg Chappell's grand dress rehearsal for World Cup 2007 was rapidly turning into a mediocre soap opera. The task ahead was even steeper; a virtual knock–out game against the reigning World Champions was still to come.

To win a must–win game, India needed to stick to the basics. Dinesh Mongia's selection out of nowhere and his promotion to No. 3 was far from sticking to the basics. India's below average bowling was also far from it. India's sluggish performance resulted in Australia's comprehensive win by 6 wickets. The magnificent Australian side shattered the hope of another Australian.

Greg Chappell's mission to outclass Ganguly's legacy had gone haywire. He wanted to better India's previous records in the ICC Champions Trophy. He ended up with India's worst Champions Trophy performance. India had three back–to–back deplorable outings to get knocked out of the Champions Trophy at the group stage itself. It had struggled outside the sub–continent this season but escaped this reality under the garb of its commanding home record. With a miserable Champions Trophy 2006, illusions surrounding India's enviable home success started to fade. The cricket crazy India now began discussing at length the shortcomings of Greg Chappell's methods. A compelling need was felt to change the team's line of thinking. India's indifferent season was at last analysed from a different and correct perspective.

The first change had already taken place at the selection level. BCCI appointed a new Selection Committee, headed by Dilip Vengsarkar. The new selection panel prepared itself to refresh the strategy of the Indian think tank. Though it did not pull the trigger immediately, it made all necessary arrangements. It waited for an opportune moment. On the shores of South Africa, India's next destination for a full tour, the Indian batting gifted them plenty of reasons to take a decisive stand. India reached 200 only once in the 4 ODIs. The inexperienced batsmen could not hold their feet against the fiery, sharp and vigorous South African bowling. The Indian team had reached a new low and the selectors found an opening to usher in a new approach. Bringing back experience to the Indian batting line up was Dilip Vengasarkar's plan of action. Bringing back experience meant only one thing and Greg Chappell was not sure he was ready for it.

THE PRODIGAL SON RETURNS

The chase of unprecedented goals through some impossible situations is the soul of any moving story. Every tale thrives on the unattainable goals as the harder it gets to achieve them, the more emotional the journey becomes. While the Indian team was struggling to find its vision, one man had his as clear as the blue sky. Soon after his unceremonious exit, Sourav Ganguly had decided the ending he wanted for his story. He had always had the last word on all subjects in his glory days. Why should this phase be any different? His was a big ego, and it had to be satisfied. He faced a daunting task though. As one of the established players in the team and the most successful captain in the history of Indian cricket, he had witnessed glorious riches in his personal and team graph. After seeing the pinnacle of international cricket, Sourav Ganguly now needed to cope with the ordeals of domestic cricket. The transition demanded mental strength more than anything else. From packed international stadiums chanting his name to empty stands and unknown grounds, the route was tough but he was a man of action. Such men always defy odds. To reach the same heights again, he was required to take a step back to jump forward.

THE EARLY JITTERS

His injury provided a pretext for the Indian team management to drop him from the first 4 ODIs against Sri Lanka in November 2005. He was virtually out of India's ODI scheme of affairs. To salvage his test place, he had to rise above the petty problems of injury and bad form and play the next best match available. In despairing hope to cling to his test team spot, Ganguly decided to play a Duleep Trophy match against the North Zone. He began well with a tremendous all–round show of 4 wickets and a fluent century. However, making a comeback into the current Indian set up was going to take more than a solitary accomplishment. As anticipated, he was dropped from the side for the remaining 3 ODIs against Sri Lanka as well as 5 ODIs against South Africa. He could sense his exit from the test team as well.

The prestigious Duleep Trophy final 2005–06 set up an ideal platform to make an impact. Unfortunately for Ganguly, one man in the opposition thought on similar lines. Zaheer Khan was Sourav Ganguly's most treasured finds of one time. Coincidentally, Zaheer Khan had also suffered the same fate as that of his mentor. Both were determined to wear the Indian jersey again. The protégé outclassed his mentor as Zaheer dismissed Ganguly for a pair. What a cruel business sport can be! A player whose career was made by the unconditional support of his captain probably ended Ganguly's comeback chances. All gates were sealed leaving Sourav Ganguly stranded. 11 days later, as he watched his home town make the Indian team's life a living hell and a finger being stuck out of the team bus window, little did he know that the same finger would carry him to the Indian team.

THE SHORTLIVED COMEBACK

Greg Chappell's show of middle finger opened a small window for Ganguly. His sacking got portrayed as a by–product of a larger political conspiracy thus bringing him unexpectedly closer to making a return. Ganguly sensed that he was one performance away. A significant score coupled with the sympathy wave surrounding him would have made him extremely difficult to ignore. The century came against Maharashtra in a Ranji Trophy match. His chanceless 159 forced the Indian team management to include him in the team for the Sri Lankan test series. The team think tank assigned him the role of a bowling all–rounder undermining the quality of his innings and overplaying his bowling potential. Sourav Ganguly knew the true reasons for his selection and how long selections based on the pressure from the fans and media could last! So even after a classy Ranji hundred, the nervousness in his batting against Sri Lanka was visible. The management subsequently dropped him for the 3rd test because he was 'too big a star' to sit on the bench. How could he beat such mindless arguments? He went to his Bengal team in search of answers. The reason offered for dropping him did not have mettle to keep him out for very long. He needed strong performances to back his case again and hence the remainder of the Ranji season became decisive for him. Though two fifties against Tamil Nadu were not good enough but the Indian team management was running out of excuses to exclude him. It resulted in another opportunity for Sourav Ganguly. He had created history across the border 2 years ago. His current visit to Pakistan provided him the final chance to save himself from being a memory of the past.

He had to justify his selection with no promise of opportunity. His irritation was bordering on despair. In his moment of desperation, he found the Lahore pitch, as flat as ever, and it excited him. He saw loads of runs in the pitch and a long–term place in the Indian team. The Indian team management had tinkered with its openers to accommodate Ganguly in the middle order but on that placid track, the opening slot was the best position to play and Ganguly realized it as soon as he set his eyes on the pitch. He tried to put across his desire more so; his need to open the innings to Rahul Dravid with all his passion and emotions, oblivious to the fact that his passionate discussion with Dravid got captured on camera. Images of an animated Sourav Ganguly talking to a rather annoyed Rahul Dravid and Greg Chappell listening on at the back, was sure to make headlines. He failed to convince Dravid and a golden chance slipped through his fingers. There was more disappointment in store as he was left out of the 2nd test on an even flatter pitch. Frustration turned into helplessness when he was selected in the 3rd test on a green pitch in Karachi. Cricketing logic said that a quality innings on such a pitch would cement his place in the team. But Sourav Ganguly was combating something beyond cricketing logic. He decided to approach it in the only way he knew, head–on. He transformed his determination into positive footwork and the pitch on which every other Indian batsman struggled; Sourav Ganguly scored 34 without breaking a sweat. His fluency infused confidence in him but just when he needed to seize the moment, an unnecessary pull shot cost him his wicket. With that false shot, the feeling sunk in. Karachi appeared to be his last test for now. His comeback came to an abrupt end. He walked into the shadows with dropped shoulders and head held low in frustration but the spark in his eyes assured his fans of one last try, one final effort.

THE COUNTY STINT

Ganguly was down but not willing to accept that he was out. The Ranji season was over which posed a worry for him. He did not have any matches to play and win back the 'India' jersey. One Australian had put him on the verge of ending his career but another one came to his rescue. An unlikely selection call to Chris Rogers for Australia–A vacated a place in the County Club Northamptonshire which sought an urgent replacement. Ganguly fit in its plan of action. Runs in England always held a premium to it. He had five weeks of priceless county cricket but many times when you get an opportunity, the anxiety to do well gets the better of you. It happens to the best of people. Ganguly fell to his anxiety in his first county game against Worcestershire. It was Zaheer Khan again who dismissed him. The dismissal also brought to fore one glaring problem in Ganguly's county stint. He had very little time to acclimatise to English conditions. His tentative second outing did not help either. 9 runs against Essex in his next match ended his unsuccessful county spell. The move to play for Northamptonshire backfired as it allowed his detractors to question his batting abilities in overseas conditions. After putting his heart, soul and body on the line for 6 months, Sourav Ganguly did not come anywhere closer to getting his 'India' cap back. In fact, chances of his comeback looked even bleaker.

WE WANT EXPERIENCE – NOVEMBER-DECEMBER 2006

The new selection panel was furious. It had tolerated India's dismal overseas performances so far because of its invincibility at home. The ICC Champions Trophy 2006, touted to be a walk in the park for the home team, turned out to be India's worst tournament of the season. Dilip Vengsarkar made up his mind to go for experience in his side. For the first time in the past 9 months, Ganguly saw a legitimate chance of making a comeback to the Indian team. His miserable county stint did not matter. His inner trials and tribulations did not matter. What mattered were his next three domestic matches. India's poor performances offered a lifeline to Sourav Ganguly. Dilip Vengsarkar had asked him to take that one last step. There was no room for failures. There was no room for excuses. The keys to his return were gifted to him. He needed to put them in the right door.

Sourav Ganguly looked anxious again in his first match and faltered. He needed a calm mind and one solid innings. He found both in his second match against the North Zone. The inning of 118 was filled with his natural timing and elegance. He was asked to perform. He did that. The ball was in Vengsarkar's court now. 91, 168, 163 and 200; India's team totals in its ODI series in South Africa provided Vengsarkar his reason to bring back experience. He seized the opportunity to bring back India's most talked about cricketer, its first true leader. Little over 10 months after his exit from Indian team, the master had come home.

HE WAS BACK AND HOW

This time, it felt surreal. Greg Chappell had no arguments to put forth. Sourav Ganguly was not in exceptional form but Greg Chappell was the last person to question the performances of anybody, given his record as the Indian coach so far. Sourav Ganguly had been once accused of faking an injury to avoid a practice game. Ten months later, he scored 83 in the practice match against Rest–of–South Africa on a hostile pitch to make his case clear. It was up to the coach to drop him but the circumstances were stacked against Greg Chappell and even he could not stop Ganguly from making his international comeback.

The moment arrived at last. Sourav Ganguly had dreamt of it for the last 10 months. He perhaps would have ranked Johannesburg last in the list of places for his return. 'None the less, he was ready to defend his inclusion once again albeit with lesser pressure. After a brilliant but brief partnership between Sachin and Dravid, Sourav Ganguly walked to the pitch to a thunderous applause. Test cricket welcomed him back with open arms. For long he had longed for the stage, the atmosphere. Nobody gave him a chance 10 months ago but here he was, taking his guard at one of the most picturesque international venues. The situation was tailor–made for a grand comeback. India's toughest nut was required to put India out of trouble as India's score reeled at 110 for 4. His positive and long strides forward, his decisive leaves and his kingly flow of the bat narrated a heroic tale. The guy had missed international cricket so dearly. With every single shot of his, he made a statement. Old habits die hard! In India's abysmal total of 249, Sourav Ganguly top–scored. That was the day when India re–learnt the true worth of determination; a quality he had imbibed in Indian cricket. He again inspired India, this time with his bat.

Yes! Inspiration! Ganguly's 51 inspired Sreesanth to produce one of the deadliest bowling spells by an Indian fast bowler on an overseas pitch. Ganguly's determination inspired another comeback kid, Zaheer Khan to take 2 crucial wickets of Gibbs and AB de Villiers. It inspired V.V.S. Laxman to remind one and all of his brilliance in the slips with 2 outstanding catches. Ganguly's majestic innings inspired the entire Indian team to bowl out South Africa for a paltry 84. His vehemence inspired India to remember the taste of overseas successes. It indeed reminded India of its ability to win overseas. Sourav Ganguly and his defiant comeback inspired India to bag its first ever test match triumph in South Africa. Sourav Ganguly had done it once again.

Though India threw away the initiative in the 2nd and 3rd test to lose the series 2–1, the series belonged to one man and one man only. The balance of power began shifting once again. Greg Chappell was losing his control in decision making. How badly he wished the last 12 months to vanish! The last year was full of disasters and as if the string of miserable performances was not enough to put him under stress, Sourav Ganguly had reappeared on the scene to haunt him. Only one event had the potential to allow him to overcome the haunting memories of the last few months. He had set his eyes on the tournament since his appointment as the Indian coach. It was his ultimate dream, the ultimate destiny; now the only way to restore his honour. India had already started buzzing. It was that time of the year. It was time for World Cup 2007; it was time for Greg Chappell to show his real merit.

CUP OF DISASTER – ICC WORLD CUP 2007

Winning the World Cup of 2007 was the focal point of Greg Chappell's presentation to his Selection Panel but things were not going according to plan for him. He had nobody but himself to blame for India's mediocre twelve months. After Sourav Ganguly's selection in test matches against South Africa, Greg Chappell very much realised that the discretion he sought in selecting his World Cup team was only an illusion. A contrasting vision and theory had gained shape in the past few months and he could do nothing about it. His 'youth only' policy was a total failure so far and the infusion of experience in the South Africa series had made a positive impact. India battled poles–apart methodologies. One outcome is always certain in such circumstances: chaos!

CUP OF CONFUSION – THE SELECTION

The 4–match ODI series at home against the West Indies served as a last chance to all World Cup aspirants to book their tickets to the Caribbean. The endeavour behind experiments in team selections and batting orders for the last two years was to assemble the ultimate dream–team. Greg Chappell filtered 14 individuals through his experiments to represent India in the curtain raiser to the most prestigious tournament in cricket. The 15th name was a nightmare for him and a pleasant shock to the country. After making an impressive comeback in test matches, Sourav Ganguly made a re–entry in the West Indies ODI series, virtually confirming his place in the World Cup Squad. How ironic was it that Sourav Ganguly was one of the first players to book his place for the World Cup!

Though Sourav Ganguly's inclusion delighted fans, some of the other names and their positions sent deep apprehension. Live pictures of Gautam Gambhir and Sourav Ganguly walking down to open the innings petrified the nation. The country harked back to World Cup 1999, the last time Sachin Tendulkar did not open for India in a world cup. The move had been an absolute debacle back then. India was about to commit the same blunder. A flat pitch, an ordinary West Indies bowling performance (India scored 338) overshadowed the intrinsic problems in the Indian batting. West Indies replied with 324 which highlighted in bold the shortcomings of Indian bowling. The second match in the series confirmed Sachin Tendulkar's role in World Cup 2007. His new position as India's anchorman of the middle order raised another equally pertinent question: who was India's new opener? Was it Gambhir? After all, he had featured in both matches. How did Sehwag fit into the scheme of things? The 3rd ODI added another opener to its list as a new opening combination of Uthappa and Gambhir made the entire opening pair saga even more mysterious. The Indian batting line up was now beyond speculations. Everybody realised that it was better to not delve upon the befuddling Indian batting order.

The Indian bowling painted an identical story. Anil Kumble's exclusion in the beginning of the series shot a direct challenge to Vengsarkar's 'experience' policy. Curiously, he got selected for the last two ODIs. Inclusion of two off spinners in the team was a direct challenge to cricketing sense. With 4 fast bowlers already in the squad, the selection of a medium pacer Joginder Sharma was bewildering, especially when Munaf Patel, India's new bowling talent failed to find a place in the squad. A 3–1 series win did not answer any of the above questions. The series, instead of deciding India's World Cup team, brought out in the open, huge differences of opinion between the Selection Committee and Greg Chappell. The selection game triggered a lot of uncertainty in players. Amidst this confusion, the Indian selectors came up with their final team. Disaster was written all over it.

The Indian squad comprised of six batsmen, two wicket keepers, five fast bowlers and two spinners. Out of the six batsmen, four happened to be specialist openers. Gautam Gambhir who featured in three of the four matches against West Indies failed to make the cut. The selection committee preferred Harbhajan Singh and Anil Kumble over Ramesh Powar, a Greg Chappell favourite. The squad was put together in haste rather than allowing individuals to fit in. India's choice of going into the World Cup with only two genuine middle order batsmen meant one of the openers along with Sachin Tendulkar was required to undergo the transition of batting in the middle order. Where did Irfan Pathan fit into the picture? Was India thinking of playing with both the spinners? Keeping either of them on the bench was going to be a contentious decision. Greg Chappell's experiments in the last two years had resulted in a total loss of structure.

THE FORMAT

The history of India's progress in World Cups emphasized one fact: India was a slow starter. In the World Cup 1996, India had lost to Sri Lanka and Australia in the Group Stage. However, fabulous wins against West Indies, Kenya and Zimbabwe had secured its entry into the quarter final. Then came that epic quarter final against Pakistan. Moments like Ajay Jadeja's onslaught on Waqar Younis or Venkatesh Prasad's response to Aamer Sohail's arrogance still give goosebumps to fans. India went on to reach the

Semi Final, where it lost to Sri Lanka.

In the 1999 edition, it had lost its first match against South Africa. Sachin Tendulkar had flown back home to perform last rites on his father. India, without Sachin Tendulkar, failed to beat Zimbabwe in its 2nd match. He came back and inspired his team with a century against Kenya. The team qualified for the next stage after losing the first two matches. In the 2003 edition, India's early struggles against the Netherlands had frustrated fans. Its capitulation against Australia in the 2nd match had made them angry. After the humiliating loss against Australia, India went on to win eight matches on the trot to reach the final.

The format of these three World Cups had allowed India to scuttle its way back after poor starts as each group comprised of 6 to 7 teams. ICC had decided to change the format in 2007, making 4 groups of 4 teams each. It resulted in only 3 matches for every team in the group stage. The number of matches at the group stage and the value attached to it are inversely related. The format was merciless on slow starters, leaving absolutely no time for recovery. Every match became a must win which meant a team like Bangladesh, capable of an upset or two, posed a stronger threat. India was scheduled to start its campaign on a potentially ominous note. Its first match was against Bangladesh.

THE NIGHTMARE

The disappointments of the Indian batting line up over the last twelve months needed to be forgotten. The World Cup was no place for failures. The big names needed to put their hands up. There were some seriously huge names in the Indian batting line up. The Bangladeshi coach even admitted before the match that a mere mention of those names was capable of heaping extra pressure on his team. His admittance of the fact did not take into account the poor form they all were going through, except Ganguly. The captain always finds himself in two minds when his batsmen are failing consistently. Chasing a total with such fragile batting posed an enormous risk; hence Rahul Dravid took a relatively smaller risk. He opted to bat first even though conditions offered assistance to bowling. Perhaps facing Bangladeshi pacers in the 1st innings seemed easier than facing their spinners in the 2nd innings. Well, at least he thought so. The flip side of Virender Sehwag's carefree batting side soon made Dravid realise his cardinal mistake.

The next dismissal exposed the fundamental hitch in India's team selection. Robin Uthappa, an opener and an aggressive batsman by nature, was playing only his 3rd ODI outside the subcontinent. An 'on–the–rise, away from the body' shot was sure to fetch him a boundary in Chinnaswamy Stadium but he was batting 9000 miles away from his home town. It took him his wicket to recognize that. Sachin Tendulkar walked in at No. 4 with a sense of reluctance. He came, struggled for 26 balls and eventually inside–edged the ball to the keeper. The Indian batsmen waited for Bangladeshi spinners, to begin their counter–attack but with Sachin's wicket, all plans of attacking the spinners went for a toss. Instead, it handed an excellent platform to the Bangladeshi spin trio to strangle the Indian batsmen.

For the next 18 overs, that's exactly what the Bangladeshi spinners did to the Indian batsmen. They were not allowed any loose balls, any easy runs. Even Ganguly struggled against the three left arm spinners unleashed by Bangladesh. Rarely had that happened before. Yuvraj Singh's impetus provided India with a hope to reach a score above 200 but his wicket along with the wickets of Ganguly and Dhoni in 7 balls, brought India right back to square one. India eventually was dismissed for 191. A below par target of 192 offered little hope to India. But Bangladesh was still a minnow, the Indian fans said to themselves. The young Bangladeshi batsmen soon introduced India to their new brand of fearless cricket.

India claimed its first wicket in the 5th over but the maturity in Tamim Iqbal's innings of 51 (7 boundaries and 2 sixes) at the other end troubled the Indian fans. India did manage to pick up wickets to restrict the Bangladesh score at 79 for 3 in 16 overs but the counter–attack which followed took the wind out of Indian bowlers. For all his experiments and vision, Greg Chappell had failed to impart one quality, believed to be his strongest asset in the Indian team; the undying Aussie fighting spirit. Rahul Dravid deployed his entire arsenal of part time spinners after seeing Bangladeshi spinners' success. However, two young Bangladeshi batsmen were determined to create history. Mushfiqur Rahim and Shakib–Al–Hasan added 84 runs and another pathetic performance to India's credit. The term 'stunned by minnows' did not convey the gravity of the loss. The real impact was on India's progress in the tournament. It now had to win both of its remaining games and the current Indian team looked incapable of doing it.

Though India's next opponent Bermuda was a World Cup debutant, there was not a single Indian fan in whose mind the thought of losing to Bermuda and getting knocked out had not crossed. The nervousness in Indian openers reflected the mood of the entire nation. Sourav Ganguly and Robin Uthappa had the responsibility to calm the nerves of a billion

Indians. Robin Uthappa! He was India's new opener in this match. After all that had happened, Greg Chappell's love for his experiments refused to die down. Uthappa's uncomfortable 5 minutes at the crease were ended by one of the most spectacular visuals of all time. Dwayne Leverock of Bermuda, weighing 127 Kilograms, flew to his right to take a catch Jonty Rhodes would have been proud of. The unbelievable sight left a country of billion shell–shocked. India lost its first wicket in the 2nd over. Virender Sehwag walking in next was sure enough to cause some more drama. India prayed it to be Sehwag's day. And thankfully, it was! His 87 ball 114 not only calmed early jitters but also ensured that India scored the highest team total in the history of World Cup Cricket. Sachin Tendulkar and Yuvraj Singh unleashed absolute massacre in the last 12 overs to score 150 runs. It gave India and its net run rate a much better look. It now needed a normal win against Sri Lanka to advance.

23rd March 2007. Greg Chappell woke up to the notion that it could be his last day at the helm of Indian Cricket. Rahul Dravid woke up to the fact that the day carried the most gargantuan test so far in his captaincy tenure. The rest of the country woke up to the possibility of India's worst performance among all World Cups. There were no predictions, no debates. No one knew what was in store. Everybody waited in anticipation and hoped that the real Indian team would somehow show up. Dravid made a daring decision to bat second. It meant India needed to soak up the pressure of chasing a total. Zaheer Khan's 1st over forced the country to time–travel to his first over in World Cup 2003 final. It was equally nervy and equally bad. India prayed that the rest of the 49 did not follow the same course as the 2003 final. Fortunately, the Indian bowlers brought back the discipline required for a must–win game and never allowed Sri Lanka to score freely. The bowlers had done their job to restrict Sri Lanka to 254. It was up to the batsmen now to rise to the occasion.

One of the toughest tasks in cricket is to curb one's natural instincts. Only the greats could do it. Robin Uthappa, a naturally aggressive batsman found it difficult to adapt to India's strategy of 'keeping the wickets in hand early' and succumbed to the pressure. Sehwag never was one for caution. His typical innings started to take the pressure off Ganguly. But then, the unexpected happened. Sourav Ganguly's unnecessary aggression and Muralitharan's brilliant running catch cost India its 2nd and perhaps the pivotal wicket as Ganguly was the only batsman who had shown some semblance of form. Before India recovered from Ganguly's horrendous shot, it received another body blow. It saw a Dilhara Fernando delivery nip back, go between the bat and pad and castle into the leg stump. The leg stump belonged to India's batting God, Sachin Tendulkar.

Within a space of 4 balls, two of India's illustrious batting stars returned to the pavilion. From that point onwards, the outcome became inevitable. Sehwag tried to postpone it but his wicket along with Yuvraj's and Dhoni's in a span of 5 overs buried all hopes. Dravid stood helplessly at the other end while his team ran helter–skelter. Everything that he feared could go wrong went wrong. One man in the dressing room had already started packing. The Indian team, comprising eminent names and exceptional young talent did not see this coming. There were plenty of signs along the road. India chose to shove them under the carpet sometimes and covered them up the other times. It lived in the bubble formed by big talks and glittery experiments. All talks and experiments failed to prevent one outcome which had threatened its existence on multiple occasions in the last couple of years but was never discussed. The unavoidable conclusion to India's most distressed campaign came on the 23rd March 2007. That was the date when India was knocked out of World Cup 2007 in the group stage itself.

The World Cup 2007 was another tournament in the long list of defeats India had suffered during the last 23 months. It had been outperformed by almost every opponent. More so, India was outdone by a constant clash of egos, an adamant coach and an unstructured team. Greg Chappell's grand vision never transpired to reality from that PowerPoint Presentation. It never really translated into a performance of any sort as it failed to account for the realities and requirements of a team sport. Sourav Ganguly was India's second highest run–getter in the World Cup, just 2 runs behind Virender Sehwag, which accentuated Greg Chappell's inability in man management and his lack of understanding of India's cricketing culture. Cricket was played on the ground and not in PowerPoint presentations and he learnt that lesson the hard way. The war, started by an explosive email to BCCI, ended with a brief one to media, "Today, I informed the president of BCCI that I would not seek an extension to my contract to coach the Indian Cricket Team for family and personal reasons." Greg Chappell left Indian shores with some painful, heart–wrenching questions – 'Where does Indian Cricket go from here?' 'Has he destroyed it beyond repairs? What will happen to Indian cricket now?'

PART III

A NEW BEGINNING

Oxford dictionary defines success as 'the favourable or prosperous termination of attempts or endeavours.' The definition dwells more on the process than the outcome. Nobody stays at the summit of success forever. The most fascinating part of any success story is the rise from the lows to unprecedented highs. World Cup 2007 pushed India to a new low. The team had no coach, the current captain wanted out, the former captain was unwilling to lead again and rumours of Sachin Tendulkar having all but quit were flying thick and fast and the worst of them all, the team had zero confidence. To swim through these troubled waters was the most important task. How to approach the revival was the most important question.

THE PLAN

India decided to start with the basics; beginning with crystallizing its vision. Greg Chappell had destroyed the structure of the team which needed rebuilding on priority but India could not afford to resort to drastic and dramatic changes which in the first place had led to Chappell's ruin. To India's advantage, it still possessed stalwarts in Tendulkar, Dravid, Ganguly, Kumble and Laxman to carry out the restructuring process. All these legends were required to raise their game to the next level. They had already done it once to pull India out of the match fixing murk. Destiny worked in a curious way. It chose them again to shape the future of Indian cricket one more time.

The process began with Dravid continuing as captain. Under Chappell, he was stifled. He was always a batsman with a quiet demeanour but as a captain, you sometimes need to be vocal. For far too long, he had allowed Greg Chappell to have his way in handling the whole Ganguly scenario or for conducting his infamous experiments. His non–interference in the Coach's methods was perceived to be his agreement. It appeared to distance him from other senior players. The coach was gone, and he found his old mates with the same motivation – the betterment of Indian Cricket.

BCCI was still trying to cope with the crisis caused by Greg Chappell. It did not wish to make a similar mistake again. India required a coach who would understand its vision and work towards it rather than forcing his ideologies. The Indian team required some time to sort itself out and a hurriedly appointed coach threatened to impede the whole process. However, India's international calendar did not afford much time. So, BCCI came up with a brilliant idea, of an interim manager. BCCI wanted someone the players trusted, more importantly, someone with an understanding of the Indian rebuilding course. Ravi Shastri was a part of a broadcasting team for years and had covered the team all this while. He was also highly regarded by the board and shared a good rapport with the players. BCCI announced Ravi Shastri as the interim manager for India's tour of Bangladesh.

For the team itself, two–fold approaches were charted. The greats still had plenty of cricket left in them. India decided to use their quality and experience in the test arena, by assigning them fixed spots and responsibilities. The middle order was packed with experience. The Indian fast bowling also called for an overhaul. Zaheer Khan had been playing international cricket for 7 years now. He assumed the duty of mentoring the young crop of Indian seamers. Anil Kumble took charge of the spin department. Along with assigning these roles, India made some painful decisions as well. The axe fell on Sehwag as his test match form had deserted him for a while. The team management put its trust in a new pair of openers: Wasim Jaffer, who had shown tremendous potential under Greg Chappell and Dinesh Karthik.

If given the task of choosing the top 3 ODI opening pairs, the pair of Tendulkar and Ganguly was as certain as gravity to feature in it. Separating one of the all–time great opening combinations in International Cricket, especially when both of them were in a sizzling form, had been a dreadful mistake. The Indian team management decided to bring them back together, but not for the Bangladesh ODI series. Instead, India opted for the Delhi duo of Sehwag and Gambhir which sent a subtle message that they were not entirely abandoned. Yuvraj Singh who had been treated like a new–comer till now, even after 6 years of international cricket behind him, was asked to step up to the challenge of spearheading the middle order. A plan was put into place for the players to get Indian cricket back on track. All of them looked hungry as ever. All of them looked determined. All of them looked raring to go.

VENGENCE IS IMMATURE – INDIA'S TOUR OF BANGLADESH 2007

An unexpected but deserved loss to Bangladesh in the World Cup 2007 had primarily catapulted India out of the tournament. For an ordinary Indian fan, a series against Bangladesh immediately after the World Cup was revenge. But Team India's focus was on rebuilding which required mature heads. A calm chase of 250 suggested that the heads in the Indian dressing room were in the right places. A disciplined bowling performance in the 2nd ODI gave India a series win. Gautam Gambhir's 100 assured India of another batting potential. India's composed series win assured the fans of its revival.

The team for the test series bore an entirely different face. The middle order of Dravid, Tendulkar, and Ganguly looked formidable to say the least. Here started the glorious phase of India's fabulous four. Sachin scored back–to–back centuries. Ganguly continued his dream comeback with another century. Dravid revisited his old self by a century of his own. Bangladeshi bowlers suffered 10 days of carnage at the hands of India's fabulous middle order. But what excited India the most was the inspirational transformation in its bowling. RP Singh impressed one and all with his consistent swing. By giving Kumble responsibility of the spin department, India entrusted faith in him once again. The legend reciprocated by running through the Bangladeshi batting line. But, the reinvention of Zaheer Khan was the most fascinating aspect of the Indian bowling. A fitter, leaner and hungrier Zaheer demolished Bangladesh to clinch the series. India returned from Bangladesh unbeaten without the slightest impression of revenge. Revenge is an immature emotion; the eager Team India stood far from immaturity. The desire to win was back, the team was back and of course, so was the famous huddle which used to give goosebumps to Indian fans four years ago.

REDEMPTION BEGINS – INDIA IN ENGLAND – 2007

India's next assignment after Bangladesh was a full tour of England. India's last visit to England for a test series had resulted in two of its most treasured memories: an elusive away test win and a chase in the final worthy of immortality. With new–found vigour and positive memories, team India embarked upon the tour which laid the foundation of their most magnificent phase of all time.

The first assignment itself posed an enormous challenge. India came across the relentless South African bowlers in seam–friendly conditions of Ireland. The Indian batting line came out with flying colours. Sachin Tendulkar, in particular, batted at his vintage best. He came close to a hundred twice in 3 matches. The Indian bowling outperformed the South African bowling and that was something! With wins in solitary matches against Ireland and Scotland, 3 practice matches and spending almost a month in Britain, India prepared itself to face the talented and formidable English team.

1ST TEST – LORD'S

Indian bowlers kept demonstrating their revival instincts throughout the Lord's Test. First, they took 8 English wickets for 46 runs in 15 overs of fierce swing bowling after England's solid start. Then they continued the good work in the second innings as well. India at 137 for 3 at stumps on Day Four in its second innings, needed to bat out the remaining overs. With rain looming large on the fifth day, it looked attainable.

Day Five began on a bad note for India as it lost both of its overnight batsmen early. The day, which was bound to get curtailed due to inclement weather, started feeling very long. India needed someone to stand up and be counted. V.V.S. Laxman was very much out of favour in Greg Chappell's regime. In India's new scheme of things, he held a key position at No. 6, which invariably ends up playing with tail–enders and a peculiar mindset and temperament is required to bat with them, which renders the position unique. The 2nd innings in Lord's test brought out this aspect of Laxman's batting to the fore. It gave India its finest finisher in test matches.

V.V.S. Laxman's partner, M.S. Dhoni was new to test cricket and his technique raised reasonable doubts on his batting capabilities in tests. Laxman took care of him with a clever mix of singles, boundaries and leaves. Laxman's calmness saw Dhoni grow in confidence in difficult batting conditions. The pair put on 86 runs and played out 29 overs. England knew it was one wicket away from winning the contest. When England finally got that wicket, two sessions still remained. Dhoni now had to bat with pure tail–enders. India had run into a similar delicate situation earlier in the match where the bowlers had brought India back into the game. It was again left to them albeit this time with the less favourable feature of their cricket, batting. The Indian team had established so far that a meek surrender was not an option. The Indian bowling trio of Kumble, Zaheer and RP Singh played out the next 15 overs. By the time India's 9th wicket fell, the dark, gray clouds closed in. The umpires offered light to India. India accepted it like a child in a candy shop. It survived. M.S. Dhoni's uncharacteristic but valiant 76 carried India through. The Indian bowlers certainly did not deserve to lose. India's batting had performed well in patches but to take the team to the pinnacle, the batting needed to be consistent. More efforts were required from the Indian team to prove its worth. That was the mission for India this season, wasn't it? – to prove its worth.

2ND TEST – TRENT BRIDGE

At the back of the Indian seamers' excellent bowling in the Lord's test, their dazzling performance in the 2nd test came as no surprise. England had no clue to the swing Indian bowlers got, especially Zaheer, a man on the path of salvation. The art of swing bowling was getting lost from International Cricket in constant search of speed. The Indian bowlers had certainly rediscovered this lost form of art. The swing bundled out England for 198 and offered a golden prospect to India. The batsmen grabbed it hard. An opening partnership of 147 runs pushed England out of the game straight away. Sachin Tendulkar again got out in the 90s, for the 3rd time in a month. The rest of the Fab–Four too scored runs. India took a lead of 283 which put it on the brink of history. All it had to do was be patient. The calming influence of Rahul Dravid was certain to provide them with all the patience they needed. England managed a decent 2nd innings score of 355 but it could not prevent India from creating history. After the humiliation, ridicule, self–doubt and anger in the last season, India led an overseas series 1–0.

England had one more chance to level the series. The Indian batsmen were not in a mood to let go. The top 8 of its batsmen got runs with an unlikely century from Anil Kumble. 664 runs in the 1st innings clinched it for India. 13th August 2007 was when Rahul Dravid accomplished his most gratifying triumph as captain. India won a test series in England after 21 long years.

The ODI series that followed saw India's most eminent openers at their attacking best. Sachin Tendulkar scored 374 runs in the series which included 2 scores in the 90s. Sourav Ganguly hammered 249 runs. Yuvraj Singh transformed himself into a dependable middle order batsman. Even though India lost a hard–fought ODI series 4–3, the team had never looked better. Indian cricket was up and going. And then, two incidents that followed the England series changed the dynamics of Indian cricket forever. Nothing would ever be the same again.

A NEW STAR IS BORN, T20 CRICKET

In the year 2001 when Stuart Robertson, the marketing manager of the England and Wales Cricket Board was assigned a mammoth task of increasing ticket sales of England's domestic County Cricket, he knew he had to come up with something exceptional. He contemplated on introducing a new format. It carried a risk as world cricket had seen the degradation of Super 6s and Super 8s. To avoid a similar fate, the format necessitated a simple structure with a different flavour. He hit bull's eye by introducing T20 cricket. It was an instant success in England and soon spread its wings to other cricketing countries. India though lived in a bubble. The BCCI, blinded by the Indian fans' obsession with ODI cricket and its mind–boggling revenue generating powers, felt that the T20 format would directly hamper the popularity of ODI cricket and hence was rather reluctant to embrace it. When the ICC started pushing the idea of a T20 World Cup, recognizing its increasing popularity, the BCCI vehemently opposed. All other countries wanted to play it and India was forced to participate in it after losing the vote ten to one.

T20 followed the same rules of 50 overs, only with 20. The compact nature of the format made it pulsating and high octave. It was essentially a youngsters' format. The Indian trio of Tendulkar, Ganguly and Dravid acknowledged the fact and formally requested the chairman of selectors not to consider them for the ICC World–T20 2007. Their absence presented an opportunity for young Indian players to perform at the highest level. But it contributed to one major headache for selectors. If Dravid was not part of the squad, then who would captain the team? Big names like Sehwag, Harbhajan, and Yuvraj featured in India's T20 squad but none of them was a permanent member of the Indian team except Yuvraj. Sachin Tendulkar had a slight suggestion, "I have talked to this fellow many times. He has an inimitable ability to lead. He is ready." Sachin's idea gave enough ground to selectors to make the official announcement. Mahendra Singh Dhoni was named India's captain for the ICC World–T20.

AN EYE OPENER – ICC WORLD T20 – 2007

India had played only one T20 game before and had absolutely no idea how to play the format. 20 overs a side reduced the chances of getting bowled out to a minimal. Batsmen played with more freedom and it usually resulted in big scores but Mahendra Singh Dhoni displayed his acute cricketing acumen when he said, "The format does not require you to start hitting from ball one. 20 overs offer you plenty of time." The thought of having plenty of time in a T20 match was absurd for many. It certainly said something about the patience of the guy. Dhoni's statement became India's strategy for the tournament.

INTRODUCTION TO THE THRILLS OF T20 – INDIA V/S PAKISTAN

India and Pakistan qualified for the next stage before facing each other in the group stage, rendering the group encounter meaningless. But there is no such thing as a meaningless India–Pakistan match. Mohammad Asif's figures of 4 for 18 (best for a bowler in a T20 game at the time) emphasized the intensity of the contest, despite it being irrelevant for the tournament. Pakistan's lethal bowling restricted India to 141. It was difficult to believe a team could lose 9 wickets in 20 overs and yet, the target of 142 posed a tough challenge.

The short duration of a T20 match ensured that both teams got the same advantage of bowling under the lights in Durban. The Indian bowlers extracted the same help from Durban conditions as Mohammad Asif did, reducing Pakistan to 103 for 6. For die–hard ODI lovers, the target of 39 runs in 15 balls with only tail–enders to come was next to impossible. However, it was an India–Pakistan encounter and moreover a T20 match. The next 15 balls introduced India to the thrills, highs, anxieties and tensions of T20 cricket. Misbah–Ul–haq's inhuman hitting took Pakistan's score to 141 for 6 in 19.5 overs. To put it simply, Pakistan needed 1 run of 1 ball. There was only one way of achieving the target for Pakistani batsmen, running like crazy. Dhoni anticipated it and took a risk of bringing his fielders closer to the pitch as it opened up the field for Misbah to play a scoring shot. What followed was a cricketing masterstroke, highlighting the young Indian team's key strength, its composure. The calmness with which Sreesanth bowled a back of length delivery to push Misbah on the back foot amazed all and sundry. Pushed back deep into his crease, Misbah was forced to run a couple of yards extra. The calmness with which Yuvraj Singh threw the ball to Sreesanth and Sreesanth ran Misbah out was startling. India v/s Pakistan's first T20 resulted in a tie. The excitement did not end there. It also led to an altogether unprecedented eventuality, a bowl out!

It was cricket's answer to football's penalty shootout. Nobody seemed sure of how to proceed. Amidst a little chaos and lots of uncertainty started India's first ever bowl out. Dhoni's choice of 3 finger spinners for the bowl–out again underlined his understanding of the game. Finger spinners have better control on their action and they get in rhythm much quicker than the fast bowlers. The selection of bowlers turned out to be the difference between the two sides. Pakistan picked 2 fast bowlers and even more absurd were their half–bowling run ups. It is very difficult to hit wickets without the usual rhythm which can be achieved only through full run ups. Indian spinners had no such worries.

Sehwag started the proceedings. While batting, his casualness had many times proved to be his bane. In the bowl–out, his ability to shun aside the pressure helped him. His off spinner crashed into the leg stump and gave India a 1–0 lead. From the second he walked to take his run–up until he bowled, Yasir Arafat looked nervous to his core. His awkward run up and a bizarre pause at the time of delivery resulted in a delivery way above the stumps, perhaps a waist high no ball in an actual match. Harbhajan Singh's well aimed quicker ball put India 2–0 in the lead. Umar Gul's correctly pitched delivery would have tested any batsman outside his off stump. He got enough away movement to probably get the outside edge. Unfortunately for him, he was in the middle of a bowl–out without a batsman to nick the ball. A wicket taking ball in a match was inconsequential in a bowl–out. India's 3rd selection was a bit of a gamble. A part timer in Robin Uthappa had the cushion of 2 hits from India and 2 misses from Pakistan. The confidence in Uthappa was visible. His bow to all sections of the beautiful Durban after his hit was testament to it. Where rest of the Pakistani bowlers now needed to hit all its chances to keep Pakistan alive, Shahid Afridi bowled a wide ball down the leg side to give India its first ever bowl–out win. India won the match in a bowl–out; it was just the kind of start ICC had hoped for. It was a start nobody in India had imagined but one thing was sure – India had fallen in love with the format instantly.

THE HITS JUST KEEP ON COMING – INDIA V/S ENGLAND

For a nation obsessed with 50–over cricket, the side almost getting bowled out in 20 overs was difficult to digest. But India's next match against New Zealand opened its eyes to new realms of possibilities in T20 cricket. New Zealand scored 190 runs in 20 overs and India almost chased it down.

Indian fans were not sure if they could handle such excitement any more. Yuvraj Singh however, was about to introduce them to the extreme meaning of excitement.

Durban had two surprises in store for Indian fans in India's next match against England – a flat pitch and a watchful Sehwag. "There is plenty of time in T20," Dhoni had said, and Indian openers followed cue. By the 15th over, the Indian openers had set up a launch–pad for Yuvraj to let loose. He just needed a little boost from his batting partner. Instead, he got one from England's premier fast bowler.

The Indian players of the time seldom got aggressive on the field. So, the images of an angry Yuvraj charging towards Andrew Flintoff stunned Indian fans. Both players exchanged a few pleasantries. The umpires controlled the situation in the end but the tension in the air guaranteed that something was about to give. Poor Stuart Broad bore the brunt of Yuvraj Singh's fury. The tale of Ravi Shastri hitting 6 sixes in an over in a domestic match was always narrated almost like a legend. Gary Sobers had also done it in the past. The latest in the list was Herschelle Gibbs (against the Netherlands). Nobody had done it against a test playing nation. 6 balls of a Stuart Broad over made a vociferous sound 6 times when dispatched to 6 different parts of Kingsmead, Durban. Broad stood expressionless. Andrew Flintoff shook his head in remorse. Yuvraj Singh scored 58 in 16 balls. India scored 218 in 20 overs. It all happened that fast.

WE MARCH AS A TEAM – INDIA V/S SOUTH AFRICA

Yuvraj's merciless attack on England took India to a virtual quarter final against the hosts, South Africa. India's young brigade had established three qualities so far in the new season. It re–emphasized all three against South Africa. First, its mission statement of 'never give up' again came to the rescue when even after losing 4 wickets early, India managed to score 153, courtesy the new kid on the block, Rohit Sharma and India's new captain. Second, was India's fielding standard, revived by Mohammad Kaif in the early 2000's but taken to an altogether different standard by the current crop. Dinesh Karthik's flier catch vouched for it. The third was a sudden rise in the number of young fast bowlers who swung the ball at good speeds. RP Singh's breath–taking spell of 4 for 13 carried India to the semi–final against the mighty Australians. South Africa's misfortune in the ICC events continued as it was knocked out of the tournament after its only defeat in the tournament.

YUVRAJ HAILSTORM – INDIA V/S AUSTRALIA

India perhaps for the 1st time walked into a semi–final match against Australia as favourites. M.S. Dhoni continued his luck with coins and had no hesitation in batting first. Indian batting followed a similar pattern of steady start till it was time to unleash Yuvraj Singh again. He came, hit the Australian bowlers to all parts of the ground, scored 70 of 30 and left. It all happened in the blink of an eye. The knock included 5 fours and 5 humongous sixes, including the biggest of the tournament at 119 meters. The shot was a mere flick of his wrists to one of the fastest bowlers in international cricket, Brett Lee. India posed a challenging total of 188 but if there was one team capable of chasing the target, it was Australia.

And as expected, Australia produced a hell of a chase as Hayden and Symonds tormented the Indian bowling. The match hinged on one mistake from either side. Fortunately for India, Sreesanth provoked a false shot from Hayden in the 15th over. The balance of the match shifted drastically with Hayden's wicket. Sreesanth's antics of thumping the pitch after taking the wicket were unnecessary but it was Sreesanth after all! Symonds' timely wicket and an extraordinary 18th over by Harbhajan (3 runs and a wicket) helped India set up the big daddy extravaganza. The final of the first ever ICC World T20 was by all means the grandest sporting event of the year. After all, it happened to be an India–Pakistan match.

THE MATCH THAT CHANGED IT ALL – INDIA V/S PAKISTAN – THE GRAND FINAL

T20 cricket presented ICC a lucrative chance to take the game to new countries. The ensuing economics of the format were not yet known. It was imperative for the tournament to be a success. An India – Pakistan final was the cherry on the cake. It could not have gotten any bigger but India's innings produced an anti–climax. It never got going and lacked momentum throughout. Everybody, including Indian players waited for Yuvraj to cut loose. But he failed. Gautam Gambhir's solid 75 gave India a respectable total of 157. A tricky target and an unpredictable Pakistani batting guaranteed a thrilling chase.

Pakistan produced one of its routine erratic batting performances. It kept losing wickets after wickets. India controlled the match from the 1st over but the presence of one man made it jittery. With 4 overs to go and 54 runs to get, Misbah–ul–Haq started doing his thing. He scored 19 in the 17th over. The 18th over was emblematic of a Sreesanth over. He was hit for 2 massive sixes by Pakistan's No. 9 batsman but finished with the crucial 8th wicket. RP Singh's tight 19th over ensured another last over spectacle. The ICC World T20 2007 had had plenty of them already but the pressure of a final makes you do silly things. Was M.S. Dhoni's choice of bowler for the last over that silly mistake? Joginder Sharma's first and third balls, a wide and a full toss which went into the stands suggested so. India's scrambled thinking handed Pakistan an opportune moment to deliver the knock–out punch but it is never as easy as it sounds in an India–Pakistan match. India–Pakistan encounters always carry extra pressure, often forcing players to commit that one cardinal blunder. The match was Misbah's to lose and he did just that. His futile attempt to scoop the ball over short fine–leg handed India its first ICC trophy in 24 years! The 'silly' move to give Joginder Sharma the 20th over did not look silly after Misbah's wicket. It reminded fans of India's former captain who used to show faith in his players in the same manner. Misbah's mis–timed scoop over short fine–leg resulted in two more important things, a stamp of approval for a billion–dollar T20 league which would change the face of Indian cricket forever and a captain destined to take Indian cricket to new heights.

A NEW CAPTAIN & AN UGLY CONTROVERSY

India was so engrossed in the thrills of T20 cricket and the euphoria of its ICC T20 title that the news of Rahul Dravid stepping down as captain took some time to sink in. Rahul Dravid had wanted to quit immediately after the World Cup 2007 but continued in the interests of Indian cricket but the decision to step down was in the making. With Dhoni's sensational success in the inaugural World T20, India identified its captain for the shorter version of the game. The selection committee declared M.S. Dhoni as the captain for the upcoming 7 match ODI series against Australia.

Few had noticed M.S. Dhoni's calm demeanour and astute reading of the game which lay beneath his hard–hitting finishing capabilities. Indian cricket was getting back on its feet. The rage of the previous season had cooled down to a large extent. India saw an opportune moment to allow a young captain to settle in. So even though Australia beat India comprehensively in the ODI series, India did not question the inexperienced captain. The

India–Australia ODI series though, was marred by an ugly, sickening but deep–rooted medieval human mind set.

Reports emerged in the local Australian newspapers about Andrew Symonds being subjected to racial abuse by the Vadodara crowd in the 5th ODI. The local police termed them as religious chants. In the 6th ODI in Nagpur, the racial abuse hurled at Symonds was captured on camera. The situation became more sensitive with each passing day but before the BCCI could react, the Mumbai crowed took matters to a new low. Disgusting placards were shown. Abusive language was directed towards the Australians. Disrespectful chants & the 'M word' echoed throughout the stadium. The Mumbai crowd usually known for its respectful attitude towards the game did its best to degrade the sport. The ICC's anti–racism code flashing on the giant screen in the ground failed to contain the behaviour. Australia decided against making an official complaint but BCCI's handling of the issue left the Australian team fuming. The BCCI managed to brush the controversy under the carpet. Skeletons of such incidents tend to show their ugly faces again. The Indian team was quite unaware that the storm was going to come back to haunt them. What happened in Mumbai was just a trigger.

FACE OF DIGNITY – A NEW TEST CAPTAIN

India, the cricket fanatic nation always fancied batting. It has produced some of the most legendary batsmen in world cricket. Bowlers were always considered workhorses. While it infuriated many Indian bowlers, one bowler enjoyed the tag and kept doing his job. The Indian selectors finally woke up to the reality that Anil Kumble was already a veteran of more than 100 tests. Dhoni was undoubtedly the one for the future but he needed to be groomed for test captaincy. Anil Kumble responded well to his ascendancy to captaincy with 7 wickets on his favourite Feroz Shah Kotla pitch against Pakistan. The 2nd test at Eden Gardens marked a special occasion: Ganguly's first test match at his home after his return. Again, a hundred thousand faithfuls gathered. They were treated with the ultimate gift. A century from Ganguly, a century from Laxman who had made Eden his second home, and 202 from Jaffer resulted in India's mammoth total of 616. The 3rd test in Bangalore marked the zenith in Ganguly's comeback story. His masterful 239, his best test score, took India from 61 for 4 to 626. It also included 169 from Yuvraj which secured his place in the test squad for the upcoming Australia tour. Overall, a run–fest series marked a good start to Kumble's captaincy career and prepared him for his next, the all–important tour of Australia. Anil Kumble knew he had to be at his very best on the field. What he would have to do off the field, he had not imagined it in his wildest of dreams.

THE CONTROVERSIAL SERIES – INDIA IN AUSTRALIA 2007-08

SYDNEY SHAME

1) "They have gone up for the catch down the leg side but Mark Benson is not interested. Even Rahul Dravid shouted there oh–c'mon. Every Indian fielder went up for the catch. Mark Benson says no. Oh dear! There is a sound there, a definite sound."
2) "Ponting is fuming and has every reason to do so. Umpire Benson misses the edge. Ponting is given out LBW."
3) "Has he gone this time? They (Indians) have all gone up. Steve Bucknor is unmoved. Not for the first time the umpires are the focal point. In fact, Andrew Symonds looked back as soon as he played it which is normally a giveaway. Yes. There was very clearly a knick."
4) "Steve Bucknor wants a confirmation, wants a referral from the Third Umpire. Well, he is out of the crease. Now, now, that foot may just be in the air. I think he might be in trouble there. Yup. I reckon he is gone. Third Umpire is Bruce Oxenford and he says not out. I don't know what to say!"
5) "Dhoni has taken the bails off obviously seeing something. Symonds' back foot is not within the ground. It's in the air and that is the reason why he has appealed. He is out here but Bucknor has not asked for the Third Umpire. Controversial decision."
6) "Rahul Dravid does not look happy. He is furious. Oh my god! I have not seen him so angry. Has he not hit it? All right! That's the reason. The ball comes off his pad. No wonder he is angry. India is at the receiving end again. This is a huge blow to India's chances to save this match."
7) "Clarke takes the catch. Ganguly waits. Benson has not given him out. What is happening here? He has given him out, has he? It seems he has put his finger up. Ganguly is asking hang on, have you given me out here? The answer is yes. Did he catch it, is what Sourav Ganguly was asking! He is not looking very happy. The top frame will indicate

to you that the ball has bounced. Rickey Ponting said he is out and that's what Benson said. Here is a man who did not walk when he was caught down the leg side. So why should his word be taken? It can not be that you are honest when you are fielding and not so honest when you are batting."

8) "How can you claim it as a catch? The ball has clearly touched the ground. Ponting is not in control of the ball. He is claiming a catch. This is ridiculous, simply ridiculous."
9) "Michael Clarke does it for Australia. He takes 3 wickets in 2 overs. Australia wins its 16th consecutive test to equal the great Steve Waugh's record. But believe you me, this will not be the talking point tomorrow."

Some of the commentary excerpts thoroughly elaborated the Sydney test which was filled with umpiring howlers and unsporting behaviour from the Australians. It eclipsed the quality of cricket produced by both the teams over the five days. Andrew Symonds' match winning 162, V.V.S. Laxman's breath taking 109, Sachin's classic 154, Sourav Ganguly's attacking 67, Harbhajan Singh's wonderful 63, R.P. Singh's delightful 4 wickets, Anil Kumble's vigilant 45 from 111 balls in the 2nd innings, Michael Clarke's web of spin giving him 3 for 5 in 1.5 overs and a test match which achieved a result just 6 minutes before the end of play; all of this took the back seat to the poor umpiring and even poorer sportsmanship from Australia. It prompted Anil Kumble, a man of few words, to utter a devastating statement," Only one team played in the spirit of the game."

In the wake of what transpired on the field, Ricky Ponting's official complaint against Harbhajan Singh, accusing him of racially abusing Symonds, did not sound serious initially. But when match referee Mike Procter found Harbhajan Singh guilty and handed him a three–match ban, all hell broke loose. For Indian fans, this was injustice, especially in the backdrop of the Sydney Test. The verdict resulted in a massive outcry of anger. For them, an Indian would never do such a thing. They had probably forgotten the horrible treatment the Mumbai crowd had subjected Symonds to. They had forgotten that Mike Procter, a South African, was perhaps best suited to deal with the racism issue. India was not willing to listen. Polls were conducted back home on whether India should withdraw from the series. The cricketing ties of two of the most influential nations in cricket appeared to be on the brink of an end. All of a sudden, a conversation which resembled a casual chat became the centre of the ugliest controversy. Did Harbhajan cross the line then? The truth never came out, as nobody including the players involved, openly spoke about it. Did India overreact in its threat to quit the tour? Was the complaint from Australia necessary, given their own philosophy of 'what happens on the ground stays on the ground'? All these important questions needed answering. Some of them were answered in a hearing behind closed doors. India eventually decided to continue the tour. A different and more pertinent question emerged. How would India react on the field? How would India react on the fastest pitch on earth?

PERTH MIRACLE

The fastest pitch on earth, that's what Perth was called. A batsman's nightmare, that's what Perth was called. The Indian batsmen knew from the moment they stepped on to the field that the nation expected, in fact demanded, a win. After all that had happened in Sydney, nobody felt more eager than the Indian batsmen to do something extraordinary. There was no second–guessing Australia's strategy: some good, hostile short pitch stuff.

Perth was probably the least favourable pitch for Sehwag to make his comeback to test cricket, but India depended on Sehwag for a good start as the captain had made another bold decision of batting first. Sehwag obliged by surviving Australia's brutal short pitch bowling. Sehwag's strike rate of 50 displayed his hunger to play for India again. After a good start, Dravid's inch perfect defence and Sachin's natural ability to score on fast pitches, took the centre stage. Both innings promised so much but folded abruptly. India's inning ended at 330; this was way short of all possibilities, considering at one point, it was on 198 for 2.

It was up to the bowlers to carry the team forward after India's late falter. The Indian bowlers had discovered the art of swing this season. All of them decided to have an exhibition of top–class swing bowling. A full–length swinging ball is any opener's nightmare. Both the Australian openers saw their nightmares come true. If quick bowling is all about playing on the back foot, the swing tests your front foot. Irfan Pathan and R.P. Singh found immaculate lengths and lovely swing in the air to which the Australian top order did not have any answer. Australia was reduced to 14 for 3.

The Australian top order failed the front foot test after which Ishant

Sharma examined the back–foot efficiency of its middle–order. Ponting and Clarke could not handle the awkward bounce Ishant derived from good length. The Indian bowlers' consistency in line and length and outstanding slip catching, consolidated India's position in the match. India maintained its intensity despite a characteristic Australian counter–attacking partnership of 102 runs in 17 overs between Symonds and Gilchrist. Eventually Anil Kumble got rid of Symonds. Symonds again waited for the umpire to give him out inspite of a clear edge. He was not playing in Sydney anymore and Mr. Bucknor was not officiating. Asad Rauf's finger went up immediately. R.P. Singh then ran through the Australian lower order, but not before getting Gilchrist out with a brute of a ball. Australia was all out for 212. India led by 118.

V.V.S. Laxman's salvaging act in the 2nd inning (79 runs) gave Indian bowlers the cushion of a big target of 413. Irfan Pathan's opening spell, in which he accounted for both the openers, set the match up for a tense fourth day. Australia's middle order was stacked with great names but India's desire to win possessed greater vigour. After Australia resumed Day Four at 65 for 2, under the grey slate of clouds in Western Australia, world cricket witnessed a long–haired young Indian bowler make a living legend dance to his tunes.

Ishant Sharma got the ball to bounce and cut in sharply from the good length. Ponting looked in two minds, whether to leave the ball or to play. Ishant's pace also hurried him. Ricky Ponting had established himself as one of the best batsmen in the history of cricket. He was not seen troubled by a fast bowler so consistently. But despite some close appeals, a few body blows and lots of play and misses, Ponting still stood at the crease and Ishant was seemingly tiring.

Sehwag: "Arey woh Delhi ke liye 9–9 overs dalata hai. Usko ek aur dede." (He bowls 9 over spells for Delhi. Give him another over.)

Kumble: "Ishant, ek aur karega?" (Ishant, can you bowl one more?)

Ishant: "Haan,karoonga." (Yes. I can.)

Sehwag convinced his captain to give Ishant one more over. After a barrage of in–swingers in his 8–overs spell, Ishant finally got one to straighten. Ponting played for the swing. Dravid held on to a simple catch and young Ishant Sharma won the toughest battle of his nascent career by putting a curtain on Ponting's miserable one hour. India now, was 7 wickets away.

The Australian batsmen tried to hang on but the wickets kept falling, one of which was Andrew Symonds', adjudged LBW despite a massive inside edge. Finally, justice was served, India felt. Kumble's uncharacteristic jumping celebrations reflected the mood of the country. How dearly India wanted Symonds to get a taste of his own medicine! When R.P. Singh clean bowled Shaun Tait, the whole of India erupted in vindication. A test win at Perth had been nothing more than a distant dream some years ago. But on 19th January 2008, India became the first sub–continental team to win at Perth. It became the first team to beat Australia in Perth since February 1997. Australia had been beaten in Australia only thrice in the past 8 years, twice by India. India again stopped Australia from winning their 17th consecutive test. It rose from the horrors of Sydney to an unexpected, unparalleled high. After conquering the fastest pitch in the world, it stared into the eyes of the world champions and asked, "Are you up for it?"

DULL ADELAIDE

The Adelaide Oval, which had given India its most iconic moment of the new millennium, was the ideal venue for India to play after its Perth heroics. India had asked Australia at Perth, are you up for it? Australia had to answer back. Yes, the Aussies were indeed up for it. They responded to India's 1st inning score of 526, which included yet another century from Sachin, with 563. Apart from Virender Sehwag's 151 in the 2nd innings, the entire match was dull and boring. At the end of the match, world cricket said good bye to one of the most destructive wicket–keeper batsmen as Adam Gilchrist hung his boots. The absence of any further controversy in Perth and Adelaide ensured speedy healing of the relationship between India and Australia. India's performances after the 1st test in Melbourne (India had lost by 337 runs.) excelled as the series went by. A very plausible win in Sydney was snatched away by factors beyond its control. Sport does not have place for ifs and buts and India never uttered them. Instead, it zeroed in on the ODI Tri–series. India had not won an ODI series in Australia since 1985. India's new captain took a long keen look at that fact; he was determined to change it.

COMMONWEALTH BANK SERIES

Greg Chappell's tenure as the Indian coach had begun with superlative ODI success but ended with sour memories of the ICC World Cup 2007. There was some kind of a renaissance in the Indian team since that World Cup. Despite its poor record in the ODIs in Australia, India fancied its chances, largely due to the new captain whose fresh approach had given the team their first ICC title in 24 years. A new leader always brings new perspective. When Sourav Ganguly & Rahul Dravid were dropped from the ODI side, India's new approach became apparent. Ganguly's exclusion evoked passion as expected. The new advent resembled Greg Chappell's philosophy, albeit there was a certain sense of acceptance this time around. Ganguly and Dravid at 35 were more precious to Indian test cricket. The cricketing logic behind the decision was reasonable. It was also done in a non–controversial method unlike the last instance. The changes rendered the Indian team an unusual look. Apart from Sachin, Yuvraj and Sehwag, no other batsman including the captain himself had ever played in Australia.

The inexperienced Indian batting was swept away for 194 in its 1st ODI. A fiery Indian bowling, continuing its good form from the test series, reduced Australia to 51 for 3, before rain intervened. Gautam Gambhir's century in the 2nd match against Sri Lanka provided a solid boost to India's batting and to the man himself. For so long, Gambhir had toiled hard in domestic cricket. His ton in Australia was heartening for those who had seen him sweat it out in domestic cricket. It was about time he climbed up the international cricket ladder. A century down–under goes a long way in announcing your proficiency. India's joy none–the–less was short–lived because of another rain–affected match. With two abandoned games, India lacked points on the table which made its next match against Australia practically a must win game.

Flashes of bowling brilliance against Australia in the 1st ODI turned into a full show of exhilarating fast bowling. India bowled with pace, with bounce, and seeing the Australian batsman jump around to fend at the balls was undeniably a first. Ishant Sharma, the kid who had given Ponting a run for his money a few weeks back, stood out with 4 wickets. The Indian batsmen however, made a modest target look like a world record chase. Only Sachin Tendulkar's two cracking straight drives that whiskered past Brett Lee at twice his bowling speed stood out from India's chase. India eventually got over the finishing line but with a big question mark. Did it commit a mistake by hurriedly bringing the youngsters in?

The question appeared more pertinent with a loss to Sri Lanka in a rain–affected match and another batting disaster against Australia (India failed to chase 203). India now had 2 washed games, 1 win and 2 losses. In other words, it found itself on the verge of getting knocked out of the tournament. The next match against Sri Lanka became a do–or–die.

Sachin Tendulkar was not able to carry his tremendous test match form into the series. Sehwag too struggled. These two needed to assume much of the responsibility and they were falling short. In a must win match, Sri Lanka asked India to chase 238 runs. India looked at its top order for stability but it got nothing. At 99 for 4, India sought some inspiration. The ODI series which was supposed to avenge the injustice of the Test series was rapidly going from bad to worse.

A team in search of inspiration always looks at its leader. M.S. Dhoni, captaining the ODI side for the first time outside India, faced the daunting task of finding some within. He was an established finisher in ODI cricket. The situation called for him to be a leader as well. Yuvraj Singh at the other end was also battling the odds. His form had deserted him in a rush. Here was a man, hitting fours and sixes at will four months back, now struggling to keep his place in the team. Cricket was a cruel sport and Yuvraj knew it better than anybody else. Dhoni and Yuvraj had more than a match on the line. Both of them desired to justify themselves. Both had a point to prove.

Yuvraj Singh responded first to the challenge. It was as if the situation freed his mind. His sweet timing came back. The sweet sound of his bat came back. Yuvraj came back indeed. His 76 runs from 70 balls turned the course of the game but the more fascinating narrative took shape at the other end where M.S. Dhoni discovered some unexplored levels of patience in him. India's hard–hitter nudged the ball around, ran singles and twos. He discovered a radically distinct side to him. He discovered a sense of responsibility. In this match at the most crucial phase of the tournament for India, he discovered a true leader in himself. The captain kept India alive in the series.

In its next match against Australia, India fell short by just 18 runs while chasing 317. The captain, it seemed, had started inspiring his team although one man appeared lost. Sachin Tendulkar's loss of form put everybody in a state of confusion. The man who, in the ongoing season, was scoring centuries for fun and was criticized for getting out in 90s, had scored a paltry 128 runs in 7 matches in the series so far. Like Dhoni, Sachin needed to ask himself some hard questions. Like Dhoni, he did and like Dhoni he found the answers.

India's bowlers brushed aside their off day against Australia in the previous match (conceding 317 runs) to display another outstanding performance against Sri Lanka in their final league match. Ishant Sharma continued his remarkable tour with 4 more wickets, restricting India's target to 180 runs. Then in walked the man. The cricketing world was buzzing with talk of his lack of form. He stood still, no feet movement, and caressed the last ball of the 1st over through the off side. The lack of feet movement worried his fans but the flow of his bat looked confident. Then came the booming square drive. Whoever was not convinced yet, surely was after the next ball. Never before was a front foot defence celebrated as much as a six. The famous flick and the backfoot drive followed next, then another, followed by a fierce cut. Soon the signature shots started coming out of his bag one by one– the flick to square leg, the cut to a rising ball, the picture–perfect cover drive straight out of the coaching manual, the paddle sweep, his proud invention. On reaching his fifty, he showed his bat to the dressing room in appreciation of its patience. With an assuring smile on his face, he carried India to the final. He had not scored an ODI century in Australia yet. Before this game he did not look like scoring it on this tour either. He set his eyes on the three finals that remained. He chose the first two finals to make his mark on the tournament.

Australia had found swing bowling difficult to play throughout the summer but in the 1st final, Praveen Kumar resorted to short–pitch bowling. Both Gilchrist and Ponting tried to attack but failed. After the top order's collapse, in a typical Aussie response Mathew Hayden and Andrew Symonds began to rebuild with massive hitting and clever running. Australia within a few overs started to take a hold on the match. That was the moment when the 'obnoxious little weed' made a striking appearance. Hayden had called Harbhajan 'an obnoxious little weed' in one of his interviews, adding another controversy to the tour. In the match, Harbhajan showed just how obnoxious he could get when he deceived Symonds in flight and forced him to hold out in the deep and then produced a false sweep from Hayden who was caught at square leg. The 'obnoxious little weed's' decisive blows restricted Australia's total to 239. It still looked tricky in the Australian conditions but Sachin Tendulkar had already made up his mind to create history against his favorite bowling attack.

If the century in the Sharjah final in 1998 was a young man's response to a challenge, the century in this final demonstrated the epitome of maturity. He looked in absolute authority from the word go. Every shot of his bore a stamp of conviction. It felt as if he had foreseen the match and knew beforehand what was going to happen. He played airborne drives against the spin of Brad Hogg over mid–off, upper cuts over the slips against an extremely fast bowler in Mitchell Johnson. All these shots carried substantial risks but when he executed them, they looked astonishingly safe. His first century in Australia became merely a formality. Sachin Tendulkar powered India through to take a 1–0 lead in the finals. M.S. Dhoni, the captain, decided to create history in the 2nd final in Brisbane. In Brisbane, India's former captain had made a telling statement in 2003; we are here to compete. India's current captain decided to take it one step forward. We are here to win.

Sachin Tendulkar's return to form was as sudden as his loss of form. He again played with supreme assurance. The young players around him started to catch the vibe. Uthappa, normally a rapid scorer, made an effort to spend time in the middle. His 99 minutes at the crease produced only 30 runs but resulted in an opening partnership of 94. Two quick wickets after the opening stand brought Yuvraj Singh to the crease in the 26th over. He had all the time in the world to build his innings. But he seemed in a hurry. He dispatched the 3rd ball he faced into the crowd over long on. Even though his timing was delightful, there was no need for such risks. Sachin was holding the innings together with absolute mastery and Yuvraj needed to support him by stitching a partnership. Better sense prevailed soon and he concentrated on taking singles. 4 overs later, the shot with which he dispatched Brett Lee's low full toss over long–on's head worried the Australian captain. The shot had two of Yuvraj's trademarks, his wonderful timing and his majestic swing of the bat. He followed it with another boundary over mid–wicket and a huge slog sweep six to Symonds. Sachin looked more thrilled at Yuvraj's hitting than Yuvraj himself. When Symonds bowled a rank half pitch ball, everybody including the Australian players anticipated it to land up in one of the stands but the eagerness to put it out of Brisbane outdid Yuvraj. He mistimed the shot and Hayden held on to a comfortable catch. The innings which had the potential to take India to a substantial total ended in a bit of a letdown. Sachin Tendulkar's disappointment was visible as he looked up to the heavens in frustration.

The possibility of a big score now hinged on him but a diving catch by Ponting ended Sachin's magnificent innings at 91. The master chose the two finals to play his two best knocks of the series but his untimely wicket dealt a considerable dent to India's aspiration of a big score. (India could score only 49 runs in the last 9 overs.) It presented Australia with a wonderful chance to level the best of three finals contest. Australia faced a couple of major hurdles though. Its batting had never got going in the Commonwealth Bank Series and India's bowling was the talk of town.

If Ishant Sharma had garnered the limelight in the league phase, Praveen Kumar certainly captured the nation's attention in the first final. He possessed a rare ability to swing the ball both ways, and the Australians had grappled with his swing in the first final. Their struggle continued in the second final as he reduced them to 32 for 3 in 9 overs. It was again left to the two big fellas, Hayden and Symonds. They again accepted the task and started rebuilding. Hayden, in particular, seemed in a vicious mood. India sought a hero to salvage the situation. The ultimate villain of the tour stepped up to the plate.

His accurate line, length and pace never allowed Hayden and Symonds to get on top of him. Both of them were in the mood of big hitting and Harbhajan Singh did not allow them to hit him at all. Pressure built and Dhoni sensed it. He brought his fielders closer than usual. Hayden pushed for a single. Symonds refused. Yuvraj did the rest. 2 balls later, Harbhajan bowled an absolute stunner. It turned, it gripped and left Symonds bamboozled. Harbhajan Singh was vindicated. He had gone through a lot of ridicule, accusations and turmoil. The Australian media had gone hard at him throughout the tour. Even the pictures of him, scratching an armpit, were portrayed as racist abuse. The crucial wickets of two of his 'mates', Hayden and Symonds, in both the finals conveyed a perfect 'adieu'.

A rear–guard action from Hussey and Hopes took Australia close to the target. Irfan Pathan was given the 50th over when Australia needed 13 runs with 2 wickets in hand. Within 4 balls, he finished the innings off and with that India capped off a miraculous journey. The road had started with annihilation in Melbourne. It had encountered grave injustice in Sydney and a stellar comeback in Perth. It had seen a legend go from the lowest and darkest end of self–belief to the highest peak of performance. Last but not the least it witnessed a leader transform into a visionary. M.S. Dhoni, India's new leader, looked determined to stand up to all upcoming challenges. He had seen what his team was capable of. The more astonishing fact was that India had finished the success story in Australia without a full–time coach. India was staring at long 2 years of continuous international cricket which necessitated a coach's services. The captain and his team required a calm, composed and competent man to drive them forward. They found a friend of a lifetime instead.

A FRIEND ARRIVES AS LEGENDS DEPART

One of the unique features that set the Indian culture apart from the rest of the world is its joint family tradition. From this tradition springs the expectation of a son to follow his father's footsteps, choosing the same profession or continuing the same business; even marry a girl like his mother. Indians are obsessed with these unreasonable comparisons with their predecessors. Going on for centuries, this outlook is so ingrained that it reflects in every aspect of our lives, sometimes even unknowingly. When the predecessor has failed, the work of the successor becomes all the more imposing.

Greg Chappell's stint had been, to be kind to him, a disaster. It had reignited an age–old debate of a foreign coach v/s an Indian coach. India had never tried the former before 2000. It was believed that for a foreign coach, understanding Indian culture and moulding himself to be a part of it and working in the domains of it was quite complex. Even though Indian coaches held a nightmarish record in the past, India had never considered trying a foreign coach. John Wright shattered all these preconceived notions. He adapted to the conditions and culture so effortlessly that when he left, India could not control its tears. John Wright's successful stint opened up an enormous opportunity for all foreign coaches, as the position of the coach of the Indian Cricket Team was the stiffest challenge in world cricket.

Greg Chappell's unsuccessful experiments and eventful off the field antics forced the Indian authority to revisit its stand on foreign coaches. India could not afford another Greg Chappell, especially when team had done so well for a year without a coach. Lalchand Rajput, India's interim manager after Ravi Shastri's tenure, made a strong case. Indian fans were sure of an Indian coach this time. The appointment of India's next coach hence, came as a serious surprise to all of them. After all that had happened under the previous foreign coach, the BCCI went ahead and appointed another former foreign player with an impeccable batting record but very little coaching credentials.

"It will be a great honour to coach the game's most passionately supported team and I can't wait to take on what I know will be one of the biggest challenges of my ongoing career in cricket." Gary Kirsten, a South African legend, veteran of 101 test matches sounded excited and thrilled on his appointment as the coach of the Indian cricket team for the next 2 years. India had witnessed such enthusiasm previously as well and its uncontrollable desire to compare the successor with predecessors made it cynical about the man though there was a noticeable tranquility in his enthusiasm. Calmness and composure were not virtues of India's previous coach. Gary Kirsten's immediate task was to free the Indian mindset from the shackles of the bitter memories left by his predecessor. His statement underlined the difference between him and Chappell. Where Greg Chappell committed himself to excellence of Indian cricket at any cost in his presentation, Gary Kirsten seemed to understand, recognize and most of all respect the passion cricket evoked in India, and that marked a good beginning.

AT HOME AGAINST HOME – SOUTH AFRICA IN INDIA

THE CHENNAI RUN FEST

Kirsten's first full–fledged series against his home country South Africa posed a stern test. South Africa had always given tough competition to India in India. Gary Kirsten had his task cut out, beginning with selecting the team. Every Indian waited with bated breath to know the Indian playing eleven, to see whether Gary Kirsten would go the Greg Chappell way. With absolute zero surprises in his team, Gary Kirsten won his first battle. India began to notice the evident difference between him and his volatile predecessor. The real battle on the field promised to be far fiercer.

South Africa's mammoth 540 asserted once again its ability to adjust to Indian conditions. The innings comprised of solid knocks from the usual suspects plus a big hundred by South Africa's newest batting sensation, Hashim Amla. He had scored 3 test centuries before his visit to India but a century in India makes careers. Hashim Amla's 159 had all the makings of becoming a South African great. India negotiated the awkward 21 overs on Day Two without losing a wicket. Wasim Jaffer played with composure. He needed to, as Gautam Gambhir was breathing down his neck for the opener's slot. As for the 2nd opener, he raced to 52 in no time, giving a foretaste of what was to follow the next morning.

Sehwag was the most difficult conundrum for the experts of world cricket. Every young batsman in the world is taught to solidify his defense, to move his feet, not to play away from body, not to go for extravagant shots early in his innings. Test cricket is the test of your patience, endurance and technique, they say. Then the man walked on the field to do the unthinkable. Unthinkable it was when he simply stood at the crease and kept hitting boundaries; no foot movement, no firm defense, just pure timing and wonderful hands. The purists and the average fans looked at it in awe when he reached his 2nd triple hundred in 278 balls. Even the South Africans could not help themselves but acknowledge and admire this ruthless yet smiling demolisher. Sehwag with his triple century became only the 3rd player in the history of cricket to have scored 2 triple hundreds after Sir Don Bradman and Brian Lara. Sehwag's was the last name experts would have imagined to feature in that list. The game of cricket never fails to amuse you. The match had only one result possible after so many runs (1498 runs in 3 innings). Both teams proceeded to Ahmedabad expecting more or less the same conditions. Both were surprised to see a bit of grass on the pitch. One team's eyes lit up while the other could only look upwards to the almighty.

JOHANNESBURG AVENGED – AHEMEDABAD

Rahul Dravid's very few memorable moments as India's captain included the Johannesburg win. India had humiliated South Africa by bowling it out for 84. The Ahmedabad pitch handed the South African pacers a marvelous opportunity to get back even. 20 overs! It took South Africa only 20 overs to decimate the Indian batting order. Dale Steyn bowled fast and straight. Ntini bowled fast and short. Morkel bowled short and got bounce from good length. All of them extracted support from a good pitch. The Indian batsmen enjoyed none. India was mauled for 76, its second lowest total at home. Dale Steyn claimed 5 wickets for 23. India had created ripples in South Africa when it had bowled them out for 84. It was time for payback for South Africa.

Anyone who believed, "If they could do it, so could we", was swiftly shaken up from their dreams. AB de Villiers's 217 and Kallis' 132 constituted a partnership of 256 runs. South Africa batted India out of the match. India managed to score 328 in the second innings, courtesy Ganguly's 87. South Africa won the test by an innings and 90 runs and led 1–0. India had to win the Kanpur Test to draw the series. The name of the venue was enough for South Africa to lose sleep and it was perhaps the only ground where India wanted to play.

THE GRAND DEBUT – KANPUR

Only the Kanpur pitch could look like a 5th day pitch on the 1st day itself. With a lightening outfield and such a pitch, both captains were dying to win the toss. Losing Anil Kumble to an injury dealt a considerable blow. No one needed a reminder of how lethal Kumble was on such pitches. It also meant M.S. Dhoni made his test captaincy debut. The coin favoured South Africa and it had absolutely no hesitation in batting first. South Africa was more desperate to bat first than India was. It wanted to avoid batting last on that pitch at any cost. It was a spinner's game and the Indian fast bowlers gave up even before putting a foot on the field. Ishant Sharma and Sreesanth's erratic lines handed the Proteas a comfortable start of 80 for 1 but on a Kanpur pitch, you never really do get comfortable.

The Indian bowlers waited for the pitch to do its trickery. The pitch obliged in the 2nd session. Yuvraj Singh's harmless ball bounced out of nowhere and took Graeme Smith's glove and thus started the South African collapse. India's part timers got extraordinary help from the pitch. The remainder of the match unfolded as expected. The South African collapse was followed by a solid first innings by Indian batsmen who were born and brought up on such pitches. India's lead of 60 on such a track was worth a million bucks. South Africa's wish to avoid batting on that pitch on Day Four and Five came true. Unfortunately for it, the pitch on Day Three looked much worse than a Day Five pitch.

Harbhajan Singh opened India's bowling, making its intentions crystal clear. The South African batsmen expected every ball to turn and do something. It is always risky to preempt on such a pitch and South Africa found that out the hard way. India managed to level the series and save the blushes. Kirsten knew that the deteriorating pitch had helped him to draw the series. He had a much better side capable of winning irrespective of the conditions. As India prepared for the Asia Cup 2008 and a full tour of Sri Lanka, he knew he would encounter similar conditions and to make matters worse, a legendary spinner. Indian batsmen always found playing spin comfortable but a young mystery spinner was emerging through the ranks in Sri Lanka to put their comfort level to test.

ISLAND OF SPIN – INDIA IN SRI LANKA

India's capitulation against Ajantha Mendis in the Asia Cup 2008 Final brought to fore Gary Kirsten's first substantial hurdle: how to tackle Ajantha Mendis. He felt the pressure of being India's coach, probably for the first time and as early as in his 3rd assignment. India drew some comfort from the fact that all the leading names had returned to the test side: the Tendulkars, Dravids, Gangulys, Laxmans. These guys had tormented great spinners like Shane Warne, Saqlain Mushtaq and Muttiah Muralitharan. A new mystery spinner would be handled with ease, India thought. This confidence was blown apart in the first test at Colombo. The legends failed to read Mendis from his hand or off the pitch. A–23–year old boy made the legends dance to his tunes. His accurate line and length did not allow any respite for the batsmen. It was beyond belief to see Sachin Tendulkar, Rahul Dravid, Sourav Ganguly and V.V.S. Laxman second–guessing the direction the ball was going to spin. It was an unprecedented scene as Mendis and Muralitharan ran through the legendary Indian middle order. Sri Lanakan spinners picked up 9 wickets in the 1st innings and all 10 wickets in the 2nd innings to hand India a colossal defeat of an innings and 239 runs.

Indian legends found themselves in the same boat as their young team mates. The struggles of the senior players to cope with Mendis threatened to hamper the confidence of the young batsmen. India could not allow Mendis and Muralitharan to dictate the terms in the 2nd test as well. For that, one of the Indian batsmen needed to clear his mind of any doubts and attack Mendis, without thinking much about his mysteries. Mendis possessed some remarkable varieties but his accuracy in line and length was the key to his success. Somebody had to take him off the line by attacking him, a job Virender Sehwag was very fond of.

The overcast conditions in the 2nd test got Jayawardene excited about his fast bowling arsenal. He gave Chaminda Vaas a prolonged spell which helped India more than it served Sri Lanka. Sehwag was given time and pace to get a flying start. He guided India to 151 in the first session itself. Both the spinners bowled only 6 overs each in the session which worked in India's favour. Jayawardene rectified his mistake by bringing back Mendis after lunch. The move straight away yielded results. He picked up back–to–back wickets of Gambhir and Dravid. Sri Lanka's under–performing seam bowling then got into the act by picking up 2 wickets in one over. Chaminda Vaas gave Sri Lanka a bonus of 2 big wickets as it was more than what Sri Lanka had asked for in the middle session. Sehwag at the other end played like he featured in a different match all together. Laxman tried to steady India's innings and with a partnership of 100, the pair of Sehwag and Laxman brought some respectability to India's total. But with Laxman's wicket, the Mendis mania wrapped up the Indian innings again. His 6 for 117 restricted Indian innings to 329 out of which, Sehwag scored 201 with 22 fours and 4 sixes. He carried his bat through the innings to become only the second Indian to do so. It was probably his finest innings as he played under extreme pressure, difficult conditions and amongst wickets falling around him. More importantly, he provided the Indian bowlers something to bowl at.

India's difficulties in facing Mendis and Muralitharan in the 1st test prompted Sri Lanka to prepare a spin pitch for the 2nd test. It carried a high risk as India itself possessed two exceptionally good spinners. Harbhajan Singh with his spin and bounce and Kumble with his accurate line dismantled the Sri Lankan batting which looked solid at one stage at 192 for 3. It handed India a lead of 37. Though the Indian batsmen again struggled against the Sri Lankan spinners, their bowling performance in the 1st innings gave it some heart to defend the total of 306 runs.

For the first time in the series, the Indian fast bowlers bowled with a sense of purpose. Ishant Sharma's 3 wickets supported Harbhajan's 4 and Kumble's 2 to the core. Indian bowling and Sehwag's brilliance saw India through, to level the series. The major headache remained though, as apart from Sehwag, every other Indian batsman struggled against M&M. Both spinners returned to haunt them in the 3rd test as India was bundled out for 249. With such a dreadful first innings score, only one result was possible.

Ajantha Mendis dominated the Indian greats in the series time and again (26 wickets in the series), and a glorious future lay ahead for him. As for India, poor performance in the 3rd series in a row raised some difficult questions. The new coach had failed to bring anything to the table so far. He knew he needed a spectacular result to get acknowledged. His next assignment was sure to provide him the platform for a spectacle. The last four series between the two giant cricketing nations had given birth to a rivalry in international cricket. In 2001, India had crushed Steve Waugh's dream. In 2003–04 in Australia, India had given Steve Waugh nightmares. In 2004, Australia had outsmarted and outperformed India in India and in 2007–08, off the field drama had overshadowed cricket. What was the upcoming series going to be about? Intense cricket, lots of tension, high quality for sure! But above all, the series turned out to be a farewell extravaganza to India's true leader, the man who had shaped Indian cricket.

LEGENDS DEPARTS – AUSTRALIA IN INDIA 2008

Sourav Ganguly stood right by the side of the pitch. He moved 2 fielders back and 1 fielder close in. Then he went to the bowler and had a chat with him. As he was coming back to his fielding position, he had the characteristic spark in his eyes and sprint in his stride. It took a while for the crowd and the millions watching the match, to realize what was happening and as soon as it did, all heads turned towards M.S. Dhoni. He was standing quietly, hands behind his back and a hint of smile on his face. In the last moments of Sourav Ganguly's cricketing career, Dhoni asked him to do it one final time. Dhoni handed over the captaincy to India's supreme leader, the man who taught India how to win, the man who introduced India to the power of self–belief, the man who rekindled India's romance with its favourite sport. It was 8 years ago, on exact same date when Sourav Ganguly had assumed charge of the ruins of Indian test cricket. Eight years down the line, the bravest soldier, the greatest fighter, a team man and a leader had decided to say his final good bye.

After the dismal test series in Sri Lanka, India won the ODI series that followed. The transformation from the whites to ODI cricket was incredible, full of confidence and buoyancy. The youngsters brought in their valor and will to command. The attitude was a reflection of the young aspiring India. On the other hand, the Indian test team lost in Australia, drew a home series against South Africa and its recent loss to Sri Lanka marked the worst performance of the season and as it always came to pass in Indian cricket, senior players were blamed for it. Anil Kumble, the man in charge, started feeling the pressure. M.S. Dhoni had captained the ODI side for almost a year now. The idea of promoting M.S. Dhoni to test captaincy was steadily gathering impetus. On 27th September 2008, in its 79th Annual General Meeting, BCCI appointed a new Selection Committee headed by Krishnamachari Srikkanth. The move initiated the process of transition. India hoped that it would be done in a civilized manner unlike what had transpired three years ago.

The first assignment of the new Selection Committee was to select the side for an Irani Trophy match. This was no ordinary Irani Trophy match though. It was the dress rehearsal for the upcoming Border–Gavaskar Trophy. The team selected for the match affirmed the perspective of the new Selection Committee. The announcement of the Irani Trophy squad came with a sense of déjà vu. The axe fell again on India's perceived perpetual problem child. Sourav Ganguly did not feature in the squad.

Memories of his infamous interview flashed back. Ganguly it was. Who else could it possibly be? This time around, the man who personified a 'not until my last breath attitude' did not have his usual ardor to prove the system wrong. He who had brought Indian cricket back to its feet had finally given in. 'One last time dada, one last time!' the nation cried. India urged him to make that one last comeback, to make that one last statement. After all, he believed in making statements, didn't he? He deserved one more chance to make his final one. The team wanted it. The nation wanted it, and thank god, the selectors sensed the mood of the nation. He was surprisingly selected for the first 2 tests against Australia. His selection relieved the nation but for how long could he continue to defy the odds? Sourav Ganguly had already found an answer to that question.

Australia named a formidable squad for the series. It had beaten India in India the last time but it was under Adam Gilchrist. Personal and team success in India had eluded Ponting thus far. This tour presented him perhaps his last chance, his final frontier. He spoke highly of his team's preparation for the tour and how hard his boys had worked. If Ponting looked all excited in his press conference, Anil Kumble's turn struck as a bit of a slump. Kumble's answers were short, abrupt and the man looked distracted. It was very unlike Kumble. The presence of Sourav Ganguly in that press conference made everybody nervous. Some of them had anticipated it to happen. None of them wanted to face what was about to happen.

"Just one last thing lads, before I leave, I just want to say that this is going to be my last series. I have decided to quit. These four tests are going to be my last. Hopefully, we will go out on a winning note," Sourav Ganguly spoke and everybody froze. He was actually leaving. He uttered the word 'quit' probably for the first time in his life. Since 2005, he had been striving to prove a point. The last 4 years had seen the best of Ganguly. He did not need to prove anything anymore. It was time to celebrate a wonderful career. The nation prepared itself to say one final time–THANK YOU.

1ST TEST – BANGALORE – THE GANGULY BOYS

Ganguly's retirement changed the entire perspective of the series. From being a fierce rivalry, the series was transformed into a farewell gift to Ganguly. When Zaheer Khan picked up Hayden on the 3rd ball of the first over of the 1st test, it looked like Ganguly's old boys were up for it. However, Australia was not going to give in easily. For India, the series revolved around Sourav Ganguly, but for Australia, winning came first. Ricky Ponting finally overcame his difficulties against Indian spinners to score his much–awaited test hundred in India and together with Michael Hussey's outstanding 146 ensured Australia of a solid 1st innings total. Zaheer Khan, Sourav Ganguly's man to go to, ended up with 5 wickets on a placid Bangalore pitch. It was perhaps his way of showing gratitude to the man.

All Indian batsmen got starts but no one went on to score big. At one point of time, India was restricted to 232 for 7. But Ganguly's boys again came to the rescue. Zaheer Khan and Harbhajan Singh put together a partnership of 80 for the 8th wicket. 'The Ganguly boys', it seemed, had decided to script the series as his final gift. He had given them all the support they had required while growing up as international cricketers. He stood behind them and many times in front of them. It was time to honour their mentor. (India managed a draw and avoided going down 1–0 in the series.)

2ND TEST – MOHALI – THE PERFECT STAGE FOR THE FIGHTER

Australia caught India unaware in Bangalore and forced it to settle for a draw. The story continued in Mohali as an inspired bowling performance from Australia led by Mitchell Johnson, saw India lose the momentum given by Sehwag and Gambhir. India at 163 for 4 was in desperate search of a fight back. The stage was set for the ultimate fighter.

Sachin followed the extra cautious approach in the beginning of his innings because of the monkey of overtaking Brian Lara he had been carrying on his back for some time now. Each run of his was getting counted. When he eventually got his 15th run, he achieved the greatest feat in test cricket batting. He surpassed Brian Lara to become the highest run getter in test cricket. Fireworks in the PCA stadium halted the match for 15 minutes, signifying the stature of the man. He always stood above the game in India. When proceedings returned to sanity, India still had a match to recover. The old teammates, the finest pair in Indian cricket, the best of buddies started doing it one more time. Both of them brought out their trademark shots. Ganguly found his natural timing; Sachin discovered his splendid foot work. Together, they took whole of India back to the late 90's and early 2000's. India time travelled to all those wonderful partnerships they had put together all those years. They certainly brought tears to the eyes of everybody watching. Good things are not meant to last forever. They reminded India one of the bitterest truths of life in the sweetest possible manner.

After Sachin and night watchman Ishant Sharma got out, India again required rebuilding its innings. At 326 for 6, India had not yet attained a commanding position. The match provided another wonderful moment. India's bright future joined hands with India's glorious past. M.S. Dhoni came and played his free–flowing game right from the word go. Ganguly allowed Dhoni to follow his natural attacking instincts as he kept his focus and defense very tight. That was his thing, wasn't it? He always protected his young players in his captaincy days, by allowing them to play naturally while he took to doing the dull job. The captain in him never went away. Here, M.S. Dhoni was his captain but Ganguly took care of him. His moment arrived soon though.

He flicked the ball to his leg side for a boundary, and then came the punch in the air. He paused and put his arms up looking at the dressing room. The dressing room stood up and applauded. All his findings, now towering names in Indian cricket, could not stop cheering. Harbhajan Singh, Virender Sehwag, Zaheer Khan looked emotional. He himself looked emotional. He had wanted it badly. His eyes said it. Dhoni ran up to him and gave him a big hug. It conveyed a lot. Ganguly had redeemed himself, one final time.

A huge 1st innings total of 469 gave the Indian spinners a cushion to control the match. Amit Mishra's surprising 5–for restricted Australia to 268. India in the second innings piled the misery on Australia through a wonderful hundred from Gambhir and a swashbuckling 90 from Sehwag. Australia was asked to chase 515. On a Day Four and Day Five pitch in India, that was impossible to achieve. All Indian bowlers shared the spoils as they bowled out Australia for 195 in the 2nd innings, winning by 320 runs, India's biggest win in terms of runs over Australia.

3RD TEST – DELHI – THE BATON IS PASSED

Anil Kumble saw M.S. Dhoni hand Australia its heaviest defeat against India. A thumping win cleared his thought process. He was now convinced beyond doubt about India's next leader. He had continued playing in the interests of the team despite his personal fight with form as India required him as a leader. It was time to go. He announced his retirement. He chose Feroz Shah Kotla, his second home where he had managed the impossible of picking all 10 wickets in an innings, to be his last hunting ground.

The Feroz Shah Kotla pitch seemed as flat as ever but to the surprise of all, the familiar invariable bounce went missing. India recovered from its early jitters as it lost Sehwag and Dravid, leaving India at 27 for 2. Gautam Gambhir absorbed the pressure and with each passing minute, he grew in confidence. Sachin was at his fluent best. A partnership of 130 between them, followed by a humongous 278 runs partnership between Laxman and Gambhir, resulted in a massive score. Gambhir scored his first test double ton. Australia had managed to keep Laxman quiet for two consecutive matches, a rarity, considering his record against them. It was about time he made runs. He responded with a double ton of his own. Australia also found scoring very easy on the pitch. All top five got runs with Michael Clarke scoring a century. The match ended in a docile draw, not the result Kumble had hoped for. It nonetheless, brought the curtains down on the career of India's finest spinner. The words courageous and resilient described his career to perfection. The lasting impression of this calm, gentlemanly figure was his spell to Brian Lara with a bandage to support his broken jaw. With 619 test wickets to his name, he was undeniably one of the greatest spinners the game had seen. Feroz Shah Kotla was over. Nagpur was about to roll. Nagpur, the place where Sourav Ganguly's career had turned upside down 4 years ago, readied itself to give him the farewell of a grand nature, the farewell he so rightly deserved.

4TH TEST – NAGPUR – END OF AN ERA

It was a match that Australia had to win to keep the Border–Gavaskar Trophy. A draw sufficed for India to claim the trophy. It would have been sweet justice after what had occurred in Australia a year ago. These were all very crucial aspects of the Nagpur match and yet nobody even bothered to pay heed to any of them. One man and only one man mattered. Sourav Ganguly, after 12 years of International cricket, set his foot on the ground in Indian whites for the last time. It was an overwhelming situation and the Indian team needed to keep its focus. Nobody knew it better than Ganguly. M.S. Dhoni, now the full–time captain of the Indian test team, won the toss and elected to bat.

It was Sourav Ganguly's master move to push Sehwag to open the innings in test cricket. Sehwag scored a blistering 66 from 69 in the 1st innings and 92 from 107 balls in the 2nd innings, as if to say Thank You.

It was under and alongside Sourav Ganguly that Sachin had witnessed some of his finest moments in cricket. Sachin Tendulkar piled up another century, his 40th as if to say Thank You.

Sourav Ganguly had promoted Laxman to the No.3 spot where he had played the innings of his lifetime, the innings which transformed his career. Laxman scored an elegant 64 in the 1st innings, as if to say Thank You.

Sourav Ganguly had picked a 21–year–old boy whose bowling action was under severe investigation, and made him his primary spinner. Harbhajan Singh took 7 wickets in the match, as if to say Thank You.

M.S. Dhoni, the future of Indian cricket, was inheriting a team which had firm foundations. It had taken Sourav Ganguly four years to build it. Dhoni ensured that the Border–Gavaskar Trophy returned to India, as if to say Thank You.

And then, the man himself! Sourav Ganguly played his cricket with his heart on his sleeves. He pulled Indian cricket out of the dark abyss of match fixing and transformed it into one of the cricketing giants. He faltered sometimes, stumbled some other times. He backed his players to the point of injustice on other players who wanted to come into the Indian team. He used his power unabashedly which bordered on arrogance, made decisions which annoyed and angered many. Sourav Ganguly did everything he did with Indian cricket at his heart, making even his fiercest rivals stand and applaud. (The Australian team gave him a guard of honour) Sourav Ganguly scored a classy 85, full of his natural timing and said Thank You to Indian Cricket.

RESURGENCE TO THE TOP – TESTS

THIS ONE WAS FOR MUMBAI – ENGLAND IN INDIA – CHENNAI TEST – DECEMBER 2008

On 26th November 2008, the sovereign nation of India felt humiliated, shaken, angry and yet helpless. In the wake of the shameful terror attacks in Mumbai, which compelled India to question and suspect almost everything, a promise by the England Cricket Team to return to India to play the test matches meant little but that did not stop England from keeping its word. It made a symbolic statement by returning to play cricket in India. England felt secure in India despite the attacks in Mumbai. The England Cricket Team put its trust in Indian security even though India did not and hence in the gloom of the Mumbai terror attacks began a test, India would never ever forget.

Sport can never be separated from emotions. The Indian fans' frustration to see India's submission for 241 in the 1st innings (in reply to England's 316) appeared reasonable. The anger India felt to witness its bowlers struggling to take England wickets in both innings, was valid. Their irritation in watching a debutant spinner, Graeme Swann, trouble India's batting stalwarts was justified. After all, India had turned to this match to seek some brief relief from the terrible scenes in Mumbai. It got none. Instead, after Four days of horrendous cricket, India had only four sessions to save the test match. The match that was supposed to bring a few smiles, had altogether gone awry, until that moment.

The advantage of Sehwag's approach to batting was that he required very little time to change the course of a match. It took him 100 minutes to turn the test in India's favour. Sehwag went berserk (83 off 68 balls) in the 29 overs that India played at the close of Day Four. It scored 131 runs in those 29 overs, reducing the target to 256 on the final day. Tendulkar had once seen one of his finest test match centuries go in vain on the Chennai ground when the Indian lower order had failed to score 16 runs! (India's last three batsmen could only manage 4 runs). Destiny worked in curious way as he faced a similar situation at the same venue again. In that Chennai test in 1999, Sachin had fallen short by just a few runs. He was not going to fail this time. After all, this one was for Mumbai.

If Sehwag unleashed a merciless slaughter, Sachin's innings illustrated the essence of patience. He looked in command of the situation even when situation appeared out of control especially after Laxman's wicket which put England firmly in the winning position. Sachin refused to buckle down. Along with Yuvraj, he built one of his calmest partnerships. Both looked in no haste, yet scored at almost 4 runs per over. They never seemed anxious in spite of the nervy Chennai crowd. With astonishing assuredness on their faces and in their batting, both kept batting. As the target came closer, the aggressor in Yuvraj started blossoming but Sachin remained in his own trance, oblivious to the proceedings at the other end. You cannot detach emotions from a sport. It was poetic justice that the boundary which gave India its unlikeliest win, also gave Sachin Tendulkar his 41st and probably his most cherished test century. This one was for Mumbai.

THIS TEAM IS CAPABLE OF ANYTHING – INDIA IN NEW ZEALAND – 1ST TEST – MARCH 2009

The Indian fast bowlers dismantled the New Zealand top order reducing it to 60 for 6. Gary Kirsten's statement, made three months before India landed in Hamilton, started making sense. After a disastrous start, Jesse Ryder and Daniel Vettori scored wonderful centuries to pull New Zealand out of trouble. Gary Kirsten was proven correct again. The Indian middle order then put three solid partnerships, anchored by a charming century from Sachin. The innings also included a stellar 51 from Zaheer Khan. India amassed 520 runs in unfavorable conditions. Gary Kirsten seemed to know what he was talking about.

In overseas conditions, where the spinner played the role of holding up one end, Harbhajan Singh's gripping off–spinners picked 6 wickets in New Zealand's 2nd innings. The target of 39 was chased with 8 boundaries. Just like that! How did Gary get it so brilliantly?

At the end of the 3rd day's play against England in that classic Chennai test, when India was staring at certain defeat, Gary Kirsten had said," This Indian team is capable of anything." India proved him right in that test itself. For anyone who wrote it off saying it was a home test, the Indian team thrashed New Zealand in New Zealand by 10 wickets by playing exceptional cricket at times and some inexplicable cricket at others, proving the man right once again.

A BOY BECOMES A MAN – INDIA IN NEW ZEALAND – 2ND TEST – MARCH 2009

Gautam Gambhir had stuck out his elbow 'unintentionally' into Shane

Watson's chest. Gautam Gambhir had stared into the eyes of Andre Neil, a man almost twice his height and given him some pure Delhi cuss words back. His ability to score at a rapid pace coupled with these instances projected his image as impatient. He was Virender Sehwag's buddy for crying out loud! How could he ever be depended upon for a marathon test innings: a long grinding test innings to draw a test match?

New Zealand dictated the first three days of the 2nd test in Napier. At the end of 3rd day's play, a loss looked inevitable and hence its dream of winning a test series in New Zealand in 41 years looked remote. India needed someone to save the match. Rahul Dravid was India's first pick. He batted for 242 minutes. V.V.S. Laxman probably stood second. He occupied the crease for 269 minutes. Sehwag for sure ranked last in that list and Gautam Gambhir featured a place above his Delhi mate. 643 minutes and 436 balls! That draws up to nearly 11 hours and 72.4 overs. The boy who had put his elbow into Shane Watson's chest in response to Shane Watson's clenched fist towards him, the boy who in a response to Andre Nel's sledging, had charged at him aggressively, stayed in the middle for 11 hours and 72.4 overs to score a match saving and eventually series winning century. Against the calm and serene settings of Napier, Gautam Gambhir, a boy, became a man.

THE ENIGMA CALLED VIRENDER SEHWAG – SRI LANLA IN INDIA – 3RD TEST – DECEMBER 2009

When one thinks of Sir Don Bradman, the sorrow of not watching him play is the instant sentiment. It is often said that two of the most important facets of batting are technique and balance. Sir Don Bradman, they say, had exquisite technique of decisive foot work and his balance while receiving the ball was exemplary. No wonder he had scored two triple centuries.

Next up, Brian Lara comes to your mind. His 375 against England was preposterous to each and every cricket follower. He had done the impossible. Then Mathew Hayden reminded us that impossible is a myth in sports. But then again, Brian Lara let us mortals delve a bit more about the realms of possibilities and impossibilities by scoring 400.

When you start analyzing the factors important for a long innings, these two gentlemen automatically become your subject for thesis. Where Sir Don makes you realize the importance of technique, balance and defense, Brian Lara throws light on the temperament one requires to stay at the wicket for three or four days and score those runs.

Now, you are ready with your thesis on how to score triple hundreds in international cricket. You have got your five fundamentals ready; Technique, Balance, Defense, Patience and Temperament. The thesis is going in the right direction until you realize that there is one more guy who has scored two triple centuries. You look at his scores, see some of his footage and that's when you tear and throw your thesis in the dustbin. That's the moment you are introduced to the enigma called Virender Sehwag.

He scored his 1st triple century against Pakistan in 364 balls which included 39 boundaries and 6 sixes. He reached his triple century with a six and scored it in only 9 hours. His 2nd triple century came against South Africa in 278 deliveries with 42 fours and 5 sixes. He again got it in 9 hours. The first fundamental of getting big scores was patience and Sehwag was miles away from it. The boundaries constituted more than 60% of his runs in that innings. Clearly, he was not interested in the 2nd fundamental of defense either. He had no text–book foot work, that is no high elbow, no going to the pitch of the ball, no straight bat defenses and certainly no leaving the ball alone. Technique, the most important aspect to huge scores did not even feature on his radar and considering he opened the innings, it said a lot. When he could think of hitting a six on 295, let alone actually hitting it, his temperament could have been a subject for a separate thesis.

So, after scoring 284 at stumps on Day Two, against Sri Lanka in the 3rd test in Mumbai, he stood on the verge of becoming the only batsman in the history of the game to get 3 triple hundreds. He was on the verge of overtaking Sir Don and Brian Lara. But the casual shot that led to his dismissal the next morning on 293 summed him up. If you did not know him previously, this was the moment you got introduced to the enigma called Virender Sehwag.

THE OTHER 10 FELLOWS – SRILANKA IN INDIA – 2ND& 3RD TEST – DECEMBER 2009

Virender Sehwag's 293 dominated all talking points and headlines but there was a test series too and there was the Indian team too. The other 10 fellows in that team also played a role in the 2–0 result. Test matches in India are invariably played in two stages. 'Win the toss, bat first and bat huge' is the first stage and 'relentless attack with the spinners' commonly follows. India took care of the 1st stage in the 2nd test by putting 642 runs on the board.

When your top 3 batsmen score centuries, it's hard to score less. The 2nd stage followed. For Indian bowlers, it was business as usual. They all shared wickets and thumped Sri Lanka by an innings and 144 runs.

Before Virender Sehwag took the revamped Brabourne Stadium by storm, Sri Lanka had actually succeeded in putting up a competing total in the 1st innings of the 3rd test. At least it looked decent before Sehwag alone scored three–fourth of it. The Indian bowlers again enjoyed the cushion of a huge score of 726. India opened its bowling in the 2nd innings with spinners from both ends which probably infuriated Zaheer Khan, India's premier speedster. He finished the match with 5 for 72.

Every soul who watched Sehwag's innings gasped over only one thought. How could a man, batting on 293, play such a reckless shot? Nonetheless, it did not stop the cricket lovers from marveling at the special talent of Virender Sehwag. No doubt, the Brabourne match was a Virender Sehwag show but India achieved another tiny piece of accomplishment after winning the match. It became the No. 1 test team. Virender Sehwag and the other 10 fellows were the best test team in the world.

NAGPUR AGAIN – SOUTH AFRICA IN INDIA – 1ST TEST – FEBRUARY 2010

What is it with Nagpur? India mulled over. Australia in 2004 at least had a green track on which McGrath and Gillespie wreaked havoc. It was a brown pitch this time. Then what exactly did Dale Steyn find in that pitch to get 7 wickets? And if the pitch was so bowler friendly, how did Hashim Amla and Jacques Kallis score 253 and 173, respectively? Why did the Indian lower order collapse in 7 overs when South Africa played 176 overs? And why did the Indian spinners require 117 overs to take 3 wickets where a lone South African spinner took 3 wickets in 38 overs in India's 2nd inning?

India had become the No. 1 test team in the world only 60 days ago. The bowlers had contributed heavily in the success. Amla & Kallis disagreed. The Indian batting was one of the most consistent and big–scoring batting line–ups in the world at the time. Dale Steyn begged to differ. South Africa's win by an innings and 6 runs put India's impeccable record at home since 2004 in jeopardy. The green pitch in Nagpur in 2004 had ravaged India. It was Nagpur again this time, with a brown pitch. While everybody was analyzing

India's mediocre performance, Team India asked only one question, "What is it with Nagpur?"

ARE YOU WORTHY OF IT? – SOUTH AFRICA IN INDIA – 2ND TEST – FEBRUARY 2010

India was barely two months old as world No. 1 and coming back from the embarrassment of losing by an innings at home required tough character and an 'X' factor. Luckily for India, the imposing Eden Gardens, the venue for the 2nd test and its high decibel crowd guaranteed India the 'X' factor it needed.

South Africa continued its momentum by scoring 228 runs for 2 at tea on Day One. The Eden Gardens had historically produced major collapses in the 3rd session and every Indian prayed for one. India's premier fast bowler along with Kolkata's second adopted son, Harbhajan Singh, obliged. Both centurions Amla and Petersen were dismissed by Zaheer on either side of the tea break, and then, the famous last session at the Eden began. It started with an uncharacteristic sweep from Kallis and ended with Wayne Parnell bamboozled by Zaheer Khan's artistry. The session resulted in 7 wickets for 38 runs which included a hat–trick chance to Harbhajan, a direct hit from Zaheer and the South African batting going into an absolute state of frenzy. The 3rd session had done its trick. The crowd got what it wanted, what it was used to seeing. The Indian batsmen now had to carry forward the initiative. Batting on a Day Two pitch in India is every batsman's delight. Four batsmen particularly enjoyed it. India amassed 643, courtesy Sehwag's 165, Tendulkar's 106, Dhoni's 132 and Kolkata's first adopted son Laxman's 143.

If there was any doubt on India's principal weapon in this match, Dhoni cast aside it by opening the bowling with Harbhajan. He brought his second spinner in the 13th over itself. Mishra got Graeme Smith on the very first ball of his spell, reaffirming India's policy of 'spin only'. Though India celebrated its success by almost mobbing Mishra, the real cause for concern walked in next. Hashim Amla had batted for 15 hours in this series up to then without offering the slimmest notion of trouble playing on Indian pitches. Amla's ease prompted India to follow a simple strategy for this innings – get the other 9 out! He for one was determined to stay in the middle and fight it out. India successfully implemented its strategy of ignoring Amla and going after the other 9 batsmen and smelled victory after dismissing Kallis. After snapping up Steyn, India required 3 more wickets to win the match and it had 55 overs left. The game plan was simple but life is not. Wayne Parnell defended 64 balls in his partnership with Amla that lasted 146 balls. Paul Harris, the next tail–ender, played out 24 balls. India began to realize the magnitude of Amla's wicket by now. The guy stayed there and guided his tail to support him. Morne Morkel, the last man, left the balls comfortably which made India more and more desperate. The game had transformed into a mind game. Amla played it better than Dhoni as he found a suitable ball in every over to change the strike. Morkel did everything that Amla was asking of him. And then an unusual event happened.

Amla hit the 5th ball of the over and Sehwag gave a chase. The South African pair settled for one but Sehwag pushed the ball over to the boundary to keep Amla on strike for that over. The plan backfired as umpires deemed it unfair fielding and awarded 5 penalty runs to South Africa. Even though penalized, Sehwag 's cheekiness got the crowd going.

Amit Mishra had his task cut out, to keep Amla on strike for the entire over. Amla, by now trusted Morkel's batting and believed he could handle Harbhajan's next over. Mishra did his bit. Morkel needed to do his. With only 12 balls left for the end of the match, India's home supremacy was on the brink of being ended. India, unbeaten in a home test series for 6 years, had 12 balls to keep it that way. Harbhajan Singh took a long hard look at Morkel and his field. The crowd was right in the game with a deafening noise. In that high decibel noise and high–tension situation, Harbhajan Singh's 3rd ball pitched on the right spot and straightened to precision. The outstretched defense of Morkel was at last beaten. The moment the umpire raised his finger, all hell broke loose. Kolkata notched up some more decibels. Harbhajan ran like a child. The team members ran after him uncertain of how to celebrate. Nobody cared though. South Africa came within 9 balls to clinch a series in India. Hashim Amla had played for another 8 and half hours but was left stranded. After just two months of being the No. 1 test side in the world, South Africa came to India's den and asked them a daunting question, "Are you worthy of that rank?" Harbhajan Singh and the team ran towards one of the boundaries and roared back, "Hell yes we are."

THE CRISIS MAN – INDIA IN SRI LANKA – 3RD TEST – AUGUST 2010

When you lose a match in two and half days, it is very very difficult to get back up and perform. After the opposition scores 520 runs in just 124 overs and you keep fetching the ball from the boundary for 9 hours, it is very very difficult to acquire a positive frame of mind to bat in the next test. When a legendary off spinner makes you look like a bunch of amateurs, it is very very difficult to face the man again. You require a very very special innings to bring you back on even terms and instill some belief in your team. Fortunately for India, it had a Very Very Special player in its team who was capable of such an innings.

After receiving a pounding at the hands of Sri Lanka in the 1st test, conceding 642 runs in the 2nd test and then facing a big total in the 1st innings of the 3rd test, India looked down and out. A mini comeback in the 1st innings anchored by Sehwag with a century, and a good bowling performance in Sri Lanka's 2nd innings (India bowled out Sri Lanka for 267), again led by Sehwag with 3 wickets meant that after being dominated for ten days, India finally had the chance to win a test match. But the hopes that Day Four raised, were dashed by its end. Needing 256 runs to win, India was 53 for 3.

The situation was nicely set up for V.V.S. Laxman to do his thing. He showed his innate composure while picking up singles and twos. His god gifted wrists worked at their fluent best. While the other batsmen groped and fumbled, Laxman had all the time in the world to play his strokes and considering he suffered from back spasms throughout the innings, his stay at crease became even more praiseworthy. His flowing innings did not offer any hint of the pain he was going through, though his eyes did every now and then. He spent an excruciating three and half hours in the middle. The moment arrived when V.V.S. Laxman, struggling with an injured back, hit back–to–back fours to bring up his century and yet another match winning 2nd innings score under pressure. Sehwag, Laxman's runner, perhaps ran his fastest run to congratulate the man. India's second innings man was now officially coroneted as The Crisis Man. His 103 in the 2nd innings allowed India to level the series 1–1.

THE TALE OF A TAIL ENDER – INDIA V/S AUSTRALIA 1ST TEST – MOHALI – OCTOBER 2010

The score of 124 for 8 felt like a nightmare. It was not supposed to go this way. For the first time since Nagpur 2004, Australia sniffed victory on

Indian shores. One could see it in Ponting's eyes. He needed two wickets to win his first test in India as captain. India required 92 runs. In walked Ishant Sharma and what followed next had never been seen before in the history of Indian cricket.

V.V.S. Laxman, struggling with a sore back, was at the other end when Ishant joined him. The pair of an injured batsman and a classic tail ender faced the monumental task of scoring 92 more runs. Laxman needed to protect Ishant for as many deliveries as possible. For that, he required facing more balls which risked the chances of aggravating his injury furthermore. But the exact contrast happened. Laxman displayed strange confidence in Ishant and gave him the strike. Ishant justified it by plunging his front foot forward and defending the fast bowlers with a straight bat. His height posed a serious disadvantage while batting as it became difficult for him to duck the bouncers and he received quite a few of them. He fended some of them, played some of them. He looked ugly while fending and disconcerted while playing but he seemed adamant to throw away his wicket. As he consumed minute after minute, Ponting grew more anxious because Laxman took care of the runs required. Ishant encountered short balls, yorkers, slow off spins, quicker spins but he refused to give in. He stood at the crease for 106 minutes, played 92 balls (71% of the balls faced by his partnership with Laxman). In those 106 minutes, he added 81 runs with Laxman. When he ultimately succumbed, he received a standing ovation from the Mohali crowd. He deserved nothing less. He was on painkillers for a troubled knee. He was short on confidence as the last few matches had not gone his way. But one thing he never lacked though was determination.

The last 11 runs were not easy though. Pragyan Ojha survived a close LBW appeal and an even closer run out attempt. Even the ever so calm Laxman lost his poise at Ojha's stupidity. It was a rarity seeing Laxman using colorful language. Ojha held his nerves in the end and saw India past the finishing line. India was pushed to the dimmest corner and yet emerged victorious. It kept Ponting winless as test captain in India. The test had comprised of a wonderful century from Watson, a masterful 98 from Sachin, 8 wickets from Zaheer, a lesson for fast bowlers on how to bowl on Indian pitches. The match had seen Sachin Tendulkar score 1000 calendar year test runs for the 6th time, a world record. Yet the match was remembered for a tall, lanky, long–haired Indian fast bowler who stood at the crease for 106 minutes. This was indeed his tale.

"I NEED TO WORK MORE ON MY BOWLING" – NEW ZEALAND IN INDIA 2010

New Zealand had last won a test match in India in 1988. It was yet to win a test series in India. It had never taken a lead in a test series in India. On 7th November 2010, New Zealand was on the brink of changing these statistics. It had reduced India to 82 for 6 (India led by only 110 runs) after a surreal in–swinging bowling spell by 36–year–old Chris Martin (5 for 25 at day end).

On 8th November 2010, India witnessed a fightback it was used to seeing in recent times involving a rearguard innings of 91 from V.V.S. Laxman. The comeback also involved another 'first of its kind' moment and highly unexpected one to say the least; Harbhajan Singh raised his bat after a test century. Harbhajan Singh always enjoyed the gift of sweet timing in his batting. He had shown sporadic glimpses of his batting skills previously but he always remained the tail ender who could give India 30 – 40 runs. The aggressive sardar in him, who would play a careless shot at any moment, always won over the batsman. His 115 in the match were filled with silky timing (11 boundaries, 3 sixes) but to the pleasant surprise of many, also with a lot of perseverance. He played 193 balls and batted New Zealand out of the game. His partnership of 163 runs with Laxman snatched a golden opportunity from New Zealand to win in India. India survived a massive scare. Harbhajan Singh added a test match century to his resume, one he was very proud of. In a week's time, in the 2nd test against New Zealand, Harbhajan scored another century, becoming the only No. 8 batsman to score two consecutive centuries. He had a tremendous support from India's No. 11, Sreesanth who in his 71 balls stay at the crease faced a barrage of short pitch balls and took most of them on his body. India went on to win the 3rd and final test very comfortably to keep New Zealand winless in India for 22 years. After receiving the man of the series award, when Harbhajan was asked in one of his interviews, "How does it feel to be the new all–rounder?" his reply was hysterical, "I need to work more on my bowling."

HERE WE GO AGAIN! – INDIA IN SOUTH AFRICA – 1ST TEST – DECEMBER 2010

In December 2010, India geared up for its sternest trial in the last 2 years. All of India's previous test series in South Africa had turned out to be a disaster. In its current tour, India did not play any warm–up matches prior to the 1st test which was growing into a trend in Indian cricket, of late. A lively pitch at Super Sports Park, Centurion, wet conditions and an un–acclimatized team were a prelude to catastrophe.

The Indian innings turned out to be more horrifying than imagined. The ball bounced, nipped around and Indian batsmen came and went. India yielded in just 39 overs and 136 runs. All heads now turned to the Indian bowling whose contribution to India's recent achievements was immense. Each bowler had contributed to its success and when in need, one or the other always put his hand up. After its trivial 1st innings score of 136, India looked at its bowling for a fightback. Instead, it received the beating of a lifetime. South Africa scored 620 runs in 130 overs. A deficit of 484 runs all but ensured a humiliating loss. Even a fighting century by Sachin in the 2nd innings could not prevent it. The No. 1 test team in the world, the team that had not lost a test series in 2 years lost by an innings and 25 runs the moment it set foot outside the subcontinent. Every single Indian cricket fan gasped in unison – here we go again.

WAS IT FATE? – INDIA IN SOUTH AFRICA – 2ND TEST

If the conditions were hostile in Centurion, the green and bouncy Durban pitch resembled hell. Only one man licked his fingers and he certainly did not belong to an Indian origin. These were more than ideal conditions to unleash the world's deadliest fast bowler. Dale Steyn demolished India in 19 overs of devastating fast bowling. He swung the ball off the pitch as well as in the air at unplayable speeds. No wonder the Indian batsmen looked relieved every time it started raining. A first innings total of 205 did not offer anything to discuss. And after conceding 620 runs in the previous test, it was possible that there would not be much to talk about India's bowling as well.

Zaheer Khan, over the years had lost speed but gained the skills to offset it. He had become a master in making the red ball do tricks on the flattest of flat pitches in India. The combination of his trickery and Durban conditions were sure to compensate his moderate speed of 130 kmph. And on top of it was his bunny taking the strike, the perfect time to make a statement. The way he set up Graeme Smith was testimony to his skills. Even Smith could not hide the grin after he edged the ball to Dhoni, acknowledging Zaheer's genius. Danger man number one was gone.

Jacques Kallis was one of those players who repeatedly scored against India, no matter where he played or which Indian attack he faced. The Indian bowlers seemed perpetually incompetent to get him out for a low score. When Ishant Sharma got his finger to a ball firmly struck by Amla, to deflect it on to non–striker's stumps, the Indian team was over the moon. Was it fate? asked the fans. Kallis' unlikely mode of run–out saved India from the painful task of getting him out. Danger man number two was gone.

What followed next was a well–pitched ball which moved away to precision and bounced to perfection. It accounted for the destructive AB De Villiers but to the utter wonder of many, it was bowled by India's most erratic bowler, Sreesanth. In the 1st test in Centurion, Harbhajan Singh bowled a lot of straighter balls and Amla kept sweeping them to the boundary. But in Durban, Amla was caught plum in front on the first straight ball that Harbhajan dished at him. Was it fate? Asked the fans. South Africa's in–form middle order was dismissed even before the score had reached 100. Harbhajan Singh then finished off the tail in 4 overs to bowl out South Africa for 131 runs. Another second innings master class by Laxman (96 off 171) gave India a tough target to defend. After reducing South Africa at 111 for 3 in its second innings at stumps on Day Three, India stood on the verge of doing the inconceivable. After a long time, the Indian team looked forward to the next day's play in South Africa.

Sreesanth got Kallis jumping and fending a good length snorter. With Kallis' dismissal to an unplayable ball came the realization for South Africa that the Day Four pitch was beyond it. When Pujara ran Tsotsobe out, India could not believe what it had accomplished. India beat South Africa in Durban on a green pitch. Despite the Centurion mauling and Dale Steyn's magical spell in the first innings in Durban, India leveled the series. Was it fate? Every Indian fan felt so.

ALMOST THERE – INDIA IN SOUTH AFRICA – 3RD TEST

Winning the Durban test was nothing less than a miracle and miracles seldom repeat themselves. India had produced two outstanding bowling performances in Durban but its batting remained dormant in the first two tests. There was no doubt that the bowlers needed to put yet another good show and they did in the dark and overcast conditions against the imposing backdrop of the Table Mountain. On a day constantly marred by rain interruptions, the Indian bowlers tested South African batsmen with premium seam bowling. It was perhaps India's best bowling effort overseas. Though it claimed only 4 wickets on the day, the sights of Indian bowling making South African batsmen jump, fend and miss the balls on a consistent basis, had not been witnessed before.

The Indian bowlers kept the pressure on Day Two as well. Jack Kallis' century, abundant with his usual panache, was not enough to give South Africa a significant score. Yet the total of 362, considering the difficulties Indian batsmen had faced on the tour playing Dale Steyn & Co. looked menacing. The bowlers had done their job. Now the time had arrived for the batsmen to rise up to the challenge. Gambhir rose to the occasion and showed the world that his marathon effort in New Zealand in 2009 was not a fluke. He played out 222 balls for his 93. Harbhajan Singh confirmed the improvement in his batting by scoring a useful 40 in difficult conditions. But the innings belonged to one man only.

At 37, Sachin Tendulkar's reflexes were the topic of discussion in the country. He had scored a masterful century in the 1st test but got out in Durban in a rather clumsy manner. But in Cape Town, he showed the world that he still retained the skills. His desire to dominate any bowling attack in the world had not diminished. And make no mistake about it, in the 3rd test he faced one of the best in the world. If the innings had a flashy moment early on where he tried to play an expansive cover drive to edge the ball over the slips, it also included a booming cover drive played to the 6'6" tall Morne Morkel. If it involved a few awkward edges induced by Dale Steyn, he also displayed magnificent cover drives to the fastest bowler in the world. If the inning had a huge let off due to an umpiring error, it also comprised cracking square cuts, authoritative pulls and a straight six to a spinner. Sachin Tendulkar's 51st test match century ensured that India did not concede a lead to South Africa. The battle of the summer was on one more time, Indian bowlers against the South African Batsmen.

Day Four spilt a surprise to all those who believed it to be a field day for Indian seamers. Harbhajan's off spin did its tricks on a Day Four Cape Town pitch reducing South Africa to 121 for 5 at lunch. Every time the ball pitched in the rough patches created by the fast bowlers; a puff of dust exploded. Harbhajan felt at home. Even Amla did not have a response. India soon reduced South Africa to 130 for 6. With the lower order of South

Africa struggling in the series and Harbhajan Singh on fire, India smelt its first ever test series victory in South Africa. It had to cross one big hurdle though. To the disappointment of every Indian cricket fan, India failed once more. Kallis alongside Mark Boucher ensured no more drama as their partnership of 103 shunned India's hopes. His 2nd ton of the match resulted in a draw. India came within touching distance of a series win in South Africa. India after a long, hard fought test series was almost there in creating the most majestic moment in Indian test match history. It was almost there.

The drawn match drew the curtains on India's test match season before the World Cup 2011. In a first, India drew the series against South Africa in South Africa. It retained its No. 1 test match ranking, courtesy its unbeaten run for the last two years. The long road had started with a surprising series win in England back in 2007. In the last 3 years, India had lost only 2 test series. It had never earlier achieved such a winning ratio. The journey that had begun in 2001 culminated in 2010 at the top of the ranking table. The team which had been engulfed in the murky atmosphere of match fixing, now reigned supreme over the test arena. M.S. Dhoni was crowned the new captain fantastic. Under him, the team took the leap from being good to being the best. Gary Kirsten, the true foil, ably assisted the team in taking that leap. Sourav Ganguly had instilled the confidence of 'being good' in his team but M.S. Dhoni imbibed the attitude of 'being the best'. India was the No.1 test team in the world. Who would have believed that a decade ago? One man's belief was transformed into reality. The dream of the original Captain Marvelous was finally fulfilled by India's Captain Cool.

ROAD TO ULTIMATE GLORY

INDIA'S RESURGENCE TO THE TOP – ODIS (ODIS FROM 2007 AND 2008)

THE OPENERS

Never in the history of its cricket had India dominated an era. A sprinkle of wins here and there, that's all it used to manage. The problem was as much of an attitude as of ability. There was a sense of reluctance in dominating as Indians often mistook dominance for arrogance. India's inability to close out matches after being in a dominating position soon became a habit. At the turn of the century came the era of Ganguly, who refused to be apologetic about being dominant. Many times, he looked arrogant as he could not back his attitude with consistent performances because he did it with a bunch of newbies. All those newbies were now reputed and experienced cricketers. All of them had the cricketing experience to graduate to the next step and the mental strength to separate dominance from arrogance. For any story to captivate its audience, a commanding opening is a must. The trio of Sachin Tendulkar, Virender Sehwag and Gautam Gambhir accepted the challenge to make the grand opening statement but without even the slightest hint of arrogance.

THE MIDDLE ORDER

In the ODI format, more often than not the middle order of the team finishes the innings and hence the success of the middle order transpires into the success of the team. Throughout the last century, India had found the task of assembling a 'complete' middle order futile. It always depended on one outstanding batsman but the rest of them used to falter. While rebuilding the Indian team, Ganguly focused on packing the middle order with a pool of talented players so that it would not hinge on any single batsman. He succeeded in his endeavor to some extent as India discovered Yuvraj Singh and Mohammad Kaif. Though Kaif could not establish himself in the team for a longer period, Yuvraj Singh's talent saw him through; but that's what he remained, a very talented player. He remained a dasher who could support the anchor but never became one himself. He never felt the need to be Mr. Dependable. But when Rahul Dravid and Sourav Ganguly were dropped from the ODI side in the early part of 2008, he became the most experienced batsman in the middle order. After his exploits in the

ICC World T20 2007, he certainly owned the tag of the main man in T20s. India's upcoming ODI season presented a splendid chance for him to make a case for the ODIs too.

For decades, India watched the Michael Bevans and Lance Kluseners of the world and fancied having such a finisher in its team. India frequently depended upon one of the top–order batsmen to take it through. It is difficult for the first four batsmen to win the match every time, but with M.S. Dhoni's arrival on the scene India got its finisher, the man who could get the job done. Batting at No. 7 is a demanding job. You either come at the crease when you have to hit big shots from the word go, or many times you are left with the tail. One needs a very strong mind and absolute control on nerves. M.S. Dhoni possessed both and hence he made the No.7 spot his own property. Whether he would be able to do it consistently as captain was the pertinent question.

What if M.S. Dhoni or Yuvraj failed to win a match or provide the late flourish? What if India needed another floater besides Dhoni? The inclusion of Suresh Raina & Yusuf Pathan answered all these ifs. A young, dynamic batsman and livewire on the field in Raina provided apt support to Dhoni. A no nonsense big hitter and a part–time off spinner in Yusuf Pathan was a suitable addition to India's talented middle order. For now, it all looked set but one careful look at it exposed a glaring absentee in that formidable middle order; the deficiency of technique required to be consistent overseas. However, India was absolutely unaware that some six months back, the Indian youth system and its U–19 World Cup winning team had already given birth to a star and a future to the Indian cricket scene, worthy of its glorious batting tradition; a player who would resolve those shortcomings. For now, the middle order needed to focus on what it had rather than on what it lacked. Yes, lack of technique was a reason to worry, but the Indian middle order possessed three qualities which took care of it for the time being – flair, power and above all, the mental grit.

THE BOWLERS

Sourav Ganguly was the first Indian captain who consistently included three genuine fast bowlers in his armory. Since India's exploits in the ICC World Cup 2003, India marked a high turnover ratio of fast bowlers. It had seen fabulous potential in Irfan Pathan wither away due to the absurd pursuit of his batting skills. It became privy to the fall of Lakshmipathy

Balaji, India's very own smiling assassin. It learnt a lesson on how stupidity could cost you an international career from Sreesanth's plummet. Amongst this chaos, one man stood resolute. Despite the injuries he suffered and the attitude problems he was accused of, Zaheer Khan stood tall. It was no wonder that Gary Kirsten and M.S. Dhoni saw in him the strongest pillar of the Indian bowling. After eight years of an international career, Zaheer Khan was finally given the pedestal of the Indian bowling unit's leader.

India carried a distinguished lineage of spin bowlers since time immemorial. Throughout the 1990's Anil Kumble bore that responsibility alone. In 2001, with Harbhajan's emergence, India was assured of another shoulder to carry it forward. Choosing between Kumble and Harbhajan always caused a headache to the captains. After Kumble's retirement, Harbhajan became the lead spinner, a role he was dying to play. India's principal spinner had the back up of 3 part–time spinners. Virender Sehwag was always underutilized as a bowler. He bowled with a classic action which allowed him to extract spin out of even unfriendly pitches. Yusuf Pathan assumed the role of holding up one end. Yuvraj Singh's very slow left arm spin needed to be more consistent.

Historically, India had always been a batting country. Its icons were legendary batsmen. It never took its bowling seriously and that was perhaps why it never enjoyed consistent success. India now had a coach, belonging to a country renowned for its fast bowling and hence understood the value of a good all–round bowling attack. Gary Kirsten decided to instill a bowling culture in Indian cricket, which turned out to be his most valuable contribution to Indian cricket.

With formidable openers, a rock–solid middle order and a hungry bowling unit, India demolished England at home 5–0 (November 2008), Sri Lanka in Sri Lanka 4–1 (January 2009) and New Zealand in New Zealand 3–1 (March 2009). Since the dreadful World Cup 2007, India had won 10 out of its 15 ODI tournaments, including a tri series in Australia. Indian ODI cricket was at the zenith of achievement. And then, two years five months and twenty days after that devastating loss to Sri Lanka in the ICC World Cup 2007, the Indian team stood on the verge of becoming the No. 1 ODI team in the ICC rankings. The game of cricket has a peculiar sense of irony. India was about to achieve the status of being the best, in the country that had handed it that defeat 2 years ago.

A comprehensive 6 wicket win over New Zealand in the tri–series held in Sri Lanka crowned India as the No. 1 ODI team. It had achieved the feat for the 1st time in its history. Being No. 1 at something was a proud achievement. It was the India of 2009, aspiring to be a potential world leader, one of the strongest economies. A No. 1 rank in its favorite sport symbolised the country's ambitions. The cricket crazy nation was in a mood to celebrate. India had clinched the ultimate glory, it felt. At the highest peak of its glorious success story of the last two and half years, M.S. Dhoni, Gary Kirsten and the rest of the team realized that the road to the ultimate glory had just started. A year and half away from it, Team India embarked upon the final leg of its journey, the journey to the ultimate redemption, a journey to the ultimate glory. The first stop on this final journey was the dress rehearsal to the World Cup itself; the ICC Champions Trophy 2009 was at hand.

ICC CHAMPIONS TROPHY 2009

Ever since Pakistan was announced as the host nation for the ICC Champions Trophy 2008, the tournament raised serious security concerns. South Africa, Australia, England, and New Zealand pulled out of the tournament which forced the ICC to postpone it to 2009. Though Pakistan was assigned the 'First Preference' as the hosts, chances of it taking place in Pakistan appeared remote. As expected, Pakistan never got a chance to host it and the tournament was shifted to South Africa. India was willing to play in Pakistan despite security problems and did not complain about playing in South Africa either as it had a good history in ICC events played in South Africa. (It had reached the final of the World Cup 2003 and had won the inaugural ICC World T20.) But just when everything looked well set up for India, three injury blows put India's campaign in jeopardy.

1) Zaheer Khan underwent a shoulder surgery. The absence of India's leading bowler in the seamer friendly conditions of South Africa severely hampered India's chances. India had a good bowling attack but without its leader, could they perform? The answer for India was a disappointing NO. It conceded 302 against Pakistan in its first match and 234 runs in 42 overs against Australia in its second. It managed to redeem itself against West Indies but by that time, it was too late.
2) Virender Sehwag's injured shoulder forced him out of the Champions Trophy 2009. India's fearless opener, who specialized in blistering starts, was not available. India had a back–up pair of openers ready.

Could it provide the initial punch that Sehwag had made a habit of? The answer was an empathetic NO. The opening pair failed to handle the pace and bounce of the South African pitches. The opening partnerships of 23 and 7 runs said it all.

3) Yuvraj Singh injured his finger during fielding practice and withdrew from the tournament. India's middle order anchor and a more than handy left arm spinner, was ruled out just two days into the tournament. Could India find a fellow to guide the middle order and also support the main spinners? The answer was a worrisome NO. Rahul Dravid, who made his comeback tried to anchor the innings but his rustiness and lack of match fitness cut short his ambitions. Virat Kohli struggled to take the leap from being a fantastic young talent to a responsible batsman. Suresh Raina tried his bit but lacked any support.

Dhoni's maiden international wicket emerged as the only talking point about India in the Champions Trophy, which summed up India's tournament. India was handicapped by injuries but great teams never give excuses. It required looking past excuses and fighting hard. India's next opponent, the reigning World Champions scheduled to play a 7 match ODI series in India, was surely not going to settle for anything less than a fight.

INDIA V/S AUSTRALIA – OCTOBER 2009

For India, ICC Champions Trophy 2009 brought disappointment. Australia won the event. Two extreme emotions set up the 7–match series nicely. India and Australia had produced awe inspiring cricket over the period of the last 9 years. Strangely enough, India had not won a bilateral ODI series in India against Australia in 10 years. It had some points to prove. Australia had some pride to protect. Another fascinating contest was about to start.

1ST ODI – THE LATE FIGHTBACK

Zaheer Khan had mastered the art of bowling in Indian conditions and hence his absence against Australia was telling as India was asked to chase 292. In a big chase, partnerships become very crucial. India's best partnership until the 40th over was 64. From the 41st over though, Harbhajan Singh and Praveen Kumar demonstrated the fighting character India had developed over the last two years. 'It's not over until it's over' was India's mantra, the new spirit inculcated by Gary Kirsten. It rained fours and sixes for the next

9 overs. The pair scored 84 runs in 9 overs. 20 of those runs came in the 49th over which reduced India's target to 9 runs in the last over. Harbhajan got India's 12th man back into the mix. The crowd was roaring. But Peter Siddle's roar was even louder when he shattered Harbhajan's off stump and with it, India's hopes. Australia bossed 91 overs of the match and yet India lost by just 4 runs. India drew some confidence from the fightback. It also needed some inspiration. The combination of confidence and inspiration always yields results. The Indian captain volunteered to provide both.

2ND ODI – CAPTAIN MARVELLOUS

The Indian top order had failed in the ICC Champions Trophy 2009 and in the 1st ODI. As Yuvraj Singh came back after an injury lay off and required time to settle in, the Indian middle order desperately desired solidity and maturity. The M.S. Dhoni of four years ago would have been unlikely to lend solidity. But he was no longer M.S. Dhoni of four years ago. He had molded himself into M.S. Dhoni the captain; from a long–haired carefree big hitter to the calmest person in international cricket. His innings which started off with strenuous running between the wickets, transformed into carnage of massive sixes and hard–hitting fours as the game progressed. Such was the maturity of the guy that nobody even noticed his change of gears. Such was the patience of the guy that he kept pushing for singles even when Ponting enticed him to hit big shots, and it did not stop him from hitting those big shots that only he could, even when fielders guarded the boundary in the later part of his innings. 'More responsibility and less flair' was the rule he had carved for himself. It takes a strong mind to play against one's natural instinct. M.S. Dhoni had developed one heck of a mind. The captain cool, the captain solid, leveled the series.

3RD AND 4TH ODI

The Indian spinners dominated on a slow and low Kotla pitch to hand India the lead in the series. The Australian pacers hit back on the fastest Indian pitch at Mohali to level the series at 2–2. The series hung on the edge of a knife. One special performance or one fatal mistake was enough to give the advantage to one team. The next match witnessed both, and both came from India's batting god.

5TH ODI – A TRIP DOWN TO MEMORY LANE, CHENNAI 1999

The 5th ODI rewound the clock back a decade. India had required 271 runs to win. Pakistan's bowling attack comprised of Wasim Akram, Waqar Younis and Saqlain Mushtaq which reduced India to 82 for 5. All its top batsmen were back in the hut, except one. A 26–year old Sachin Ramesh Tendulkar with an injured back was not yet finished. A sore back did not stop him from playing some extensive cover drives. It did not stop him from playing delightful flicks and straight drives; from stealing singles and running like his life depended on it. It did not stop him from scoring one of his finest test match centuries. However, it did stop him from winning the match. India fell short by 12 agonizing runs. (Sachin got out when India required 16 runs.) The match that saw the Indian crowd give a standing ovation to the Pakistan team, is till date remembered by Sachin's 136. Alas, even after a decade, the ghosts of that match would not let India rest.

In reply to Australia's 350, India reeled at 162 for 4. It had lost all the big hitters but 36 years old Sachin Ramesh Tendulkar was not ready to give in. He brought out the attacker in him, the one he had hidden under the guise of maturity and age. The aggressor chose his favorite bowling side. (it was his 9th ODI century against Australia, most by any batsman against any opponent.) His 175 was full of his old self, filled with lofted shots; the way he used to play them earlier and his coming down the wicket to the spinners and hitting them for huge straight sixes made India nostalgic.

Just when India felt invincible due to Sachin's heroics, there came the costliest blunder of his innings. He failed to middle his cheeky attempt to loft the bowler over short fine leg. The ball went straight up in the air and he was caught by short fine leg. Sachin Tendulkar got out when India needed 19 runs. India lost the match by 3 runs. It gave Indian fans another Chennaisque memory. Sachin Tendulkar alone scored half the runs required and yet India lost. The match was labeled as Sachin's 175 immediately. It shot a serious warning to India. Cricket is a team game. The Australian team, despite Sachin's brilliance, was now leading the series 3–2.

6TH ODI – EARLY MORNING BLUES

And it soon became 4–2 as in the land of the rising sun, in an early 9:00 am start to the game, the Australian pacers cut through the Indian batting line up and Australian batsmen chased down the score in 41 overs. For the series that had produced five nail biters so far, Guwahati delivered an anti–climax. India after those two fabulous years of ODI cricket lost the second ODI series in a row. The memories of its sudden downfall in 2004 made fans uncomfortable. But there was some comfort in the fact that the Champions Trophy was an injury marred tournament. India had played quality cricket against Australia and to lose such a series was definitely not a shame. The start of the road to its final destination was not ideal. India needed to shake off these losses. The mood of the nation deserved to be elevated. And nothing could do it better than brutal batting extravaganza.

THE BATTING EXTRAVAGANZA

SRI LANKA IN INDIA – ODI SERIES – DECEMBER 2009

A summarized result of the match flashed. India won the match by 3 runs on the last ball. Without considering factors like the venue for the match or the players who took part in the match, a plain reading of the line suggested it to be a tight match in which the Indian bowlers had done a good job. But given that the match was at Rajkot, a normal score was out of question. Sri Lanka must have played well then, to come close to a target of somewhere around 325, the average 1st innings total on the ground. But then, if Sehwag scored 146 off 102 balls, Sachin 69 off 63 balls and M.S. Dhoni 72 off 53 balls, India must have scored over 325 for sure. Then one realized the severity of the outcome of the 1st ODI at Rajkot against Sri Lanka. India had scored 414 in 50 overs and Sri Lanka had replied with 411.

After a dwindling start to the road to the ultimate dream, India was desperate to get back to its winning ways. It also wanted to draw the disappointed crowd back into the action. The Indian batsmen obliged. World Cricket had already seen a successful chase of 438. Sri Lanka almost repeated it, courtesy a spectacular 160 from Dilshan and a class–apart 90 from Sangakkara. The desperation to win showed in Zaheer Khan's celebration after he affected a modest run out. It showed in the way Sachin rejoiced at his catch of Angelo Mathews. The win even made Captain Cool jump with joy. India's hunger and desire to be at the top was palpable. The theories of complacency were washed away. Team India was back to winning ways.

Rajkot is perhaps India's best batting pitch. Nagpur though is not far behind. A batting paradise at Nagpur ensured a M.S. Dhoni special and another high–scoring match. Considering 414 seemed getable in the last match, a target of 301 did not offer much. Sri Lanka chased it down quite comfortably. Two matches in the series produced 1428 runs. Who would want to be a bowler in such adverse conditions? The key to success in such an environment is to bowl as a unit. The Indian bowlers' combined efforts restricted Sri Lanka to 239 in the 3rd ODI. For the Indian batting line up, it was a stroll in the park. Things returned to normalcy in the 4th ODI as Sri Lanka scored 315 and India reached it without a fuss. A series loaded with runs erased the memories of early fumbles in the campaign. It is difficult to muse over the forgoing losses when your batsmen score 1275 runs. The Indian batsmen gave Indian fans a generous Christmas gift. Sachin Tendulkar was about to give them an even greater new year's gift.

SOUTH AFRICA IN INDIA – FEBRUARY 2010

"He is the first man on the planet to get a double hundred in ODIs and it's the superman from India," Ravi Shastri elocuted another of his lines which etched in the heart of every Indian fan. Sachin Tendulkar at 37, scored the 1st ever double hundred in the history of limited overs cricket (25 Fours, 3 Sixes). At 37, he batted through the innings in the simmering conditions of Gwalior. The most important aspect of his innings was that it came against one of the best bowling attacks in World Cricket, South Africa. India could now finally forsake the pain from Saeed Anwar's 194 against it.

21st May 1997! Chennai! Pakistan elected to bat and lost its first wicket in the 2nd over which remained India's only bright moment of the match. The rest of the 48 overs saw a pure massacre. The way in which Anwar dispatched the Indian fast bowlers into the stands stunned Indian fans. That era was not used to such a savage attack. How he toyed with the Indian spinners made the Indian fans fume with anger. As the innings progressed, anger turned into embarrassment. The helplessness on the faces of Indian bowlers could not be veiled. For those 48 overs, there was a constant expression of dismay on the face of every Indian fan. A score of 327 in a 50 overs match was unheard of in that era. An individual score of 194 was never seen before. After 13 years of painful waiting, Sachin Tendulkar finally put behind the dreaded figure of 194. Sachin Tendulkar's double ton in the 2nd ODI assured India the series win.

The Indian batsmen came to party in grand style. The campaign had started with 2 series losses but now was leveled with 2 series wins. After 4 series in the penultimate voyage, India's record stood at 50%, hardly acceptable to the standards of the current Indian team. This team pursued goals that would set it apart from its predecessors. The team had already set its target. One trophy had eluded India since 1995. It was time to regain it and end the drought of 15 long years.

ASIA CUP 2010

The Asia Cup 2010, repackaged into a compact tournament, comprised of only 4 countries, Sri Lanka, Pakistan, Bangladesh and India. After the set of one round–robin matches, the top 2 teams qualified for the final. Every team had 3 matches to secure its place in the final. India, historically a slow starter, never enjoyed such short tournaments. World Cup 2007 was the classic example of it. To occupy the No. 1 spot in anything, you need to conquer your weaknesses. The new Team India, marched on by a fantastic leader and managed by a brilliant coach, vowed to get rid of its inability to perform in short format tournaments.

INDIA V/S BANGLADESH

The ball had swung and seamed under the lights in the tournament's 1st match between Pakistan and Sri Lanka. India, who had to bat second under lights, realised that it needed to restrict Bangladesh's score. It produced the first breakthrough in the 3rd over through Praveen Kumar. After the early set back, the Bangladeshi batsmen succeeded in negotiating the Indian fast bowlers for 13 overs before Ashish Nehra, playing his 100th ODI, punched a telling blow to Bangladesh when he picked both the set batsmen in consecutive overs. The Bangladesh innings never recovered from it. Sehwag's 4 for 6 finished the tail off. India bowled out Bangladesh for 167. The Indian team's energy distinctly separated the current team from the old India which used to go through the motions in these early matches of a big tournament. The first match of the Asia Cup 2010 was a smooth ride. India made the first and most substantial announcement – we are here to win.

INDIA V/S PAKISTAN

India–Pakistan matches never fail to produce sizzling moments. This match also did its bit when the visuals of an angry Gautam Gambhir charging towards Kamran Akmal were displayed on the screens. The delicately poised situation probably brought the angry men out of both of them. India, while chasing a challenging total of 268 against a lively Pakistani bowling, required

101 more runs with 8 wickets in hand. Pakistan hoped for one wicket to get back into the game. The tempers were high but Dhoni with a smile on his face, pushed Gambhir away. That was an astonishing gesture. How could a man stay so calm in such an intense moment!

The loss of temper resulted in the loss of wicket for Gambhir. Pakistani spinners saw a window of opportunity and got the foot stuck in. In the next 9 overs, it dismissed 3 Indian batsmen for 39 runs and like any other India–Pakistan match, this match took a 360 degree turn in no time. India went from being favorites to facing a defeat, mainly because one of the 3 wickets was of India's finishing genius. M.S. Dhoni's wicket reminded India that he too was human. He left Suresh Raina and Harbhajan with an unlikely task of scoring 49 runs in 29 balls but those who had followed India–Pakistan matches for a while knew one thing beyond doubt. India–Pakistan matches always produced more than one 360–degree turns.

If the first ball of the 46th over gave Pakistan a wicket, the 3rd and the 6th gave India 10 runs, courtesy a superbly placed four and a slog sweep six. The next over became critical. Harbhajan Singh faced Shoaib Akhtar. The over had the potential to finish the match as Akhtar's ability to bowl those tow–crushers to tail–enders was not a secret. To India's advantage came Harbhajan Singh's natural timing and his ability to hit a length ball a long way. Harbhajan Singh did exactly that with a huge six over long on. No fast bowler likes a tail ender hitting him for a six. Shoaib Akhtar followed it up with a fast bouncer which stirred up another heated moment, this time between Harbhajan and Shoaib.

Suresh Raina at the other end scored 10 more runs with a four and a six. It looked like his amazing composure was going to give India a memorable win but the moment of madness struck him when he tried to steal an unnecessary run. Even his peculiar full–length dive was not enough to save him from a direct hit from Kamran Akmal. India needed 6 runs from 4. Praveen Kumar took strike with any of the three results possible. Pravin picked up 3 runs in the next 2 balls. India required 3 runs of the last 2 balls. There was not a single Indian who did not think of Javed Miandad's six at that precise second.

Harbhajan took leg–guard. But as the bowler was about to deliver the ball, he moved a step inside, swung his bat and middled the ball to the sweetest spot on the bat, and then roared to the maximum capacity of his lungs. He provided India its very own Miandad moment, winning the match by hitting a six. He did not forget to acknowledge his friend, Shoaib Akhtar while roaring. The Indian team which always faltered in short tournaments booked a place in the Asia Cup final with a game in hand.

INDIA V/S SRI LANKA – FINAL

When your innings starts with the run out of your most prolific batsman of the series, it's perhaps a sign of things to come. Without Gautam Gambhir, the Indian batting looked lost for ages. Eventually India managed to score 268 which was a competitive score, if not a winning one. The Indian bowlers, who had had a mixed tournament so far, now became the deciding factors in the big finale. The conditions favoured them. All of them possessed skills to use the conditions well. All they needed was a boost to lift their performance.

They received the required push in the 1st over itself. Praveen Kumar dismissed the ever so dangerous Dilshan. It was a lucky wicket on an ordinary ball. If Praveen Kumar found luck, Zaheer found some movement of the pitch and with a fabulous in–cutter to Tharanga, found his off stump too. The recent history of India–Sri Lanka encounters suggested that two of the most prolific batsmen joined hands after Tharanga's dismissal. Mahela Jayawardene and Kumar Sangakkara were Sri Lanka's last chance to salvage the match. Ashish Nehra had some other plans though. It took him 7 balls to break the backbone of the Sri Lankan batting order. He grabbed Jayawardene, Mathews and Sangakkara in those 7 balls. The result was done and dusted there itself.

India finished the formality in the 45th over. M.S. Dhoni won India their 1st Asia Cup in 15 years. India had always faltered in Asia Cups despite invariably entering the tournament as favourites. In the last three very special years, India had won many tough tournaments on its road to being No. 1, and now by winning the Asia Cup 2010, India was officially crowned as the Asian Kings. Only one significant test remained before it took on its mission to win the coveted Cup. In the land where India had never tasted a bi–lateral series win, the Asian Champion, the World No. 1 team was scheduled to start the penultimate chapter of the epic journey.

INDIA IN SOUTH AFRICA – 2010-11

Whenever India thought of a bi–lateral series in South Africa, a few iconic moments (most of them were terrifying for an Indian fan) came to the mind. Tendulkar's flying off–stump introduced India to Alan Donald. Alan Donald's angry eruption at Dravid made the entire nation furious except of course Rahul Dravid himself. In 2001, images of Sachin Tendulkar cleaning the seam of the ball and the subsequent ball tampering charges levied on him hurt India. Sreesanth's lethal bowling performance in its 2006–07 tour handed India its first test win in South Africa. And who could forget the grand re–entry of Sourav Ganguly in International Cricket in 2007!

Despite some wonderful moments, ODI success in the country always eluded India. In fact, it never went into an ODI series in South Africa as favourites. Things were different this time around though. India went into the series as the World No. 1 and after an outstanding test series in South Africa. For the first time, India believed it could win.

1ST ODI – THE FAMILIAR STORY

Its one thing to believe you can win and all together a different thing to actually win. The confidence of being the best changed nothing for India. For the entire length of the first ODI, a familiar story unfolded. The South African middle order milked the Indian bowling just like its predecessors had done all those years. India's much talked about bowling leaked runs, especially Ashish Nehra (61 runs in 6 overs).

For India, the target of 290 looked tough from the word go. Dale Steyn's pace softened up the Indian batsmen and Lonwabo Tsotsobe cashed in on the tentative Indian batsmen. Of late, India had gotten out of such old habits, courtesy one or the other player who would pull it out of such a mess. Unfortunately for India, nobody stepped up in the first ODI. There were sparks though. Virat Kohli once again gave glimpses of his talent with 54. Suresh Raina once again reminded everyone of his prowess of big hitting but these were few and far in between. To win in unfamiliar conditions, India wanted a closely–knit performance. To do that, someone had to assume a leading role. With the place in the 2011 World Cup squad up for grabs, India was sure to find one.

2ND ODI – THE UNLIKELY HERO

What does one pray for when he knows that the next match might be your last chance to feature in India's 2011 World Cup Squad? First, you hope to get selected for the match. Next you hope for an early wicket to calm your nerves. A crucial wicket at a delicate time strengthens your case. The icing on the cake is a tense over which finishes the match for you. Yes! That's a dream match for any World Cup probable. Munaf Patel, India's surprise selection for the ODI series found all his wishes come true in the second ODI.

First, the Indian batting gave him an insipid total to defend. The opening spell becomes pivotal in defending low scores, more so if the opening batsmen are Hashim Amla and Graeme Smith. Hence, to get rid of Amla in the 2nd over of the match was a bonus for India and a reincarnation of sorts for Munaf Patel. When he came back for his second spell, South Africa had recovered from the quick wickets and only required 39 runs to win. Now was the time to strike the crucial blow. Now was the time to deliver his best ball. His precisely landed ball straightened, and took the inside edge of Graeme Smith's bat. He had taken the wicket which had the potential to turn the game around.

Even after the good disciplined bowling by the Indian bowlers, South Africa inched closer to the target to reduce it to only four runs when Munaf Patel returned for his third spell. India required two wickets. South Africa had 8 overs to score two runs. Zaheer had only one over left which made it imperative for Munaf Patel to take at least one wicket in that over. He took two to finish off the South African innings and give India a marginal win by just 1 run.

Munaf Patel had arrived on the scene when India was desperately in search of a genuine fast bowler who could bowl yorkers. Munaf possessed pace and ability to bowl yorkers. He became an instant success but lack of fitness and sluggish fielding slowly sidelined him. A groin injury threatened to put a full stop to his stint in the Indian Cricket team. His surprise selection in the South Africa ODI series presented him the last chance to put his case forward for a selection in the World Cup squad. Munaf Patel bagged the man of the match award and with it, sealed his berth in India's World Cup squad. His bowling figures of 4 for 29 gave India its first win in a bilateral series in South Africa in 5 years.

3RD ODI – BATTLE FOR NUMBER 7

Suresh Raina's emergence resembled so much to Mohammad Kaif's. Kaif, more than a handy batsman at number 7, left an enduring mark with his splendid fielding and energy. There was a certain sense of amiability to Kaif and his undying spirit. Suresh Raina stood a notch above Kaif in fielding.

He had greater batting abilities than Kaif. He had received a rare word of praise from India's former coach Greg Chappell. Yet, Raina struggled to transform himself from a good talent to an exceptional player. His recent string of scores of 30s threatened to jeopardise his place because a big fella kept knocking on the door.

Despite showcasing his potential in U–16 competition and his subsequent ascendance to the U–19 and the Ranji Squad of Baroda, Yusuf Pathan sought a mentor, a guide to cultivate his potential into execution. He was determined to play for India but time was running out. Then, in the summer of 2008, in India's glitzy sporting extravaganza, he found words of wisdom from the legendary leg spinner. Under Shane Warne, Yusuf Pathan found his gate pass to the Indian national team as he set the IPL's first season ablaze. A series of subsequent low scores made him sit out of the team in late 2009 but he never gave up. Shane Warne had instilled the Australian spirit in him. His perseverance paid off. When you score a hundred in the first innings (108) and a double hundred in the second innings (210) of a significant match (2010 Duleep Trophy final), you make yourself hard to ignore. He conquered his first battle and re–entered the Indian Cricket team. Now began the second battle, a battle for the No. 7 spot with his buddy Suresh Raina.

After a clinical bowling performance by the Indian seamers followed by another collapse of its top order, the scene was well set for Raina and Pathan to make an influential impact. At 93 for 5, Pathan walked in. Raina already looked good for his 14 with a couple of charming boundaries. But Pathan stole the show. After hitting a boundary each to Steyn and Duminy and two to Botha, came the over which confirmed Yusuf Pathan's inclusion in the World Cup Squad. The first six he hit, Dale Steyn tried to catch and nearly succeeded. For the next two, he stood and watched the ball soar over his head out of the ground. Yusuf Pathan's three sixes in an over changed the entire complexion of the game.

Yusuf Pathan's quick scoring provided Raina ample freedom to pace his innings. But 6 overs later, Raina squandered his chance to make an impression. Another score in the 30s put his chances in serious doubt. Yusuf Pathan's 59 gave India a lead in an ODI series in South Africa for the first time in its history. Pathan clearly won the first round of the battle for India's number 7. Suresh Raina's place in the World Cup Squad was guaranteed but a place in the playing eleven now came under threat. Yusuf Pathan's belligerence added an element of suspense over India's number 7. He gave Indian fans something to discuss, albeit for just 5 days.

5TH ODI – A WIN IN A LOSING CAUSE

The ODI series (2–2 after South Africa won the fourth ODI) seemed a closely fought contest but the reality was far from it. The Indian bowling had occasionally marked its presence but largely took a sabbatical. Munaf Patel's brilliant spell in the 2nd ODI and Yusuf Pathan's destructive innings in the 3rd ODI gave India its two victories. In all the four matches, the Indian top order had flopped miserably. When South Africa asked India to chase 251 in the 5th and the deciding ODI, in overcast conditions, the result appeared a foregone conclusion. The South African pace attack blew away India's top order as expected. India lost 8 wickets for 119 in 23 overs. In the lost cause, Yusuf Pathan decided to have a bit of fun. The next 13 overs saw brutal batting at its very best. It did not matter who bowled to him; whether it was Robin Peterson's slow left arm or Faf du Plessis' part–time leg spinners; whether it was the world's tallest bowler Morne Morkel or the world's best bowler Dale Steyn, he kept hitting sixes. India was certain of an embarrassing defeat after the early stages of the match but eventually lost by just 33 runs. Yusuf Pathan's 105 (8 fours and 8 sixes) guaranteed him a place in India's playing 11 in the World Cup 2011. India lost the match and the series 3–2. This was the closest it ever came to winning an ODI series in South Africa. Despite losing the series, this was India's best performance in South Africa.

The ODI series in South Africa ended a memorable season. An unexpected and famous win in the Australian tri–series had caused a revolution. It had provided India its next captain. The captain then along with a fantastic coach rebuilt a team of young cricketers around some of the most reputed names in world cricket. The past 3 years had witnessed a legend rediscover himself all over again. India saw one of the game's supreme leaders say good bye to world cricket. A legendary leg spinner departed from international cricket. It had witnessed India's unbelievable home dominance. Few of the 'Sourav Ganguly Guys' came of age to carry the team on their shoulders during this time. In this period, India had registered some of the most impressive overseas wins. Team India had found the mental strength to successfully take that one step forward which Ganguly's team had failed to do. By consistently performing at the peak of its abilities, Dhoni's Team

India managed to deliver the most fruitful three years of Indian cricket.

Of course, India faced hiccups on the way. But now was not the moment to mourn wasted possibilities. It was not the time to discuss past failures. The hour had finally arrived. After the debacle of the previous World Cup, India had resurged to the summit of ODI cricket. Yes! It came out shining from every challenge thrown at it, overcoming the disappointments of 2007 and successfully focusing all its energy on the future. India's success story established the power of perseverance, hard work and the ability to dream. But what is the pinnacle if you do not hold the symbol of it? What is the significance of being the best if you do not conquer the toughest and most treasured competition? Are you really No. 1 unless you win the most important trophy in World Cricket? Are you really successful unless you win the most coveted prize? Fifteen individuals were selected on 17th January 2011 to uncover the answers. These fifteen individuals were selected to fulfil the long pending desire of an entire nation and a national icon. The nation had rejoiced the last three years of glory, victories and self–esteem. These years symbolized passion, hunger and determination. The next two months represented the ultimate redemption. After the dark abyss of match fixing, after the resurrection and restoration as a recognizable force, after an unexpected downfall, a dictator regime and the lowest ebbs of self–belief, after the magnificent journey to the top, India found itself two months away from its final redemption. It was ready to embark upon the final leg of its voyage to destiny. India prepared for the Cup of salvation.

EPILOGUE

On 2nd April 2011 at around 10:49 pm, Mahendra Singh Dhoni launched Nuwan Kulasekara into the stands and with that monstrous hit, India concluded one of the grandest stories in international sports. It took India 11 long years to redeem itself. 11 years ago, when Indian cricket suffered a humiliating crisis, when the trustworthiness of Indian cricket was brought to the stands and was asked some humiliating questions, a team had stood up to take the challenge of bringing the nation's lost prestige back. The captain along with his team had pulled India out of the credibility crisis but could not complete the ultimate task. M.S. Dhoni, India's most successful captain, built on the strong foundations given by India's first true leader and realized the nation's dreams of a worthy coronation. While the entire country celebrated India's ultimate redemption, one man was nowhere to be seen. Perhaps somewhere in a quiet corner, Sourav Ganguly reminisced, "We are finally here!"

AS I SAY GOOD BYE

'It wasn't a waste of time' has not been easy. As a subject, I didn't know how to structure this book. What should I include and more so what do I leave out? It has taken me five years to come up with this final version. I still remember the day when I compiled the prologue of the book. As naïve and arrogant it may sound, I needed only fifteen minutes to put it on paper. I thought, "How difficult could it be?" There, I was pompous. The next sixty months made me realize that I was naïve as well.

To write a book which covers 11 years of a sport, I needed an extensive research. Thankfully, there is one platform which carried all the statistics, news and articles. It became my 'one stop shop'. ESPNCRICINFO is the sole source of all statistics, factual stories which are part of this book. I was once cribbing to my wife about the amount of research I was required to do and how frustrating it was. She replied, "What research? All you do is log on to ESPNCRICINFO." It struck me at that moment, and I was amazed at the vastness of ESPNCRICINFO's data library. This book could not have seen the light of the day if it wasn't for ESPNCRICINFO. For that, saying thank you will not be enough. I am ever so grateful to ESPNCRICINFO for building such a vast and detailed database that I could write a 250–page book referring to only one site. I thank you from the bottom of my heart for making this happen.

In 1992, my father decided to move to Malvan, a small coastal village in Maharashtra. Education in such remote places is always a major concern and my mother was very wary of it. But to my advantage, Malvan had a school, an educational institute which already had a history of 80 years when I enrolled. My mother had convinced me to become a Chartered Accountant by then and for that, I needed a strong foundation. A.S.D. Topiwala High School provided exactly that, a strong footing. I have had so many brilliant teachers in those eight years but as it always happens, you have your favourites. Barve Sir was mine. His lessons infused confidence in me to think of writing a book in English. I could write this book because of the belief he instilled in me. As a small–town boy, I carried all inferiority complexes that one could possibly have. As I spent some years in Pune, I started overcoming them one by one. But to overcome them, I required patience. I thank A.S.D. Topiwala High School, my school, for cultivating important values in me. I cannot complete this book without mentioning Parulekar Sir, Khanolkar Sir, Avasare Sir, Girkar Sir (He was my drawing teacher and he made me realise that drawing was not my cup of tea by giving me 7 out of 50 in 6th standard.), Valanju Sir, Prabhukhanolakar Sir and Prabhu Sir. The list is unending and I thank all of you for shaping me up the way I am.

As a child when you are fragile and impressionable, there is always a possibility to form some strong and baseless opinions. With cricket evoking so much passion, I grew up hearing some of the most outrageous comments such as about Sanath Jayasuriya having a spring in his bat or the extra muscles in Shoaib Akhtar's forearm. In the chaos of such insipid opinions, one man's acute reading of the game helped me look for cricketing reasoning. Balkrishna Parulekar – (Bal Mama), helped me understand the game of cricket. We had watched the ICC World Cup 1992 together. I was just seven and I don't remember the matches at all but his opinions and understanding of the game left a permanent mark. Bal Mama invoked the true passion for cricket in me and this was and will be his biggest contribution to my life.

As a kid, I was a difficult child to handle for my mother and it did not help that I was hugely fanatical about the one thing my mother hated the most. I had lost count of the number of times she had said, "Cricket is not going to help you in life." She was right to certain extent; at that time, I did not have the courage to tell her that I wanted to play cricket and take it up as profession. She wanted me to be a Chartered Accountant. My father had wanted to be a Chartered Accountant himself but he could not due to some circumstances and it was her dream to make me one and fulfill my father's wish. I missed her the most when I finally got through the final examination of Chartered Accountancy. As I finish this book, I cannot explain how much I miss her. Of the many things that I failed to share with her while she was with me, this would be the least important. Yet I want her to know that cricket has helped me beyond anybody and anything. I wish she was here to read it. And I am sure, even after knowing nothing about the 'stupid game', she would have enjoyed every single word of it. This book would not have been a possibility without my father who let me form my opinions whether or not they contradicted with his.

Following the game is one thing; writing about it is altogether another. There is one man, my roommate, who unknowingly encouraged me to write. Sandeep Shelke a.k.a. Sandy, is another person to whom I am so very grateful. I am also very thankful to Kabir Mandrekar from whom I had received good positive feedback on my articles.

When I say that I have been writing this book for the past three and half years, I don't mean to say that I have slogged every day and night. In fact, after finishing the first draft of Part I and halfway through the Part II, I lost interest. The words stopped coming, and I started to get absorbed in my daily life. There came a time when I had abandoned the idea of finishing the book. And then– I watched a Marathi movie which had the leading pair of Ketaki Mategaonkar and Prathmesh Parab. The age of the leading pair hit me really hard. Ketaki Mategaonkar at an age of 20 and Prathmesh Parab at an age of 21 years had the maturity and commitment to be the leads in a feature film. It shook me to the core and brought me out of my lethargy. For the next seven days, I did not understand what had hit me. On the 8th day, I took a decision and on the 9th, I started writing again. I don't know whether the film–makers of 'Time pass' meant it to be an inspirational film, but it indeed inspired me to complete the unfinished job.

As I come to the end of it, only one person is left to say my thank you to. She was the one who gave me the idea of writing a book. She was the one who gave me that all important first push to start writing. While writing, I never cared for the grammatical mistakes. I just kept writing, thinking that the mistakes can be corrected afterwards but the flow of writing must be maintained. As it turned out, I made some fifty mistakes a page. And who corrected them all? Certainly not me! My wife had to go through the pain of correcting all of them. She did it, sometimes willingly, sometimes with unimaginable irritation. But through the agony and frustration, she stuck to her job and kept correcting one mistake I made after another. She has corrected and re–written so many lines in the book that I probably should officially name her the co–author. But that is not her only contribution. Every single word that I wrote, I read to her on the same day. Anybody who knows my wife can tell you that patience is not her virtue. I don't know where she drew it from while I kept reading my drafts to her out loud at even the ungodliest hours. Her struggle and battle against her patience while I read page after page showed me how important this book was for her. Her criticism and frank opinions were hard to digest but easy to incorporate. It is her love and efforts that has transformed my dream to reality. With all my heart and love, I dedicate this book to her alone. It would not have started without you. It would not have finished without you. It certainly would not have been possible without you. Thank you, Kanchan.

REFERENCES

PART I

PROLOGUE

1. Excerpts of Manoj Prabhakar Interview – Outlook India.com.

2. Excerpts of alleged conversation between a London–based NRI, Sanjay Chawla, and the South African cricket captain, Hansie Cronje – The Hindu – Online Edition on 08.04.2000

3. Partial Text of Hansie Cronje's confession – Rediff.com – 08.06.2000

4. Excerpts of Statement issued by BCCI – BBC Sports Online–05.12.2000 and The New York Times–06.12.2000

PART II

BATTLE FOR CONTROL

1. Harsha Bhogle's day end interview with Sourav Ganguly as telecasted on ESPN/STAR SPORTS on 15.09.2005 – PAGE NO. 149

2. Greg Chappell Email – as published on www.snh.com.au

3. "Indian cricket has to move forward and for that, both the captain and coach have to work together and a professional working relationship has to be maintained. Both Chappell and Ganguly have told the committee they will work together." BCCI Official statement after the meeting in Mumbai on 27.09.2005. PAGE NO.158

4. "It would be inappropriate to leave an experienced player like Ganguly out of the team and keep him on the bench". – Kiran More's official statement after Selection Committee Meeting on 14.12.2005. PAGE NO. 161

COPYRIGHT ACKNOWLEDGEMENTS

Particulars	Links
Included in Prologue – Manoj Prabhakar Interview	https://archive.fo/20120913231940/http://www.outlookindia.com/full.asp?fodname=19970611&fname=-COVER+STORY&sid=2
Included in Prologue – Hansie Cronje Telephone Conversation Transcripts	https://www.rediff.com/sports/2000/apr/07trans.htm
Included in Prologue – Hansie Cronje Confession	https://www.rediff.com/sports/2000/jun/08cronje.htm
Included in Prologue – BCCI Statement banning 4 Indian Players	https://www.nytimes.com/2000/12/06/sports/IHT-azharuddin-and-4-others-are-punished-for-cricket-match-fixing.html
A quote by Frederick Douglass	Power concedes nothing without a demand. It never did and it never will
Sourav Ganguly Interview with Harsha Bhogle	Transcript of the interview telecast on Star Sports India in 2006
Greg Chappell Email to BCCI	https://www.smh.com.au/sport/cricket/text-of-greg-chappells-email-20050926-gdm4xo.html
Various Commentary quotes	From actual match Commentary